*C*lose your eyes, take a deep, easy breath, and imagine yourself holding a small black stone, a smooth river pebble. In your imagination, let this stone grow until you are standing on it.

You're not alone. Before you is a golden light, and in this golden light, you see the goddess Isis. "Are you willing to enter into meditation with Me and My Sister Goddesses?" She asks.

As you say yes, you soon become aware of a circle of goddesses, all the goddesses with whom you will soon meditate, all dancing on this black stone. Seventy or more goddesses stand with you on your black stone, seventy goddesses who will lead you into new places and new ideas, perhaps into a new life ....

As the poet saw the world in a grain of sand, so can you know how the universe danced in an ordinary black stone. Dance with the goddesses. Breathe in their spirit and energy, absorb their wisdom and creativity, as you welcome them into your daily spiritual practice ....

About the Author

Dr. Barbara Ardinger is a Witch, teacher, and freelance writer/editor who lives in Long Beach, California, with her two cats, Schroedinger and Heisenberg. She is the author of *A Woman's Book of Rituals and Celebrations*, *Seeing Solutions*, and *Granny Gosle's Tales*, as well as multitudinous magazine articles, technical projects, book reviews, and Goddess novels in progress.

Barbara holds a Ph.D. degree in English Renaissance literature and has also studied the Tarot, Reiki, numerology, color, healing, the Qabalah, drumming, and Aramaic origins of the Bible. She has received a third degree initiation in a hidden occult order, was given the Green Tara initiations by Dagmola Jamyang Sakya, and is a member of the Fellowship of Isis.

To Write to the Author

If you wish to contact the author or would like more information about this book, please write to the author in care of Llewellyn Worldwide and we will forward your request. Both the author and publisher appreciate hearing from you and learning of your enjoyment of this book and how it has helped you. Llewellyn Worldwide cannot guarantee that every letter written to the author can be answered, but all will be forwarded. Please write to:

Dr. Barbara Ardinger
℅ Llewellyn Worldwide
P.O. Box 64383, Dept. K034-5
St. Paul, MN 55164-0383, U.S.A.

Please enclose a self-addressed, stamped envelope for reply, or $1.00 to cover costs. If outside U.S.A., enclose international postal reply coupon.

Goddess
Meditations

Barbara Ardinger, Ph.D.
Foreword by Patricia Monaghan

1998
Llewellyn Publications
Saint Paul, Minnesota 55164-0383, U.S.A.

FIRST EDITION
First Printing, 1998

Cover Design: Anne Marie Garrison
Cover illustration: Claudia Connelly
Interior illustrations: Wendy Froshay
Editing and interior design: Astrid Sandell

Library of Congress Cataloging-in-Publication Data
Ardinger, Barbara, 1941–
    Goddess meditations / Barbara Ardinger; foreword by Patricia Monaghan.
      p.   cm.
    Includes bibliographical references and index.
    ISBN 1-56718-034-5 (pbk.)
    1. Goddess religion. 2. Meditation. I. Title
  BF1623.G63A73   1998
  291.1'4--dc21   98-39623
                                                CIP

Publisher's Note: Llewellyn Worldwide does not participate in, endorse, or have any authority or responsibility concerning private business transactions between our authors and the public. All mail addressed to the author is forwarded but the publisher cannot, unless specifically instructed by the author, give out an address or phone number.

Llewellyn Publications
A Division of Llewellyn Worldwide, Ltd.
P.O. Box 64383, Dept. K034-5
St. Paul, MN 55164-0383, U.S.A.

Printed in the United States of America

Other Books by Barbara Ardinger

A Woman's Book of Rituals and Celebrations
(New World Library, 1992; revised paperback edition, 1995)

Seeing Solutions
(Signet New Age Book, 1989)

Dedication

First, as always, to my son, Charles. A published poet, he understands the struggle it takes to get the words right and, though he often thinks it's a little weird, he gives me honest feedback on my writing.

To my father, Harold Rohne, who died while I was writing this book. From the time I was able to hold a pencil, he encouraged me to write and praised my juvenile stories.

To my friend, Rose Sheppard, who has given me a thousand gifts, both tangible and intangible, the best of which is her friendship. Some of the meditations in this book are my gifts to her. Rose also died while I was writing this book. Bright blessings to her!

Acknowledgments

I am always grateful for the friendship and support of my community.

Timothy Roderick talked me into getting back to my proper work for the Goddess and actually writing this book. Tim is a Gardnerian High Priest and in many ways a lot more structured than I am, but we do knockout rituals together and are taking the *Barb 'n' Tim Show* (a lecture on Witchcraft) on the road.

Patricia Monaghan said she'd "be delighted" to write the foreword. Pat wrote *the* definitive book on goddesses. The whole time I was writing this book, her *Book of Goddesses and Heroines* sat beside my keyboard. I'm glad she's done a new edition; my copy is getting pretty ragged. It's the book I open when I need to know who's a healing goddess, a household goddess, goddesses for germination and the seasons and the elements, and goddesses for just about everything else under our Mother Sun.

Holin "Badger" Kennen edited the manuscript. She made me write more clearly so I won't embarrass myself in public, and she also explained the processes of spinning and weaving for the Protection meditation. Holin is writing a book on drumming, and I'll get to edit it for her. My *Artist's Way/Vein of Gold* community, facilitated by Valerie Meyer (Eagle Heart), paid attention to me when attention needed to be paid.

Nancy Amaris proposed the Queen as a life-stage between Mother and Crone. Anna Cassidy explained the great spiritual value of blowing bubbles. Paul Cummins told me about Wonder Woman's history. Frances Daws feng shui'd my home and became my friend. Judy Dienst explained "cording" as a part of cutting ties. Judith Kali Evador shared her concept of BodyKnowing. Jeanine Just teaches seminars on core values; five of mine are included in the Great Goddess meditations. Sandra Lange helped me select the five runes for Hel's meditation. Patti and Chuck Leviton shared their expertise in guided imagery. Shira Paskin and Karima Seabourne suggested images I adopted. Marsha Smith Shaw answered some unanswerable questions about esoteric lore. Kitari Om, the StarWalker, shared information she's collected on alternative chakras. I am enormously grateful to all of these people, but my interpretations of things they told me are my own responsibility, not theirs.

Although some of my friends did not participate directly in the creation of this book, they deserve to be acknowledged simply because they keep on believing in my work. They're the ones who made sure I remembered to eat and pay bills. Understanding that writers can be really grumpy caterpillars until their books are hatched and begin to fly on fragile verbal wings, these good friends also plucked me out of my computerized cocoon from time to time just (I suppose) to see what I was doing. My gratitude goes to Georgia Amos, Mark Boling, Elizabeth Cunningham, Judy Dienst, Patricia Kelly, Ron and Sandra Lange, Merry Neitlich, Anne Niven, Sandra Richmond and Dareelle Foster, Judy Semler, Suzan Walter, Tom Tokunaga, and Kathleen Zundell.

I give ten thousand thank-yous to Dagmola Jamyang Sakya for her prayers and to Theo Clark for investing in me and for a thousand more things.

I'm also grateful to Nancy Mostad, Astrid Sandell, and the other folks at Llewellyn for their enthusiasm about my work.

Finally, I thank Dr. Mark deDubovay and Gilda Lubis for chasing the energy dragons up and down my arms and around my back.

Contents

Illustrations

Goddesses

Figures

Tables

Foreword

Once upon a time, there were temples to the goddess everywhere. Some were marble-pillared and decorated with statuary; some were primal groves bisected by murmuring streams; some were cut from the living rock; some were carved into open meadows. Some were never permanent structures, but sacred spaces created through rituals that honored the land and its fruitful energy. In these temples, our forebears gathered to celebrate and worship, to offer thanks for a good harvest and to petition for help with life's many challenges. In these temples, feminine energy was acknowledged and made manifest.

These temples still exist in many lands, in places where honoring the goddess—usually together with the god as her consort or son—is still part of the fabric of life. Durga's chariot still travels the length of Indian cities; the songs to Dewi Shri are still sung in Balinese towns; Japanese visitors still bow at the white silk curtain that hides the secrets of Amaterasu-omi-kami; the pipe given to the Lakota people still is passed with reverence and honor.

But in many lands the goddess temples have disappeared. The flame of Celtic Brighe was snuffed hundreds of years ago in Ireland, and her shrine at Kildare is no more. Or the temples have been changed, sometimes beyond recognition. Great French cathedrals honor the Christian Virgin at sites where the primal goddess of birth was once worshipped. The Parthenon, Athena's great sanctuary in the town that bears her name, is now a historic site rather than a gathering place for those who worship the goddess of wise protection.

For many of us, the temple of the goddess exists now in our homes and in our hearts. And there she truly lives. We gather friends to celebrate new versions of feasts that once were public ceremonials; we pray or meditate on the feminine divine, attempting to live wisely in Her ways. We create sacred spaces in our gardens; we hallow our automobiles with dashboard altars of feathers and stones; we deck our bodies with significant symbols that attest, to the knowing eye, the course of our experiences of worship. The lost temples of the goddess are re-created each time those who honor Her call out one of her many names, in the silence of the mind or in the singing of the voice. Here is a book that helps in that great rebuilding—a book that offers multiple opportunities to invoke and re-create the greatness of the divine feminine. Wise and witty and whimsical and warm and wild, these meditations open the way for the heart and spirit to reconnect with goddess energy. And in doing so, Barbara Ardinger's words create again the sacred space for that energy to re-enter the world.

—Patricia Monaghan
author, *The New Book of Goddesses and Heroines*

The Goddess Meditates

In the moment
before days begin to be measured,
I dance
       alone
and love
       alone
and find myself

in one of *those moods*.
I cry aloud,
Connection! I cry,
Empty space must now be filled!
And so I squat down

in my secret place
(before there is any place).
I sit upon deepest red and farthest purple
and watch the way my breathing goes.

    One

         Darkness dreams our spinning grandmothers
         and Light begins her quickening walkabout.

    Two

         Sun and Moon call forth their chariots
         and planetary rulers assume their thrones.

    Three

         Holy Wisdom picks up her basket of seeds
         and wings and waves and trees begin to sing aloud.

    Four

         beehive, silver egg, and drum begin to tick
         and my wine-dark womb opens.

In the void
before the earth is peopled
I see
    community

and touch
    community
and find myself

well filled with lovingkindness.
I laugh aloud,
Connection! I laugh,
Sacred space is forever filled!
And so I rise up

from my secret place
(and now the world is born).
I dance its four corners, dance its deepest center,
and witness all the ways my loving goes.

Introduction

Winged Isis

Nearly everyone I know meditates with some regularity. Some people have been given, or made up their own, mantras. Others focus on the deep power of their own breathing or on the stillness of a candle flame. Still others do moving meditations as they walk through the park or along the beach. When my friends meet in groups, they do guided visualizations for world peace, for community health and well-being, or for their personal abundance. They often name or invoke goddesses as they set their intention for their rituals or meditations.

Although most of the books of Goddess spirituality contain meditations and guided visualizations focusing on pentacles, the ocean, specific intentions and goals, and inner or otherwise invisible beings, and there are many books about meditation per se, until now there have been few books entirely and specifically devoted to meditations upon the Goddess of Ten Thousand Names.

Goddess Meditations therefore presents unique meditations created for women and men to use in their efforts to find a place of centeredness and serenity in their lives, both alone and in groups, either in rituals or informally.

Because most of the readers of this book will be familiar with meditation and guided visualization, this is not a beginner's how-to-meditate book. Nevertheless, it opens with a chapter on meditation, breathing, and visualization, and several of the more useful how-to books are listed in the bibliography. I have also indicated useful places to pause in each meditation. Use these, or find new places to pause that are more comfortable for you. Because many people who meditate do so before their altars or as part of rituals, chapter 2 addresses those topics. Building an altar and participating in a ritual are not, however, necessary to meditation, and if such things make you uncomfortable, try them in a safe place to see if you can change your comfort level.

Chapter 3 presents nine meditations on the ancient and future Great Goddess, our Mother/Creatrix. The meditations deal with issues that come up again and again in our lives: love, protection, gratitude, trust, community, creativity, spirituality, wisdom, and priestess power. They're core values in my life; I'm sure you're dealing with them, too.

Twenty-six of the meditations in this book are based on the natural cycles of light and dark that we see and experience every day of our lives (as well as every month and every year), in our emotional cycles, and metaphorically in our personal year from birthday to birthday. Meditations are given for both "light work" and "dark work."

Light work (chapter 4) is done in and for the daytime; the new, waxing, and full moons; spring and summer; growth, blooming, and bearing fruit; and moving out into the world again. Specific light work meditations include attracting love and abundance, celebrating, meeting your Fairy Goodmother and making three wishes, and finding your own strength and courage. Three of the meditations in this chapter are moving meditations.

Dark work (chapter 5) is done in and for the nighttime, the waning and dark moons, fall and winter, rest, planting metaphorical seeds of intention in our lives, germination or incubation, and withdrawing for a time from the world. Specific dark work meditations include cutting the ties that bind us to people we no longer need in our lives, dumping old toxic tapes, meeting our shadow, incubation and rebirth, and the widdershins spiral. Please remember that dark work is in no way negative. As Timothy Roderick writes, it is:

> a natural, spiritual state that simply exists, like the blackness of space. It is
> nothing to fear. It simply is. And awareness of this darkness waxes and wanes
> like the light of the moon or like the rising and setting of the sun.[1]

Chapter 6 presents seven chakra goddess meditations. I have linked goddesses to the chakras especially for this book, and these meditations, which deal with issues of survival, relationships, willpower, love, communication, intuition, and understanding, are true magical encounters.

Chapter 7 presents the Goddess Pillar Meditation. Although it is based on Israel Regardie's Qabalistic Middle Pillar Meditation, which uses five traditional names of Jehovah and is Judeo-Christian in design, the Goddess Pillar Meditation uses goddess names and is Neo-Pagan in design. Whether done in a group or alone, the Goddess Pillar Meditation is powerful. I know this through my own experience, as I've done the meditation myself and led it in large and small groups. I also remember that when I created it for a class I was teaching several years ago, I received several phone calls the next morning. I listened to reports of extraordinary dreams and visions, and one woman said she hadn't slept at all.

When we do the Goddess Pillar Meditation, we stand between the Pillars that hold the veil between the worlds. Descending the Pillar, we sound the names and call the powers of five great goddesses into our physical, emotional, mental, and spiritual bodies. Ascending the Pillar, we project those powers out into our communities and into a world that cries out for the nourishing powers of the Goddess.

Sometimes we want to do "pure" meditation instead of guided imagery. Chapter 8 consists, therefore, of twenty-seven brief suggestions and inspirations for this type of work. You can meditate with a goddess, an idea, an attribute, a clue. You can start with a word or phrase and take off from there. Topics include Darkness, Light, the four elements, the four seasons, and the Virgin, Warrior Queen,[2] Mother, and Crone aspects of the Goddess.

The goddess meditations in this book will keep us all mindful of the ancient Great Goddess and Her 10,000 manifestations, old and new, classical or Found. The meditations are intended to enrich the lives of women and men who follow a spiritual path and practice the presence of the Goddess.

Let Us Now Begin: Isis

This is an introductory meditation.[3] Its purpose is to give you the flavor of the goddess meditations to follow and get you started.

Before you begin, however, go out and find a garden planter where the architect has used Mexican or Japanese river pebbles in the landscaping. You can also find these stones at landscape supply stores and some import stores. You'll recognize these stones right away. They're usually oval and flattish and either sort of steel gray or black. Select one stone, preferably a black one and preferably one that fits comfortably in the palm of one hand. If landscapers where you live don't use these particular stones, find another rock that fits the description. *Do **not** use a stone you purchased at a metaphysical store.* The idea here is to use an ordinary stone.

Bring the stone with you to your meditation place. Hold it in your hand, feel its curves, feel how it is both hard and soft at the same time. Hold your stone throughout the meditation.

Isis is the Great Creatrix, first daughter of Nut, Mother Sky Who is Heaven. Isis, Queen of Heaven and Earth, was originally Auset (or Aset), and Her hieroglyph meant "throne," for the Pharaohs of Egypt lived in Her lap. Goddess of grain, of water, of the moon, She was married to Her brother, Osiris, Lord of the Earth and the Underworld. It is possible that Isis has been worshipped longer and by more people than any other goddess: in Egypt from time before time (or at least from the fourth century B.C.E.), in Greece, in Rome, throughout the Mediterranean lands, and today throughout the world. Her last temple in Alexandria was destroyed in 391 C.E., by those who obeyed a Christian Emperor, and the last recorded Isian festival was held in 416. In 1976, the Honorable Olivia Robertson, her brother, the late Lawrence Durdin-Robertson, Lord Strathloch, and his wife founded the Fellowship of Isis. Thus is the Great Creatrix loved and honored again throughout the world.[4]

In the Roman novel *The Golden Ass* (written during the second century), the Goddess speaks:

> I am Nature, the universal Mother, mistress of all the elements, primordial child of time, sovereign of all things spiritual, queen of the dead, queen also of the immortals, the single manifestation of all gods and goddesses that are.[5]

It is fitting that Isis begins our goddess meditations.

The Meditation

Sit comfortably in a peaceful place and close your eyes. Take two or three deep, easy breaths and let your fingers caress your black stone. Take another deep, easy breath and let your body relax and let your mind become more and more creative.

In your mind's eye, see your black stone, first as you found it lying among its kinfolk in a planter or garden or driveway. Relive the intuitive nudge that led you to pick up that individual stone. Know that this is a most ordinary stone, a common stone, a plain stone, and it has no symbolic or occult significance whatsoever.

Pause

Suddenly there is a golden light on the horizon in front of you. As you watch, this golden light becomes brighter and warmer, and after a time you can glimpse a figure inside the light. The figure advances, and soon the Goddess Isis is standing before you, and Her golden light shines upon you. It shines on you, around you, above and below you, in you, and through you. You must stand in the presence of the Goddess; in your imagination stand up. Because anything can happen in the universe of our meditation, you are still holding your black stone, the Goddess is holding your black stone, and you and She are standing together upon your black stone. Your plain, ordinary, common black stone has become the earth, it has become the platform of the Goddess.

"I am the universal Mother," Isis says to you. "I am the sovereign of all things spiritual. Are you willing to enter into meditation with Me and My Sister Goddesses?"

If you are willing, tell Her so.

Pause

"That is good," She replies, and She opens Her arms wide, as if to embrace the whole world, and bids you look around.

And you become aware that you are no longer alone before Isis. There is a circle of goddesses around you, and in this circle are all the goddesses with whom you will meditate in this book . . . Shekinah, Athene, Brigid, Tara, Aphrodite, your Fairy Goodmother, the Fates, Grandmother Spider, Baba Yaga, Oya, Sarasvati, Sophia, and the Great Goddess Herself.

Pause

Seventy or more goddesses stand with you on your black stone, seventy goddesses who will lead you into new places and new ideas, perhaps into a new life. And behind them? Still more goddesses. The great Ladies of all the world's pantheons. Goddesses from the past and the future. Found Goddesses. Goddesses named and unnamed.

In the Middle Ages, scholars used to ask, How many angels can dance on the head of a pin? Ask yourself, How many goddesses can dance on an ordinary black stone? You already know the answer: All of them.

As the poet saw the world in a grain of sand, so can you know how the universe dances on an ordinary black stone.

Spend as much time as you want to dancing and being with the goddesses. Breathe in their spirit and energy, absorb their wisdom and creativity.

Pause

When you come back from this meditation, you may want to keep your black stone in your pocket or pouch or put it on your altar.

Since writing this meditation, I have collected ten black stones, which I keep on top of the chest where I store my magical supplies. Sometimes I'll carry one in my pocket. Each stone is oval, each is less long than my thumb, each is unique. One has spots like ghosts marching across its face, another has streaks like the trails of comets, one has markings like waves, another is covered in brownish clouds, others look like starry skies. You, too, may gather such a collection of treasures.

I hope you enjoy both your stones and the meditations in this book.

Endnotes

1. Timothy Roderick, *Dark Moon Mysteries* (St. Paul: Llewellyn Publications, 1996), p. 5.

2. My friend Nancy Amaris has suggested the Queen as a fourth personification of the Goddess. Some of us just don't jump directly from Mother to Crone; we need an intermediate stage when we're powerful and beautiful. Modern life being what it is, I added Warrior to Queen. See also Elizabeth Davis and Carol Leonard, *The Woman's Wheel of Life* (New York: Viking Arkana, 1996), pp. 4–8.

3. My thanks to my friend and editor, Holin Badger Kennen, for suggesting this meditation. As she described the metaphorical properties of the black stone, she nearly put me into a trance during our phone conversation. So I gave her the stone.

4. Sharon Kelly Heyob, *The Cult of Isis Among Women of the Greco-Roman World* (Kinderhook, NY: E. J. Brill, 1975), chapter 1. For information on the Fellowship of Isis, see the resources at the end of the book.

5. Graves, Robert, trans., *The Golden Ass* (New York: Farrar, Straus and Giroux, 1951), p. 264.

1
Time to Meditate

Inanna

Many and various are the consciousness-altering activities that fall under the label "meditation." There are techniques taught by the heavily advertised commercial schools and gurus of meditation, including all the "mind probe" and "mind control" seminars. There is Transcendental Meditation. There is sitting *zazen*, which is as close to perfect stasis as I've ever been, and there is prayerful meditation. There are chanting and drumming and moving meditations. There are "trips" and hallucinations, vision quests, sensory deprivation, and trance channeling. There is meditation that focuses all of our attention on words or images, and there is meditation that focuses on nothing.

I'm sure that all of the foregoing can produce beautiful and useful experiences. I have, in fact, tried many of them at one time or another.

"But—" I can hear you protesting "—wait a minute. Some of these things are not meditation at all. Some of them are entertainment. Some are religious practices."

You're right. Nevertheless, I have heard people claim that every activity (and more) on my list is a meditational technique.

To find a satisfactory definition of meditation, therefore, I turned first to my favorite resource, the dictionary,[1] where I learned that as a verb, "meditate" entered the English language as early as 1560. The word comes from the Latin *meditari*, "to reflect upon, to study, to ponder." In 1560 (shortly before Shakespeare was born), "meditate" meant "to exercise the mind in (especially devotional) thought or contemplation." *The Oxford English Dictionary* gives a later definition of meditation as **the continuous application of the mind to the contemplation of some religious truth, mystery, or object of reverence, as a devotional exercise.**

Here's a definition I like! ***The continuous application . . . .*** Meditation doesn't work if you do it only once. Ideally, perhaps, we should endeavor to live in a constant meditative state, but modern life being what it is, spaced-out people on the freeways would cause major problems. Don't meditate, therefore, while you're driving.

"Continuous application" reminds me of the definition of meditation given by John Welwood in his introduction to a lovely book titled *Ordinary Magic*. Meditation, he writes, is the practice of mindfulness, awareness, or presence. It is:

> the practice of becoming more fully awake and present [and] nothing more esoteric than that . . . . [It is] the spice that brings out all the varied flavors of human existence, the doorway to rediscovering the inherent magic of being alive . . . . Meditation is extremely down-to-earth because it helps us connect with the actual textures of our experience, in all their variety and profundity.[2]

Although mindfulness has wide application, as demonstrated by the thirty-five essays in *Ordinary Magic*, my intention is *to practice the presence of the Goddess*.[3] This is a phrase I borrowed from *Practicing the Presence of God*, which was written four hundred years ago. Its author, a monk named Brother Lawrence, practiced the presence of his god every moment of every day, whether he was cleaning the monastery's ovens or repairing shoes for his brother monks or sitting in the chapel.

When we practice the presence of the Goddess, we likewise take Her with us everywhere we go. She is with us while we're washing dishes, cleaning the toilet, standing in line at the post office, shopping for groceries, doing our homework, surfing the Net, making love. When we practice the presence of the Goddess, we remain mindful of Her presence. Wherever we go, there She is. And Welwood is right: this is not esoteric at all. It is, indeed, down to earth, for it means being grounded in the Goddess.

. . . of the mind . . . Meditation is, of course, a mental process. Even moving meditation exercises the mind as well as the body, the movement often being somewhat trance-inducing. Repetitious movement, like walking or drumming, keeps the body and the left brain busy and frees the right brain to do whatever it does. Meditation is, of course, a largely right brain process, being not full of words but flowing with images and feelings.

. . . to the contemplation . . . thinking about, looking at, observing. Contemplation is a quiet and solitary work. The religious life is traditionally classified as either active or contemplative, with the former referring to working out in the world and the latter referring to a cloistered life of prayer. Academic life can also be contemplative, and it's been demonstrated that even business life needs its contemplative moments. Meditation is an effective stress reduction technique.

. . . of some religious truth . . . In these days of worldwide fundamentalist revivalism, religious "truth" is thunderously proclaimed from every pulpit. But it's hard for true believers to recognize someone else's truth, and it's especially hard to acknowledge the fact that truth comes in many forms. So I'll speak forth my religious truth. *My truth is the truth of the Goddess.* My truth is Her reappearance upon the earth and in the hearts and minds and bodies of Her daughters and sons.

. . . mystery . . . It seems to me that religious truth is, essentially, a mystery. That is, it can't be captured by words or held in the rational mind. Mystery is questions, not answers, and it can't be measured, weighed, cut open, analyzed, or programmed into a computer. Nevertheless, even though we can't really hope to do so, we keep on trying to understand the mystery. One way to do this is to still the mind's "endless monkey-chatter" and listen to that famous "small, still voice" that is our intuition, our soul, our holy spirit.

. . . or object of reverence . . . Like believers of many faiths, we pagans collect jewelry, statues of goddesses and gods, works of art, and innumerable spiritual *tchotchkes.* We don't worship these things, of course, but we do respect them. They are objects of reverence that help us focus, still our minds, and begin to meditate.

. . . as a devotional exercise. Dion Fortune has written that there are two spiritual paths: occult science (ritualism) and mystic art. I myself have been on both paths, having at one time been an officer of a Grand Lodge that practiced ceremonial magic. I got bored with ceremonial magic, though, and as a solitary Witch, I do fewer and fewer rituals and more and more meditation.

Not to worry, however. Fortune says that:

> a mystic is simply an introvert occultist and the occultist an extrovert mystic. Both aim at the same goal, though they seek it by different methods. The difference between them is of temperament, not of ideal.[4]

Whether you do rituals or simply sit before a little altar with your eyes closed, therefore, you're participating in a devotional exercise.

I also looked for other definitions of meditation. I asked around, even went to the library. I'll summarize what I learned. Meditation is a process whose aim is to quiet the body so the mind can work creatively. It tames the left brain so the right brain becomes free. It alters our consciousness by moving our attention out of beta brainwaves, which are used in our normal alert states as we move about the world, and into alpha brainwaves, which make us more creative and artistic and intuitive. Meditation is not the same as thinking, nor is it the same as praying, though it can perhaps be triggered by either. Some people distinguish meditation from prayer by saying that the former is listening, whereas the latter is talking.

Visualization

Most of the meditations in this book are guided visualizations, appropriate to be done alone or with a group. Generally speaking, my preference is for *guided visualization*, also called *guided imagery*. That's because I have a vivid imagination and like to see what's going on, whether it's going on in the outer world or in my own head.

I'm not alone. Look at the metaphysical magazines and you'll find dozens of ads for cassette tapes of guided meditations. While some are quite good, others are guaranteed (if not intended) to put you to sleep. Guided imagery is a valuable tool used by psychologists, psychotherapists, and other healers of all schools, from high touch to high tech. One of the professional organizations for those who use guided imagery is the American Association for the Study of Mental Imagery.[5]

Over the years, as I have conducted rituals, meditations, and guided visualizations, people have come to me and protested, "I just don't see what you're telling us to see. My mind doesn't work that way." Some people are like that. They don't have great inner visual acuity. I suspect that this has something to do with left-brain dominance, which is the only kind of thinking we learn in school.

What I tell these people is not to worry about seeing or not seeing and to *act as if they are seeing*. If you're one of these people, then, *relax. Pretend that you're seeing images in your mind*. Imagine that you are imaging. With enough practice, you will begin to see with your mind's eye, but until then use your other senses internally—hear, feel, taste, smell in your imagination.

Likewise, if you're one of those people who see only in black and white, *pretend you're seeing in color*. Act as if the tape in your brain is a full-spectrum tape. (You might even, in your imagination, install a television set in your head and visualize adjusting—or pretending to adjust—the color to full contrast.)

Guidelines

Because you are probably already familiar with meditation, the following paragraphs are given as reminders.

Posture

I have read somewhere that the Buddha taught four meditational postures: standing, walking, sitting, and lying down. That's pretty all-inclusive. If we're not already in one of these postures, we're moving from one to another and getting ready to meditate, or at least be mindful. It means that wherever we are and whatever we're doing, we can be meditating.

Many of the how-to books advise us to sit up straight when we meditate because when we lie down it's too easy to fall asleep. I'm not sure sleeping is a problem, however. When my son, Charles, was nine years old, he attended a week-long "mind probe" seminar with me. He got bored right away with all the far-out "woo-woo" talk and made a tent out of two folding chairs and my raincoat. He slept through most of the seminar. And he seemed to learn as much as any adult who stayed awake.

When I lead meditations and visualizations, therefore, I generally say, "If you fall asleep it's OK. Your unconscious will get what you need and your body will thank you for the rest." And while it's true that most people consider falling asleep while meditating counterproductive, others actually use meditation to get to sleep. For the sleep-deprived, that is a major benefit of meditation.

If you prefer to lie down while you meditate (and intend to stay awake), lie on your back, hands at your sides, without a pillow under your head. This keeps your spine straight.

If you sit, don't fold yourself up so much that your feet and legs fall asleep. Concentration becomes fragile when aches and pains keep noodging at you. I think it's best to sit on a comfortable chair that helps you keep your spine erect. Keep your feet flat on the floor and your arms on the arms of the chair or in your lap. Many people say you should never cross your arms or legs during meditation. I do it all the time, however, and it's never seemed to do any harm to my meditating.

Equipment

You don't need any equipment to meditate. It is not necessary to purchase expensive meditation videos (how do you watch them, anyway, with your eyes closed?), subliminal tapes, bioelectric shields, tachyon meters, meditation goggles, special clothing, or master-wave-producing meditation machines. All you need are yourself and your concentration.

If you meditate alone, however, a tape recorder will be handy. You can record the meditations and play them back for yourself. Record the meditation if you're part of a group, too, unless someone volunteers to read the meditation—and thus loses out on participating in it.

Breathing

I believe that the most important meditative tool is *breathing*. We use our breathing to transport ourselves into the alpha state where the magic happens.

Some people say that breath is the very foundation of life. Breath is *prana* (Sanskrit), *ruach* (Hebrew), *rookha* (Aramaic), *pneuma* (Greek), *spiritus* (Latin), *chi* (Chinese), *ki* (Japanese). When we breathe in, we are inspired, and when what we "breathe in" is more than the air around us, we are inspired to write or sing or dance or do whatever we love to do. When we breathe out, we expire; the last time we expire, we pass into another world.

Breath is thus more than air entering and leaving our respiratory system. It is, the esoteric teachings maintain, the very essence of life. Some teachers teach us to breathe in color and direct the color to various parts of our body for energy or healing. Singers and other musicians, especially horn players, must learn breath control in order to master their instruments. Actors and professional speakers also learn breath control early on. It is not surprising, then, that techniques for breath control are common to most of the esoteric schools and traditions.

Here are two breath control techniques that I teach.

Fourfold Breathing

The most effective controlled breathing technique I know comes from *pranayama yoga.* This technique is fourfold breathing. (Some people use other counts, like six in and six out, or nine in and six out.) Fourfold breathing even works by itself as a kind of wordless meditation and is especially useful for lowering blood pressure when we're angry, anxious, or frustrated.[6]

Here's how. Breathe through your nose.

1. To a measured count of 4 (approximately one second per count), inhale. Inhale for the *whole count.* Don't stop inhaling at 2 or 3.
2. To the same measured count of 4, hold your breath.
3. To the same measured count of 4, exhale. Again, exhale for the *whole count.* Measure out your breath so it comes out even.
4. To the same measured count of 4, hold no breath.

Repeat this cycle three more times, for a total of four fourfold breathing cycles, then return to normal breathing.

No matter what—fourfold breathe. You can do it anywhere, whether you're alone or in a group. Breathe when you have stage fright before an interview, a presentation, or a test. Breathe when you're afraid. Breathe when you want to increase your self-confidence. Breathe when you're embarrassed, sad, bored, or angry. Breathe when you can't sleep. If there is a panacea on earth, I believe that fourfold breathing is it.

Deep, Easy Breathing

Whereas fourfold breathing energizes and relaxes us simultaneously, deep, easy breathing is strictly for physical relaxation. When the body is relaxed and running on automatic, the mind is free to work more creatively.

Deep, easy breathing is exactly what it sounds like. Breathing through your nose, take a deep breath that fills your lungs but does not make you hyperventilate. Don't strain to take in air. Use your diaphragm and fill your lungs from the bottom to the top. Hold this breath for a second or two or three, then exhale with the simple ease of a sigh. Do this two or three more times, then return to normal breathing. You'll probably find yourself afloat in alpha brainwaves.

Inductions

Many people prefer to be guided in a detailed introduction into a meditative state. This guidance is called an induction. To save time and space in this book, I have not written a new induction for every meditation. If you prefer to use an induction, however, two follow. You can memorize or tape record them and go directly from the induction to the meditation of your choice.

Moving Through the Rainbow

Take a deep, easy breath and see and feel yourself surrounded by a beautiful red light. Red is the color of life itself. Red is the color of strength, of will, of groundedness. Enjoy this red light and feel it moving throughout your body, helping you relax.

Pause

Now see and feel yourself surrounded by a brilliant orange light. Orange is the color of solar energy and emotions. Orange is the color of sexual energy, appetites, and social abilities. We need the energy of orange in our lives. Feel this orange light permeate every cell of your body as your body relaxes and your mind becomes more alert and creative.

Pause

Take another deep, easy breath and see and feel yourself surrounded by a beautiful, cheerful yellow light. Yellow brings intellectual energy and learning to our lives. It brings personal power and self-confidence. As this yellow light flows throughout your body, you feel more relaxed and your mind becomes more alert and creative.

Pause

Take another deep, easy breath and see and feel yourself surrounded by a beautiful green light, the green of fine emeralds and fresh spring grass. Green symbolizes love and empathy and healing. It symbolizes abundance and the intelligence of love. As this green light floods every cell of your body, your body continues to relax and your mind continues to become more alert and creative. Feel this green light soaking through your body, bringing its loving, healing, abundant energy into your life.

Pause

Now see and feel yourself surrounded by a beautiful blue light, the blue of a cloudless spring sky. Blue is the color of communication, speech, artistry, and creativity. It is the color of loyal sincerity. These are qualities that enhance our lives. Feel this blue light filling every cell of your body as your body continues to relax and your mind continues to become more alert and creative.

Finally, see and feel yourself surrounded by a beautiful, shining purple light. Purple is the color of transcendence, meditation, power, and influence. It's the color of royalty, nowadays royalty of the spirit. As this purple light floods through and around and into every cell of your body, your body is now fully relaxed and your mind is now fully alert and creative. You feel better than you have ever felt before.

Mystical Solar System

Take a few deep, easy breaths and imagine that you have traveled to a mystical solar system whose planets you will visit one by one.

Imagine first that you are standing on the planet Venus. Venus is an emerald green planet, and you feel her energy pouring into you. Her energy is the energy of love, pleasure, harmony, and nature. Feel the energy of earthly love flowing into your body as your body becomes more relaxed and your mind becomes more alert and creative. Take another deep, easy breath.

Pause

Now imagine yourself standing on the planet Mars, the red planet. Mars is filled with strong energy: assertiveness, passion, fortitude, individuality. Feel this strong energy pulsing around and through you as your body becomes more relaxed and your mind becomes more creative. Feel the strength of this planet become part of you. Take another deep, easy breath.

Pause

Now imagine yourself standing on a giant, deep purple planet. This is Jupiter, whose energy promotes justice, enthusiasm, optimism, and expansion. Feel this energy of growth and expansion surround you, permeating every cell of your body as your body becomes more relaxed and your mind continues to become more alert and creative.

Pause

Next imagine yourself standing on another giant planet, this one as black and quiet as the deepest cave. This planet is Saturn, whose energy gives you your sense of duty and responsibility. Saturn gives you discipline and a knowledge of limits. Feel this Saturnian energy, which provides a necessary balance to Jupiter's energy. Let it flow into your mind and body as your body relaxes still more and your mind becomes still more alert and creative.

Pause

Imagine yourself on an indigo planet now, a planet whose surface is a deep blue-purple, almost black. This is Uranus,† whose energy pushes you to evolve and awaken to your true freedom. Uranian energy drives you to the unexpected events of life. This is the energy of the visionary, the one who sees afar and ahead. Feel this wonder-filled energy pulsing through your body. Feel it fill you as your body becomes more relaxed and your mind becomes more alert and creative.

Pause

Finally, imagine yourself on the planet Neptune, an electric-blue planet whose energy brings the ability to visualize and be creative. Neptune's energy helps you dissolve the old and imagine the new. It is the

† Pronounced YUR-uh-nuss.

energy of divine love and cosmic creativity. Feel Neptune's envelope and inspire you, as you know that your body is fully relaxed now and your mind is fully alert and creative.

Safety

Here is a safety paragraph with an intent you should internalize early on. Even if you're in the most secure, most private space you can find, it's good to program your mind to know the following.

Take a deep easy breath and know that your body will become very relaxed and your mind will become alert and creative. Know that you are in no one's power but your own and that no one will ask you to do anything that might embarrass you. Know also that if something were to demand your attention, you could return from the meditative alpha state to the alert beta state. You could open your eyes, get up, and take prompt action. No outside noises will disturb you. You are safe. You are beloved.

Returning to Normal Consciousness

It is also useful to have a regular formula to return to normal consciousness with. I have found counting backwards most helpful and have used the following many times:

I'm going to count backwards from 10 to 1. With each number you will come closer to normal consciousness. You will remember as much as you need to remember, either consciously and immediately or something will pop into your mind when you need it. Please be sure not to open your eyes or speak until the count is finished. You don't want to disturb anyone.

Ready? With each number, you will come closer to everyday awareness.

10, you're starting to return to the mundane world. 9 . . . 8 . . . 7, you're getting closer to ordinary consciousness. Remember—don't open your eyes or speak yet.

6 . . . 5 . . . 4, you're almost back.

3, you can move your fingers and toes now. Wiggle your fingers and toes.

2, you're ready to be back. Stretch if you want to.

1, you're back! Stretch again and open your eyes when you're ready. You have returned to ordinary awareness.

Grounding Yourself

As soon after meditating as it's convenient to do so, ground yourself. If you want to sleep tonight, you *must* ground yourself. You must release the energy you've been working with and stop its cycling and recycling through your brain and body.

One way to do this is to kneel or sit on the floor and put your hands palm-down beside you. Visualize the excess energy flowing through your body and out through your feet and hands. Let the excess energy drain out through the base of your spine and into the earth. If you've had an especially profound and far-out meditation and are still floating, it might also be helpful to have someone you trust brush your aura. That is, ask a friend to hold her hands or a feather an inch or two from your body and tune in to your personal energy field, or aura. Then she should gently and lightly sweep her hands or the feather through your aura to ground its excess energy. This aura brushing should be downward and focus especially around the stomach and solar plexus.

After you've let the excess energy ground itself in the earth, eat earthy food. I find saltines to be the best things to eat because they're bland, salty, and simple. They're comfort food. Also good are corn chips, pretzels, potatoes (mashed, baked, potato chips), and bread. You don't need to eat much, but these earthy, "peasant" foods work very effectively to get you down to earth.

A note to vegetarians: fruits and salads will not ground you. Eat solid food!

Endnotes

1. Except for the definition to follow from the *Oxford English Dictionary*, all definitions and etymologies are taken from the *American Heritage Dictionary of the English Language*.

2. John Welwood, ed., *Ordinary Magic* (Boston: Shambhala, 1992), p. xviii.

3. See my *Woman's Book of Rituals and Celebrations* (San Rafael, CA: New World Library, 1995), Part I.

4. Dion Fortune, *The Esoteric Orders and Their Work* (St. Paul: Llewellyn Publications, 1978; originally written in 1928), p. 138.

5. See the Resources at the end of the book for more information.

6. My friend Anna Cassidy, a psychic and spiritual counselor, says we can blow bubbles. As we dip the bubble wand into the soap, we are inhaling. We are forced to exhale slowly as we blow the bubbles. Plus, she adds, the bubbles bring so much joy to other people.

2
Altars and Rituals

Athene

Although this is not a book of rituals, I know that some of us like to set up an altar and do an occasional ritual. An altar can bring a wonderful point of focus to a meditation; a ritual can give it a magical framework. Together, they place your meditation within a devotional structure.

If you have never built an altar, why not try it now? If, like me, your home is full of altars, maybe you can squeeze another one in for a Goddess meditation. If you're nervous about going to a public ritual or can't seem to get invited to an "outer court" ritual, you can do a simple ritual at home, all by yourself. Even if you're not sure you want to—even if you prefer "pure" meditation—I believe that an altar and a ritual are worth trying at least once.

Altars

An altar you build for a goddess can be simply beautiful—both simple and beautiful. The following paragraphs describe how to create an altar. But don't copy what I have done. Use my ideas for inspiration and create your own unique altar.

Suppose, for example, we want to set up an altar to Athene, one of the goddesses to whom I am devoted. When we look Her up, we learn that She's the Greek goddess after whom the city of Athens was named. Although the original Athene was possibly Black African, or at least Egyptian,[1] the Goddess with whom we are most familiar is the European warrior maiden whose statues were made by Greek and Roman sculptors. The most famous story about Athene is that She was born, full-grown and armed for war, from the head of Her father, Zeus. The archetype She represents to us today, therefore, is an activist, a warrior goddess who is comfortable in the world and work of men.[2] Early on, however, She had been a domestic goddess, symbolized by the "implements of domestic crafts: the spindle, the pot, and the loom."[3] Other famous stories about Athene relate Her comradeship with Odysseus (She protected this cunning scoundrel and led him home from Troy); Her contest with Poseidon over possession of Athens (as the producer of an olive tree, She won); Her supposed punishment of Arachne for the latter's weaving a cloth that illustrated Olympian love affairs (after Arachne hanged herself, Athene turned the princess into a spider); and Her guidance of Perseus as he slew Medusa (She received and thereafter wore the Gorgon's snake-haired head). It's also important to remember that every midsummer in ancient Greece, Athene's statue was taken out of the Acropolis, carried in procession to the sea, washed, and dressed in a newly woven robe. Finally, the Greeks associated the owl and the oak with Athene.

When we build our altar to Athene, therefore, we consider all of these associations and decide which ones and how much we want to include. When I created a small altar to Athene a few years ago, I placed my nine-inch golden reproduction of the statue by Phidias in the center. Next, I added a small clay snake and a small owl carved of rhodocrosite. Then, because She's the goddess of wisdom and, by extension, writing, I added a fountain pen.

That's one possibility. Someone else I know found a photo of the goddess in a magazine, mounted it on a piece of yellow posterboard beside an owl feather and the Queen of Swords from an old Tarot deck, laminated it, and then hung it on her loom, framed by a skein of fantastic yarn. Another woman found a little porcelain statue of Athene, which she kept near her potter's wheel. She brought fresh flowers to the goddess every few days.

Pick the goddess you want to honor or petition with your meditation, do some research to find out what ideas, animals, or objects are associated with Her, and build your own altar. In addition, you can set crystals, fresh flowers, and candles on your altar.

Where will you place your beautiful altar? How about a single shelf in your bedroom, the top of a bookcase or dresser, or an end table or TV tray? I've put altars on hanging shelves, one of them glass (3"x8") mounted on wrought iron brackets. After I got my computer, I put an altar on my old typing table for a while. I've put altars on old orange crates, on my dining room table, on my mother's cedar chest, on the bottom shelf of my television stand. I have friends who have put altars in an empty fireplace, on the mantel above the fireplace, in a little kitchen-window greenhouse (and surrounded the opening with tiny Christmas tree lights), on top of a filing cabinet, even on a narrow shelf above the toilet.

Yes, you can put an altar *anywhere*. If you think the other people who live with you might disapprove of an altar to a goddess, choose an inconspicuous shelf, perhaps in your bedroom or workroom. Find a postcard that shows a goddess or a woman who reminds you of one. One of my friends found pictures of goddesses in expensive art books, made colored photocopies of them, mounted them on cardboard, and laminated them. You can do the same. Then bring Her a fresh flower in a simple vase, which you set on one of your grandmother's doilies. That can be enough.

Your altar is limited only by your imagination, which is limitless.

The meditations in chapter 3 are dedicated to the Great Goddess, the Eldest One who has ten thousand names and no name. You may wish to begin by building a Great Goddess altar. To represent Her, I use a reproduction of the so-called Venus of Willendorf, now generally referred to as the Great Mother of Willendorf or the Willendorf Goddess.[4] She is the oldest sculpture of a human figure on earth (approximately 35,000 years old) and about four inches tall. She is thus the perfect size to hold in your hand as you meditate. For your Great Goddess altar, I suggest a Willendorf Goddess and fresh flowers. You can also use anything else that reminds you of the ancient Great Goddess. Objects from nature are especially appropriate: a rock with a natural cleft in it or a rock you paint spirals on, a forked twig or piece of driftwood, a cowrie or conch shell, an apple sliced in half horizontally to show the pentacle of seeds . . . the list is endless.[5]

If you're feeling more ambitious, you can build a shrine[6] to your goddess. Perhaps you're familiar with shrines for saints in Roman Catholic churches. Shrines are actually much older than the standard-brand churches admit, however, and Neo-Pagans are reclaiming them. A shrine is generally larger than an altar, a more dramatic environment. The goddess (or god) is often ritually dressed or decorated (I've given several of my bracelets to my goddesses, who wear them as necklaces), and offerings are generally made to the deity—fresh flowers, *milagros*[7] to represent what

ɔddess or want to give thanks for, or food (especially fresh fruit
shrine is often framed or housed (old wooden fruit crates are
and can hang on the wall. Or it may well cover an entire tabletop.
ɛ your shrine as fancifully as you wish with ribbons and lace, beads,
ɔ and crystals, pictures and photos, drawings you and your children
ɔund objects, and (again) anything else you can think of. A shrine is a
ɔication, a work of love, and a work of art.

Ritual

A ritual is a repeatable and often-repeated action that has a specific meaning and an
intention. Ritual is often dramatic, often retells an old story,[8] and can include
singing or chanting, dancing, drumming, mime, and other activities such as planting seeds, burning small pieces of paper upon which wishes or spells have been
written, or hands-on healing. Both the actions and the words serve to put the people doing the ritual into an altered state of consciousness. This altered state gets us
in touch with the invisible powers with whom we work. The invisible powers may
be intrinsic (our subconscious, our creativity) or extrinsic (goddesses, angels, elemental spirits, and others).

Ritual is both a process and procedure. Generally speaking, a ritual follows these
seven steps:

1. Purification of the participants and the space to be used.
2. Casting (closing) the circle within which the magic work is done
   by invoking the powers, entities, or deities of the four directions
   and the center.
3. Stating the intention or purpose of the ritual.
4. Guided trance work, visualization, or meditation to focus the ritual
   intention in the minds of the people and the universe.
5. Raising power/energy by drumming, chanting, visualization, or some
   other technique.
6. Grounding the power/energy.
7. Opening the circle, after which the participants either go home or hang
   out together as long as they like.

It is possible to use any of the meditations in this book in ritual. The title of
each meditation identifies its intention. If you're familiar with ritual-making, create
a ritual to go around your meditation; if not, a brief generic ritual follows. You can
plug your chosen goddess and meditation into this generic ritual and use it as a
template upon which to create your own rituals. If you're doing this ritual alone,
read all the parts yourself, and be sure to read aloud so your unconscious can listen
to your words. If you're doing the ritual with a group, assign the parts ahead of

time so it flows as smoothly as possible. Do not worry, however, if something goes wrong. The Goddess does have a sense of humor; She is seldom offended by the dumb things we mortals do.

Unlike the hierarchical arrangements we find in the standard-brand churches, rituals generally take place in circles. If you have created an altar, place it on a low table in the center of the circle or at the north side. Decorate it beautifully. If you're working with a group, let everyone present decorate the altar with fresh flowers, crystals and stones, goddesses, and other treasures. Many times, people like to place their jewelry on the altar; this blesses both the altar and the jewelry.

It is important to clarify your intention ahead of time so that you can state it clearly and in positive terms. You need to state it as simply and directly as you can, without negatives. That is, say, *I am brave* instead of *I feel no fear.* This same principle is used in stating affirmations.

Be sure to give yourself an hour of uninterrupted private time in a private place. Turn off the phone and the TV and lock the door. Announce ahead of time that no one is to bother you; while you are unavailable, they must solve their own problems.

Decide ahead of time whether you're going to use an induction and the countdown return or only the meditation. Decide ahead of time if one of the participants will read the induction, meditation, and return. Understand that that person will not be able to meditate. A better decision might be to tape record the induction, meditation, and return, leaving adequate quiet time on the tape.

Music enhances a ritual wonderfully. There are numerous recordings of chants,[9] and you might also find classical music or light jazz to be appropriate.

It can be helpful to take a ritual bath before a ritual and dress in clean, comfortable clothing. A ritual bath usually involves herbs in the bathwater (wrap the herbs in cheesecloth or you'll have a mess) and is done by candlelight. The idea is to make yourself both physically and emotionally clean.

A Generic Ritual

Note that this is not a complete and polished ritual but an outline designed for purposes of illustrating how a ritual goes. Although you can fill in the blanks and have a perfectly good ritual, it's really just a frame upon which you can build to create a ritual that is truly yours. Both stage directions and spoken words are included.

Again, take some time *before* you begin the ritual to clarify your intention. If you feel unsure of yourself, write it down so you can read it aloud during the ritual without forgetting anything important.

Begin the ritual with purification. One nice way to do this is to take your kitchen broom and sweep a circle on the floor where the ritual is to take place. For a largish group, the circle may be nine feet in diameter, but if you are working alone or with two or three friends, or if your room will not accommodate such a large circle, make it whatever size works for you and be sure to sweep in a clockwise direction. If you're on carpeting, sweep an inch above the carpet; what you're sweeping is energy, not dirt.

You can also use incense, sage, a smudge stick,[10] a flower, or a feather to purify your space and the people with you. Moving clockwise around the circle, use the incense or flower or feather to sweep the energy into order. If you're doing this ritual alone, use the tool to demarcate the circle. If you're working with a group, use the tool to brush the aura of each person standing or sitting in the circle. If you want words to say during purification, say something like this:

> **I use this sacred *(name of tool)* to cleanse and purify my circle. May this space be blessed for the work to be done here and may my *[our]* working be blessed.**

To cast the circle, invoke (call) the powers of the four directions: east, south, west, and north.[11] Stand in the north or in the center or walk clockwise to face each direction, starting in the east.[12] If you're working with a group, let someone sitting or standing in each direction speak the invocation for that direction. Please add your own words as you are inspired to do so.

Facing the east, say:

> **Powers of the East, Goddesses of Elemental Air, I call you into this magical circle. Holy Powers, please be with me *[us]* and bring me *[us]* your magical gifts of intelligence, intuition, and discernment. Welcome.**

Visualize goddesses or angels or other beings entering your space or a breeze blowing clockwise around the circle. Facing the south, say:

> **Powers of the South, Goddesses of Elemental Fire, I call you into this magical circle. Holy Powers, please be with me *[us]* and bring me *[us]* your magical gifts of passion, inspiration, creativity, and "fire in the belly." Welcome.**

Visualize goddesses or angels or other beings entering your space or magical flames leaping around the circle. Facing the west, say:

> **Powers of the West, Goddesses of Elemental Water, I call you into this magical circle. Holy Powers, please be with me *[us]* and bring me *[us]* your magical gifts of love, spirit, and steadfastness. Welcome.**

Visualize goddesses or angels or other beings entering your space or waves or a stream of water washing around the circle. Facing the north, say:

Powers of the North, Goddesses of Elemental Earth, I call you into this magical circle. Holy Powers, please be with me *[us]* and bring me *[us]* your magical gifts of groundedness, roots and growth and blooming, and manifestation. Welcome.

Visualize goddesses or angels or other beings entering your space or earthworks, trees, or plants growing up to surround the circle.

Now, standing in the center (unless that's where your altar is) or in the north, invoke the goddess for your meditation. You can raise your arms, hold flowers or some other magical tool, or simply stand as you speak. Although you can use the following invocation, it is better if you speak from your heart. Great rhetoric and drama are not necessary; sincerity is.

Blessed *name*, I *[we]* call you to my *[our]* circle. Beautiful name, you are strong, wise, and compassionate. Great Goddess, I *[we]* honor You always and ask for Your help in my *[our]* meditation today *[tonight]*.

Declare your intention as part of this invocation. State it in present tense with no negative words. Here are two examples. The first might be for the Wonder Woman meditation (see "Light Work," chapter 4):

My intention is to find and honor my strength and courage. Inspired by Your voice and led by Your hand, I am strong and brave. I can endure these hard times in my life and learn what I must learn from them.

The second example might be for the meditation to the Fates (see "Dark Work," chapter 5):

My intention is to sever all bonds and connections between me and my former friend *name* and to release him *[her]* to his *[her]* own karma. I am free from all entanglements with this person, past, present, and future.

If you're doing the ritual alone, you might sit comfortably before your altar and pull the energy, or let it flow, from the Goddess' heart to your heart.

When you feel the presence of the energy (or the Goddess), ask everyone to get comfortable. If one of the participants has agreed to read the induction, meditation, and return, let her begin now. If you're using a tape, turn on the tape recorder now.

Because this is a meditative ritual, you should raise quiet energy. Energy doesn't have to make you sweat, it doesn't have to raise the roof. Raised energy can be sweet and gentle. If you dance, do only gentle movement. If you drum, don't get carried away. Choose a simple beat that is slower than your heartbeat. If you chant, chant softly. A more effective technique might be visualization. See the energy flowing in a web around and through your circle. You might even visualize the energy radiating out from the center altar like the spokes of a wheel. If this is a group ritual, all can join hands and feel the energy moving from person to person. Raising the energy allows everyone to internalize the meditation.

Ground the energy using one of the techniques given in chapter 2. Sometimes "cakes and ale" are served at this time. "Cakes and ale" (a term from Gardnerian Wicca) means light refreshment, today as often as not cookies and wine or juice. (Always have a non-alcoholic beverage available for those who cannot or do not drink alcohol.)

After the energy has been grounded and everyone is back, eyes open and paying attention, ask if anyone wants to share what they have experienced in their meditation. You can go around the circle or let people speak up when they feel able to do so. Never force anyone to share, however. Some things are too personal to be spoken aloud.

It is good to honor the Goddess and the earth at this time. Everyone saves a bite of cookie or cake and a little bit of wine or juice to return to Her. You do this by collecting the food in a napkin and the liquid in a special glass. After the ritual, take them outdoors. Pour the liquid on the grass or near a flower and leave the food for whatever critter comes to eat it.

Finally, open the circle, beginning in the north and moving through west and south and back to east. Opening the circle is releasing the energy and thanking everyone present, both visible and invisible. Here are two examples of how to open the circle:

A. Standing in the center, say:

> I *[we]* give thanks to all present. Goddesses, gods, angels, humans, fairies, elemental powers and beings, animal companions—I *[we]* thank you for sharing your energy and bringing your holy gifts to me *[us]*. Leave this space if you must or stay if you will. Our circle is open but unbroken. Merry meet, merry part, and merry meet again.[13]

B. Standing in the north, say:

> Goddesses and other powers of the north, I *[we]* thank you for being present in this circle. Go if you must or stay if you will.

Standing in the west, say

> Goddesses and other powers of the west, I *[we]* thank you for being present in this circle. Go if you must or stay if you will.

Standing in the south, say:

Goddesses and other powers of the south, I *[we]* thank you for being present in this circle. Go if you must or stay if you will.

Standing in the east, say:

Goddesses and other powers of the east, I *[we]* thank you for being present in this circle. Go if you must or stay if you will.

Standing in the center, say:

Our circle is open but unbroken. Merry meet, merry part, and merry meet again.

Most people who do rituals now adjourn to the kitchen for refreshments and impressive conversation (i.e., to find out who knows which Important People and who knows more Esoteric Stuff than someone else; someone is bound to be impressed). Sometimes it's potluck—real food—and sometimes it's snacks. Be sure that earth foods like breads, potatoes, or corn chips are included in case anyone needs further grounding.

If you keep a journal, record your meditation as soon as you can conveniently do so. Write down what you saw, heard, smelled, or otherwise sensed, how or what you felt before and after, any other details that you don't want to forget.

It's often useful, in fact, to have notes on your rituals and meditations. If you want to do the same one again, your notes will tell you how the altar was set up, how the intention was stated, what goddesses were invoked and what invocations were used, how the energy was raised and grounded. When such notes are systematically made, the journal becomes a Book of Shadows, which is the "traditional" term for a secret book that also contains spells and charms.

Endnotes

1. See Martin Bernal, *Black Athena* (New Brunswick, NJ: Rutgers University Press, 1987), for a discussion of racism in classical studies.
2. See Jennifer Barker Woolger and Roger J. Woolger, *The Goddess Within* (New York: Fawcett, 1987), chapter 2; and Jean Shinoda Bolen, M.D., *Goddesses in Everywoman* (New York: Harper and Row, 1984), chapter 5.
3. Patricia Monaghan, *The New Book of Goddesses and Heroines* (St. Paul: Llewellyn, 1997), pp. 41–42.
4. You can purchase exquisite reproductions from Star River or JBL Statues. Ordering information is given in the back of the book. You can also buy goddess figures in metaphysical bookstores and museum gift shops, and you'd be surprised what you can find in thrift shops and garage sales.

5. For inspiring examples of present-day Goddess art, see Gloria Orenstein, *The Reflowering of the Goddess* (Elmsford, NJ: Pergamon, 1990). You can adapt some of the ideas shown in this book.

6. For more information, and photos, see Dan and Pauline Campanelli, *Circles, Groves and Sanctuaries* (St. Paul: Llewellyn, 1992), chapter 2. Other chapters discuss and illustrate indoor and outdoor altars and other sacred spaces.

7. *Milagros* ("miracles") are silver charms from Mexico. They represent body parts (arms, legs, torsos) healed or in need of healing, animals, and other symbols, like suns and moons.

8. You may remember the saying that if it's "my belief," it's religion, whereas if it's "your belief," it's myth. Thus I prefer to say "story" in a context like this.

9. See Resources.

10. To me, a chronic asthmatic, smoking incense and herbs—especially sage—are air pollution. Please be aware of the health and feelings of other people when you use something that smokes.

11. The order of elemental powers given below is the standard Gardnerian order. You can assign the elemental powers to other directions. My preference, for example, is East = Fire, South = Water, West = Air, North = Earth. Other people use other systems. See my *Rituals and Celebrations*, chapter 5, for more information.

12. Stand and move if you're working with a group. If you're alone, you can remain seated.

13. This is a common "traditional" benediction. It's nice for everyone to hold hands and say it together. It can also be sung. The tune is on *Ancient Mother*, by Robert Gass and *On Wings of Song* (see Resources).

3
Great Goddess Meditations

Cybele

I've seen a wonderful green T-shirt that proclaims, *I Worship the Ground I Walk On.* If that's not an annunciation of the Great Goddess, I don't know what is.

She is our Primal Mother, the Eldest One whom our earliest ancestors, no matter where we came from, honored and worshipped. When I try to visualize this most ancient Great Goddess, the image I see is the Willendorf Goddess (Figure 1, page 30).

Here is an ocher-covered female figure with gigantic breasts, belly, and hips, but no face, and still she's the perfect size to hold in your hand while you meditate. You can run your fingers over her generous curves, feel her abundance.

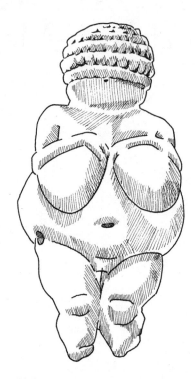

Figure 1. **The Willendorf Goddess.**

Before all other goddesses, this little Mother was with us. Before all other goddess figures, this is the one to have.

In the book that accompanies her wonderful *Amulets of the Goddess*, Nancy Blair writes that the Willendorf Goddess is the "divine Creatrix"

> whose mystery resonated deeply in the hearts, minds and magic of early peoples. The feet of most of these early Goddess sculptures are pointed, possibly to stick in the earth—establishing a sense of place where cosmic forces could be generated, focused and grounded. A Divine Female presence was the core of religious, artistic, psycho-sexual, and ceremonial expression for possibly the first 200,000 years of human life![1]

In a series of novels and short stories that I'm working on from time to time, I call this primal goddess Great Mother Earth. The heroine of one of the novels repeats the stories her grandmother told her:

> She told me every story our people knew, every old story of Great Mother Earth and Her First Daughters. She told me how the Great Mother carried the egg of the universe in Her great womb, how that egg cracked open one day and its yolk became the spinning sun. How the Great Mother touched

Herself with desire and bore the earth and all the peoples on it. How She formed and fed Her creatures with Her own blood and milk and saliva. How She still sleeps under the mountains and behind the stars and upon the elements. How She dreams the ways of the world, dream-spinning the world's holy universal web.

Although this is a cosmology I invented, the goddess I beheld in my imagination was the Willendorf Goddess. I was inspired by the ovular works in feminist spirituality—books by Merlin Stone, Monica Sjoo and Barbara Mor, and others. I was inspired even more by the work of Marija Gimbutas, whose great spirit has led so many of us to think and dream and write and draw and bring the Goddess back to modern civilization.[2]

Under the heading "Mother Creator, Great Goddesses," Monaghan lists ninety-five goddesses. Sampling her list, we find Aditi, Cerridwen, Danu, Eve, Frigg, Ganga, Isis, Madder-Akka, Obatallah, Omecihuatl, Sedna, Waramurungundji, and White Buffalo Woman.[3] Great Goddesses come from every continent and probably every culture. For your altar and your meditation, you can choose a Willendorf Goddess, one of these goddesses, or any of the remaining eighty-two listed by Monaghan. Or perhaps you'll want to buy red clay and create your own Creatrix.

The issues addressed in the following meditations are the big ones in our lives. I believe that they are, or should be, the core values[4] by which we live our lives on the planet. I believe that they're also the lessons we've come here to learn.

1. Love
2. Protection
3. Gratitude
4. Trust
5. Community
6. Creativity
7. Spirituality
8. Wisdom
9. Priestess Power

Notice that there are nine values here. As three times three, nine is one of the most magical of numbers. It's the number of the Muses. Numerologically, nine signifies the end of a cycle and is the number of selflessness, compassion, wisdom, and dedication to others. Like the Major Arcana of the Tarot, these nine values describe the path we who practice the presence of the Goddess are walking. We begin with three basic, inward values, values of nurturance and comfort. We might call these three the values of the young one, the Maiden. Next we grow up and move outward into our community, our work, and the world. We might call the second triad of values the values of the Mother. Finally, we move into the spiritual realm, and the last three values we might call the values of the Crone. In many traditional settings, when people completed their earthly work of raising a family and working their work, they became elders who shared the experience of their lives with their people and were teachers, counselors, and priestesses or priests for the tribe as a whole.

As I created each Great Goddess meditation, I struggled to find images and words that worked for me. As I wrote and meditated and rewrote, as I tried each meditation out while I was lying in bed at night, I found that bit by bit, one day at a time, *something*—Someone?—began to work on me. As I continue to meditate in the presence of the Great Goddess, I feel my life getting better.

I hope these meditations work for you, too. I hope they help you along your path through your life.

Remember, you can do these meditations with or without an altar. You can do them as simple morning meditations or weave them into rituals with drumming and dancing under the full moon. You can meditate indoors, in your special room or sitting on your coziest chair, or outdoors in your garden or sitting under a friendly tree. You can do these meditations by yourself or with a group.

My intention is for us to do them together, which explains my use of the first person plural pronouns. We may not be meeting in person or at precisely the same time by the clock, but be sure of it: we *are* meditating together in Her presence and in Her time.

Love

Sit quietly, either with your altar or elsewhere, indoors or outdoors, in a place that makes you feel comfortable and peaceful. Before you close your eyes, look around. What is it about this space that brings comfort and peace to your spirit? As you ponder answers to this question, take a few deep, easy breaths and let your eyes begin to gradually close. Let your body become relaxed.

Pause

Let us focus on the qualities of our space that make us feel comfortable and peaceful. We don't have to name them yet. We can simply *feel them*. Feel the comfort. Feel the peace around us. This is sacred space. Let the eyes of our imagination begin to see both the tangible and intangible things that create comfort and peace. Let's explore this sacred space with our internal senses.

What is here? What makes our space sacred? Is it the altar? The polished stones, the sea shells, the fresh flowers? Perhaps, like me, you have wonderful original art on your walls, nothing famous, but pieces your friends did, pieces you found at a fair and fell in love with, pieces you yourself created. How does art make sacred space? Whenever I meditate or do a ritual at home, my two cats come to help. How do our furred friends make our space more sacred? The room where I write is sacred space to me; is your workspace sacred?

Pause

Let us begin to understand what sacred space is. We look around and, even in the city, see space that looks empty. We look up into the sky and see space that looks empty. Scientists are telling us that the atom is perhaps ninety percent empty space, which means that, as we are composed of atoms, we're mostly empty space. Twenty-odd years ago, Itzhak Bentov wrote:

> It seems that the real reality—the microreality, that which underlies all our solid, good, common-sense reality—is made up . . . of vast empty space . . . .[5]

Pause

Back in the 1930s and '40s, Stewart Edward White wrote that the "unobstructed universe" is filled with consciousness, which is "the one and only reality."[6]

Space, which looks empty to our physical eyes, is filled with consciousness. Let us call that consciousness *love*. Can we agree that love is sacred? In all the space between the stars, as in all the space within the atoms within our bodies, there is love. It's infinite love. It's our Mother's love for us. It's the love that creates and protects. It's the love of unbroken and unbreakable bonds. Thus is consciousness sacred, thus is space sacred, thus are our bodies sacred, thus is the earth sacred. Thus is every space sacred space.

If we can be still now, we can feel this love touching the tops of our heads. Perhaps love emanates from our altar and the figure of Great Goddess. Perhaps it emanates from the pattern of the Great Goddess that we hold in our consciousness. Perhaps it arises from fresh flowers and other treasures on our altars. Feel the love of the Great Goddess that comes from nowhere and everywhere—that comes from Her consciousness—and surrounds us.

Pause

We can feel the love of the Great Goddess touching the crown of our head, our third eye, our eyes, our nose and mouth. Perhaps love comes from the air around us. Perhaps it rises in our auras, but remember, we are always moving within the aura of the Great Goddess.

Let us feel the love of the Great Goddess as it flows into our throats, into our chests, our bellies. Feel it streaming down each arm, into our hands, even into our fingernails. Her love is filling all the spaces in us. It doesn't really matter where we believe the love of the Great Goddess comes from. It originates in Her, as all things originate in Her. It holds every one of us lightly in its embrace.

We can feel Her love moving through our lower body, our sexual organs, down our thighs, knees, down to our toes. There is no part of us that is not saturated by the love of the Great Goddess, no space in us that is empty. Feel Her love under your feet as I feel it under mine, and know that the infinite Mother-love of the Great Goddess supports us every day, in every way.

Pause

You are loved. I am loved. You are Her best-beloved child. I am Her best-beloved child. We are Her most precious children, all of us. Wherever we are, we are in sacred space because there She is too.

Stay with that realization as long as you want to. After you return to normal awareness, keep it with you. Become aware of manifestations of Her love in the everyday world where we work and play and have our being. Become mindful that all space is sacred space.

Protection

Sit quietly and take a few deep, easy breaths. Did you have a blanket when you were a toddler? Close your eyes, take another deep, easy breath. What did that blanket look like? What color was it? Did it have a satin edge that you could rub against your cheek at night to lull you into sleep? Take another deep, easy breath. Did you drag your blanket along everywhere you went during the day? How did you feel when your mother insisted on washing it? How long did your precious blanket survive? Or do you still have it, folded carefully and put away somewhere safe?

In our imaginations, let us bring our security blankets out of those boxes in the back of the closet. Unfold your blanket. Pet it. Feel the fibers, the weave. Find the old familiar stains, the rips, the places where it started to fall apart twenty or more years ago. Hold your security blanket to your heart and remember how safe you always felt when you had that blanket. I felt the same way with my blanket.

Let's put our security blankets around our shoulders. Miraculously, they easily expand so that we can be wrapped all around. You are wrapped in your blanket, I in mine. Or maybe it's the same blanket, the same security.

Pause

We are protected. This childhood blanket is the armor the Great Goddess has given us. Though its physical form may be old and raggedy and ripped in places, it is impregnable. Nothing can touch us when we are wrapped in our security blanket.

Here is the blanket the Great Goddess has made for us.[7] She pastured Her sacred sheep in great green fields and tended each ewe and lamb and ram. She led them into the fold each night and out to Her fresh fields each dawn. When the year turned to spring, She sheared Her precious sheep, and then She sorted and washed and carded the pure white wool.

Pause

She spun the thread with Her own fingers, and every turn of Her golden spinning wheel added the strength of spider webs to the thread

She spun. She wove this blanket for you and for me with warp threads colored by the warm west wind and the rich black earth and with woof threads colored by singing fire and deep, still waters.

Pause

The Great Goddess cut and stitched our blanket with the tools of The Fates, and then She bound the edges with the satin of Her own beauty. And at last She decorated our blanket with the nobility of cats, the joy of hummingbirds, and the determination of turtles. Each of us is wrapped in the security of the blanket the Great Goddess has made for us.

No matter what happens to us—we've got our blanket. We can wrap ourselves up, we can wodge it up into a pillow and cradle our aching heads. We can make our blanket into a tent and crawl inside, or we can tie the ends and wear it as a cape as we transform ourselves into super-heras and fly above any villain.

Pause

The Great Goddess has made a security blanket for each of us. She has given us Her great protection. It's true. No matter what—we are protected. She protects you and me and all Her children.

Sometimes it is necessary for us to walk through shadowed valleys. Sometimes we must go alone into lions' dens and pits of vipers. We must go into the worlds where envy and competition prowl, where cut-throat people lurk. We must go where the Wild Things hunt.

We can take our blankets with us. Wrapped in the blanket the Great Goddess has made for us, we can go anywhere. Let us wrap ourselves in the elemental powers the Great Goddess has woven into our blankets, knowing that we are protected. Let us remember that wherever we go She is there to protect us.

When you come back to ordinary consciousness, try to find your "real" blanket. Does it look any different now?

Gratitude

Before you sit down to meditate, find a penny,[8] preferably a bright, shiny one. Hold it in your left hand during this meditation.

Close your eyes, relax, and take a few deep, easy breaths. As you sink into a relaxed state, let penny ideas noodle through your mind. "Penny wise and pound foolish." That optimistic old song, "Pennies From Heaven." "Penny plain and tuppence coloured." "A penny for your thoughts." A bittersweet verse by Conrad Aiken:

> All lovely things will have an ending,
> All lovely things will fade and die,
> And youth, that now so bravely spending,
> Will beg a penny by and by.[9]

Pause

A penny used to be worth something. Nowadays, most people don't even bother to pick one up when they see it on the sidewalk. Take another deep, easy breath, and in your imagination find yourself walking along a familiar street.

Glance down. There's a penny! We can pick it up and hold it in our hand. Be penny wise and give thanks. Let us consider this nearly insignificant coin, a coin that doesn't buy much anymore. This little copper coin is a special gift from the Great Goddess just to you, just to me. Give thanks.

We need to be penny wise and consider the wisdom of the penny. It knows it's small, and so it is humble. It also knows its power, however, and it knows that in one individual there is power, there is wisdom. It knows that when individuals come together, there are greater power and greater wisdom. When you and I come together, there are greater power and greater wisdom. Give thanks for this humble lesson. Let us both give thanks that we have come together again.

Do you remember the song? "Every time it rains, it rains pennies from heaven." Every time it rains, it's raining untold wealth in small blessings. This was a favorite song during the Great Depression, back in the days when a penny was a lot of money.

Pause

What is a penny from heaven today? An almost insignificant blessing. But it's the tiniest blessings that touch our hearts most indelibly. Consider the small blessings we receive. A kind word from a coworker. A friend's arm around our shoulders and his or her attention when we need it. A smile from a stranger. Something unexpectedly beautiful we glimpse for a minute or two. The cat contentedly washing her paws on the sofa beside us. We receive small blessings, and we give them, too. Give thanks to the Great Goddess for your pennies from heaven as I give thanks for mine.

Pause

"Penny plain and tuppence coloured" refers to a children's game in Victorian England. The stage sets of popular plays were re-created in miniature, like paper doll books, and children made up their own plays. Colored paper doubled the price. What does your inner child play with? Mine will play with nearly everything. I have a toy car on my altar, a wind-up crab on my desk, a Slinky in my magic chest, a glow-in-the-dark spider perched on my computer terminal. Give your child-self the gift of a penny and let that penny represent joyful things to play with—ribbons and streamers and windmills and marbles and Slinkies in all the colors of the rainbow. Let's give our child-selves Technicolor dreams and give thanks, too, to the Great Goddess that we may play.[10]

Pause

What are your thoughts worth? What are mine worth? What is the value of our dreams and daydreams? Of our reverie and reasoning? A penny for your thoughts, dreams, ideas, creativity? Now that we know what a penny is really worth, give thanks to the Great Goddess that we can think, dream, and create. Let us always keep a penny as a token of gratitude.

"All lovely things will have an ending." We understand the cycles of creation, destruction, and re-creation, of course. We understand how lovely things will fade and die. We know that the Wheel of Fortune turns and turns again. One who was king may be reborn a peasant, the peasant may be reborn a bishop, the bishop may be reborn a Witch, the Witch may be reborn a merchant, the merchant will be reborn . . . . Our lives cycle endlessly around the Wheel of Life. Let a penny represent that wheel, and let it represent the Wheel of the Year, too. Let it show all the cycles of being, and let us give thanks to the Great Goddess for our lives today and for the cycles of all our lives. Though we fade and die, we are part of Her cycling cosmos. We'll meet again.

Pause

In your imagination, look at the penny again. Feel the copper penny in your physical hand. Remember all the blessings in your life and give thanks to the Great Goddess for them.

When you return to everyday awareness, put the penny in your pocket and carry it with you to remind you to give thanks every day to the small blessings the Great Goddess rains upon Her children.

Trust

Close your eyes and take a few deep, easy breaths.

Did you ever dream of flying? Do you remember when your dream-self soared above the mundane world? Take another deep, easy breath. Do you remember how you flew? How you spread your arms and flew as effortlessly as a hawk in thermal currents above a meadow? Take another deep, easy breath and—look! We've got wings. My wings are the snow-white wings of a dove. I know someone who has stately angel's wings.

Pause

What kind of wings are yours? Did you simply grow feathers along your arms? Or have you acquired the powerful wings of an eagle, the silent wings of an owl, the elegant wings of a heron, the rapid wings of a hummingbird? Notice how strong our wings are, and how beautiful. We could fly anywhere on these invincible wings.

And now, yes, we are flying. Feel yourself rising as effortlessly as the breeze. Just feel it—we're swooping up through the air and dancing on clouds. We're zooming and gliding, we're spiraling up and down. What else can be so much fun?

Pause

And here are the birds. Some of them stare at us in surprise. How can mere people fly? But other birds swoop and glide with us, flying at our sides, perhaps speaking to us. Here's a robin, there a wild goose, and over there, a raven. Look around you again. What birds are flying beside you? With our wings came the ability to understand the language of the birds. What do they say to you? Fly beside the birds awhile and listen to their wisdom.

Pause

But how is it possible that we can fly? What powers our wings? What is the source of our flight? It's the air, and it's more than the air. We fly upon of the breath of the Great Goddess. We fly supported by Her power. Every day, She supports us. Swoop and dive though we may, She will never let us fall. Trust Her.

Let us trust the Great Goddess. Let us feel Her sweet breath lifting our wings. Let us feel Her powerful arms holding us up. Know that wherever we may go, even as far as the farthest corner of the earth, even as far as the stars above, She is carrying us. Trust Her.

Look down. There—you can see your room, your house, your apartment building. And over there—I can see my home. As we soar in a sky as blue as the beginning of the world, we can look down and see our community, our city. With amazing telescopic vision, we can see our families and friends. With amazing X-ray vision, we can see through roofs and ceilings. We can see other people meditating. We can see their altars, their circles, their rituals. We can see how many people have wings, how many are learning to fly, how many trust Her.

Pause

Whoa—we've got problems ahead. Downdrafts. Thunder and lightning. What if we fall? There are sharp rocks down there to cut and tear us. Alligators to eat us up. A bottomless abyss to swallow us. Poisonous people to wound us, body and soul. What if our wings fail?

How could they fail? Our wings are gifts from the Goddess. Trust Her.

Pause

Rocks, hard weather, alligators, abyss, poisonous hatred—yes, they're down there. But where are we? We're flying with the wings of the Great Goddess. We're safe in Her sweet breath, in Her strong arms. We must remember that we are always safe in Her arms. We must remember that no matter how bad it seems, no matter how hard it gets, She guides our wings and holds us safely in Her arms. Consider some of the rocks and alligators in your life. The poisonous people. The challenges and tests that always come into a life on earth. How do you endure? How do I endure?

We endure because Her mind is guiding us. Her breath is lifting our wings. Her strong arms are holding us. Trust Her.

Pause

Let us resolve to let Her intelligence guide us through all obstacles. Call it a small, still voice. Call it your own intuition. Call that voice what you will, but remember that it's Her voice, and what She tells us is the truth. Trust that voice and know that She speaks clearly if we will only listen.

Pause

Let's soar up into the empyrean now, leap up above earth's sky. Feel the cosmic winds. Glide in those great winds, knowing that it is She who blows the winds and She who lets us glide. We're flying among the stars and comets. Starstuff is sprinkling around us. Do you remember the starstuff? It's Her breath, Her milk, Her essence. It's the starstuff that built the cosmos. You and I are made of that same starstuff. We are all of us made from Her essence.

And look. We are not alone. Among our friendly birds, here are other flyers. More and more people are with us here in the sky. As we look around, we can suddenly see hundreds, thousands of people with wings. Multitudes of people are flying around us. We're all made of the same starstuff, and we all fly together. Let us join hands with other flyers, join hands and fly together, fly in circles and spirals. We'll fly around the stars, fly through comets' tails. We'll fly through the Milky Way and recall the old stories that it was formed from the milk of Her breasts.

Pause

We'll fly together, soar and sing, and remember that we're all supported by the power of the Great Goddess. You're not alone. I'm not alone. Trust Her.

Pause

Fly as long and as far as you want to, trusting Her, and when you come back down to earth, fold up your wings and continue to trust Her. Walk with Her. When you go to work, keep Her in your heart. Wherever you go, trust Her. No matter what happens, remember that we have flown with Her. Remember that She is always with you, as She is with me and with all of us who love and honor Her and call upon Her.

Trust Her.

Community

Sit comfortably, close your eyes, and take several deep, easy breaths. When you feel relaxed, call into your mind the familiar image of the fishing net. See a vast net that stretches up and down, as far around as you can see, every knot a sparkling star. See yourself in the center of this shining net, see that the stars glitter around you, but know that each of us stands at the center of that same net. The stars revolve around each of us, they shine for each of us. This net has as many centers as it has knots that are shining stars.

This net, these stars—this is our community. And the Weaver of our net is the Great Goddess.

Let us gaze upon our net and see who the Goddess has woven into our life today. Look at the closest circle of stars and name them:

- *name* , who cheers me when I am sad.
- *name* , who holds me when I am weary.
- *name* , who feeds me when I am hungry.

Let us name the sisters and brothers who are closest to us. Let us call out the names of our dearest friends and be grateful that the Goddess has brought us together.

Pause

Let us understand, also, that no community is built at random. No community comes together by chance, for a wise Goddess gathers Her children with purpose and humor.

Let us continue to name our friends:

- *name* , who walks beside me.
- *name* , who plays beside me.
- *name* , who works beside me.

Pause

The word "community" comes to us from the Latin *communis*, "common." A related word is "communion." One meaning of "communion" is "a sharing of thoughts or feelings." With whom do we brainstorm our best ideas and reveal our most intimate feelings, if not with our community? Another definition is "a religious or spiritual fellowship." We are, all of us, part of a vast community that lives in the lap of the Goddess.

Look again at the net of our community. Consider the light of each star. See how far it shines, how it touches the lights of other stars, just as our fingertips touch when we reach from a distance. We find comfort in the touch of a friend, in the feeling of those fingertips. Touching joins us, it links our auras. We are lighted by all the stars around us and we share the light. That light is thought, it is feeling, it is sisterhood and fellowship. It is community.

The Goddess creates our communities, and in our communities we share our ideas, our passions, our hopes and disappointments. We share comfort and criticism. We share our work and we share what is in our heart.

Pause

Look again at the net. The stars shine, and the lines of the net shine too. See how they pulse like veins and arteries. They carry the life-blood of our spirit throughout our community. These lines carry our philosophies, our core beliefs.

The Goddess creates Her communities. Let us name more of our friends:

- *name*   , who stands by my side.
- *name*   , who speaks truly with me.
- *name*   , who listens when I speak.

Pause

The Goddess creates Her communities, and they are as ever-changing as they are enduring, as elastic as they are stable. We grow, and our thoughts and hearts' desires flow along differing lines. We grow and find that one who was once our friend is no longer with us. We grow and blossom and find that we have grown into new communities. Bless the communities of former friends and know they have found their best places.

Look upon our community. Look around and see the faces of the people the Goddess has brought to us. See their hearts, see their minds, and know that our community has purpose. Know that our community is blessed by the Great Goddess.

After you have returned to ordinary awareness, give thanks for community. Resolve to keep your community in peace and harmony until its work is complete. Know that new communities will form at their proper times. Know that the Goddess will continue to weave Her vast net and that community will always be with us.

Creativity

Sit quietly and close your eyes. Take several deep, easy breaths and begin to let the idea of "creativity" float into your mind. When you are doing your creative work, what do you do?

Take another deep, easy breath, and another. There are many goddesses of creativity. There are goddesses who inspire the trees and flowers to grow, goddesses who push the grain up through the ground, goddesses who tell the fruit to ripen. There are goddesses who invented writing and mathematics. There are goddesses of smithcraft and cooking. There are spinners and weavers and potters. There are poets and singers and dancers.

Creativity is ever-flowing. Inspired by the Goddess, it flows in streams we cannot predict, in rivers that may travel into the farthest lands. Every instant of every moment of every hour of every day, creativity is flowing.

Pause

In your imagination, see us standing together in a meadow. Not far away are the mountains and behind us is the forest, but here the earth is soft and moist. If we are quiet, we hear a slight sound. It's the giggling of a spring. It's tiny, this baby spring, hardly more than a few enthusiastic drops bubbling up from the earth, but this little splash of water is determined to create a baby brook. This is such a tiny spring, such a tiny brook that an acorn boat might dam it from bank to bank. Nevertheless, it bubbles up. This baby stream is outward bound. It already knows it's going somewhere.

Let us take this stream as our symbol of creativity. Let's follow this stream and see where it goes. Begin walking along this baby stream. Here, where it rises from the earth, it's not much. But walk awhile and see how the water sparkles. When we are first inspired, our ideas are only drops and bubbles and splashes, and we may not think they're very much. As this tiny spring rises, so does our creativity arise from the belly of the Goddess.

Pause

As we walk, we find other tiny springs rising out of the earth and joining our original stream. New streams flow from the forest, some from other parts of the meadow. Each new spring adds more sparkles, more giggles, more bubbles, and the stream grows wider and deeper. Soon it's as wide as the span of your arms. And here is another source of water. Runoff from the mountains leaps down in waterfalls and cold, clear brooks that also flow into our stream. Now the water not only rises from deep under the land, but it also flows down from snow that once fell on the mountaintops. So does our creativity spring from many sources. We know that, ultimately, all these sources are one, and that the Great Goddess is that one source.

Pause

Let's keep walking.

Our stream of water is a full-fledged creek now, in some places too wide to jump over, in some places deep enough to dive into. And suddenly—suddenly we see the insects, the frogs, the fish, the water birds, the aquatic animals. Our creek is supporting a food chain! So does our creativity feed itself, so does it support beings—ideas—that feed each other.

As we travel beside our creek, we find other creeks feeding into it and it grows wider and deeper. Trees line its banks in many places now, and reeds and bushes and flowers. We can see where animals come to drink, where children come to play and sail over the water on tire swings. Our creek is becoming a stream, and soon we come to the first bridge. Let's cross the bridge and find out what's on the other side. It's a small village. Some of the people in this town use our stream as their source for drinking water, just as other people have dug wells. All the water, however, and all our creativity has the same deep source.

Pause

Here sunlight touches the water. Look at its play on the water, at its flash and sparkle on the wavelets moving downstream. How beautiful that watery light is, how inviting. It's the light of inspiration, illumination from our local star. And beneath the light on the surface? Deep in the water it is dark. The light strikes the water, but below is the nurturing darkness, darkness that harbors unknown creatures, darkness that flows around all obstacles. So must our creativity, warmed by the light, harbor unknown ideas that rise in our work and flow around all obstacles to our work.

But look again—see how the sunlight is no longer on the water but suddenly *in* it. See how the stream has absorbed the light, how deeply the water glows. Not for long, of course, only for an endless instant. So are we sometimes possessed by our creativity, obsessed by it. So are we sometimes swallowed by the light of our creativity. These are the times when the writing writes us, when the drawing draws us, when the work works us. As we stand together on the shore and watch the light playing on our stream, let your mind dwell on a time when you were absorbed by your creativity. Let your mind understand that you can return to that sacred space whenever you want to.

Pause

Let us rise into the air now and fly. Our stream continues to grow, and now it's a small river. Looking down, we can see where it is joined by another small river, and another, and if we look upstream, we can see their sources: tiny springs, tiny brooks, mountain runoff. So many distant sources, so many unexpected sources feed our river. So many distant and mysterious things feed our creativity. So many unexpected ideas and materials flow into our minds and hands. We may never know where they all come from.

Our river becomes a mid-sized river now, deeper and darker, and it flows through towns and cities. Its water is used by more and more people. We have come a hundred miles or more. Other mid-sized rivers feed into our river.

Pause

Let's rise higher and look down again. Why, this is a major waterway we're following! It's a wide, swift-flowing river into which flow other wide, swift-flowing rivers. Our river now supports large cities and major industries. Barges and other boats move up and down the river. Our river cuts through a continent. During its winding travels it has cut bluffs and made grasslands into swamps, it has cut through obstacles that would dam a smaller river. Sometimes it floods, and the devastation to farmlands and low towns is unthinkable. But when it floods it also deposits rich black soil on those farmlands. The people of ancient Egypt understood this paradox. They depended on the annual flooding of their river and celebrated new fertility every summer.

When we consider the strength and persistence of water we understand why it is an elemental power. Water flows around all obstacles. It carves its way through the hardest, toughest stone until it reaches its goal, the sea. It carries rich black earth from all the lands it passes through and gives that wealth to all the other lands along its shores.

Consider your own creativity and know that it can become as wide and deep and strong as this river. It can produce major projects.

Pause

For remember—even the mighty Mississippi River is composed of endless drops of water. The Mississippi River begins every instant of every day as a tiny spring in a northern state. And every drop of the Mississippi River flows southward into the sea, which is the source of life on earth.

From a tiny spring to mighty rivers to the oceans that cover most of the earth, we are washed in creativity. After you return to ordinary awareness, remember to give thanks to the Goddess for water. Give thanks to Her for Her ever-flowing, ever-growing creativity and for ours, which echoes Hers.

Spirituality

Our intention in this meditation is to explore and affirm our spirituality, and our image is a familiar and comfortable one: a tree. Before you begin, spend some time selecting the kind of tree you want to represent your spirituality, magic, or intention. Table 1, below, lists nine common trees and some magical powers attributed to them.[11] If one grows nearby, it might be nice to sit under the tree of your choice while you meditate. People who are attuned to the spirits of nature often hear (or feel) these spirits talking to them. Although I can't say I've ever held a conversation with a tree, I know them to be very wise.

Apple	Love, healing, garden magic
Ash	Protection, prosperity, sea rituals
Bamboo	Protection, luck, wishes
Birch	New beginnings, purification
Juniper	Protection, love, health
Maple	Love, longevity, money
Oak	Protection, health, money
Pine	Healing, protection, money
Willow	Love, divination, healing

Table 1: **Common Trees and Their Magical Attributes.**

Sit quietly, close your eyes, and take several deep, easy breaths. Visualize your selected tree. See it as tall, healthy, and ensouled.

Let us consider the tree. Let us walk around it, lay our hands on its trunk and feel the smoothness or roughness of its bark. Whether this tree looks delicate and pliable or is so large that three people together cannot reach around it, it stands where it stands and is (so to speak) a pillar of its community.

Here is the true Tree of Life, not the Qabalistic Tree, which, being rooted in heaven, is upside down. This is a tree whose roots sink deep into Mother Earth, whose trunk is a genuine pillar of strength, and whose branches and leaves reach as high as the sky. This is the authentic Tree of Life, not an intellectual diagram, for it supports life on earth. Insects, small animals, and birds may live in or near this tree. The transpiration of its leaves gives us oxygen to breathe. Fruit and nut trees feed us, most trees give us bark or leafy branches for shelter, and their wood builds our best houses and furniture. Trees give us music when they lend us their wood for drums and woodwinds. After its death, the tree becomes compost to support the creation of new life.

Pause

Let us become very small now and enter the root system. We burrow deep into the earth. Here is the major tap root, here the auxiliary roots, here the fine hair-like rootlets. Deep or shallow, roots hold the tree securely in its place and pull nutrients into it. Just so, we remember that we are rooted deep in the love of the Great Goddess. She holds us in our place in our community. Our roots in Her give us our daily spiritual bread: the certain knowledge that we are grounded in Her.

Pause

Let us move up into the trunk of the tree now. Here is a miracle of circulation, a miracle of timing. Each tree knows when it's time to send its sap upward, and, gravity notwithstanding, the sap does rise. There may be holes in the trunk of our tree for birds or squirrels to live in, there may be insects traveling up and down, mistletoe and orchids may infest its crown, but this tree lives peacefully and grows as it grows. Let's feel our own circulation as we stand inside this tree. Our energy rises and falls every day, old thoughts and other parasites infest us, and still we grow. We and this tree and the Goddess—we're united. Let's spend a few minutes feeling the comfort and inspiration that such knowledge of unity brings.

Pause

Take time to explore the rings of the tree. Used by scientists as trustworthy calendars, tree rings record the history of the place where a tree lives. Is it possible that we, too, in a sense have rings? Think about the experiences of your life. I know that each experience I've had has added something to me, visible or invisible. The rings of my experience create a record of my whole being, of my every age. Our rings may be invisible, or perhaps they manifest in our auras. They're the ageless rings of our spirituality.

Pause

The oldest being on earth is a bristlecone pine, the youngest may well be a seed just sending up its first tender shoot. Is it possible that each of us is as old as that pine? And as young as the seedling?

Pause

Finally, let us climb up to the branches and leaves. Whether the leaves of this tree are evergreen needles or wide deciduous leaves that turn color and fall, every day of their lives they create the miracle of photosynthesis. Just so, every day of every one of our lives the Goddess re-creates us as Her small miracles. We are grounded in Her. We stand strong. But like the bamboo and other seemingly fragile trees, we also bend when we must. We stretch upwards into the heavens.

Like the branches and leaves of a tree, we cast shadows around us and create shelter for the people we meet. We need to consider what kinds of shadows we cast. Welcoming shade protects from too much light and heat, whereas other kinds of shade are ominous. Do we give safe shelter? Are the people who come to us sometimes struck by lightning? A lightning bolt can split a tree in half and kill it. As we learn from Card XVI of the Tarot, The Tower, a lightning bolt of sudden insight can open our minds and souls and kill outworn ideas.

Let us sit awhile beside our tree and contemplate the elements of our spirituality—love, healing, new beginnings, the consciousness of abundance and good fortune, new insights struck from old thoughts. Let the tree speak. What will she teach us today?

Pause

Let her speak finally of community. A tree may grow in a forest and be a member of a long-lived family. A tree may grow in a garden or near a house and serve as the guardian of flowers, as our silent guardian. A tree may grow near city streets and serve as a vision of the natural world for those whose vision seldom reaches beyond the concrete. Wherever she grows, a tree brings oxygen, shade, and blessing to our world.

Black Elk said of his vision:

And I saw the sacred hoop of my people was one of many hoops that made one circle, wide as daylight and as starlight, and in the center grew one mighty flowering tree to shelter all the children of one mother and one father. And I saw that it was holy.[12]

Wisdom

Of what does wisdom consist? It is cerebral knowledge? Is it booklearning? Is it common sense? Street smarts? My dictionary says that wisdom is "understanding what is right, true, or lasting." Is wisdom a big, complicated concept? Is there a universal wisdom?

You know, that's too abstract for me. It's too unwieldy to be useful.

Let's bring it down to a more personal level. Of what does *your wisdom* consist? Of what does *mine*? It's easy to say what we think we know, and we talk all the time as if we really knew something. But perhaps the essential wisdom the Goddess has given us is simple wisdom. Perhaps we need to speak simply from our heart to our mind and then through our mouth.

Poets and philosophers can discern metaphorical qualities in any object. To symbolize our wisdom, therefore, let us choose a common sea shell, the spiraling chambered nautilus.

Sit quietly, close your eyes, take several deep, easy breaths, and visualize the shell of the chambered nautilus. It fits comfortably in the hand. Its outer surface is ivory with the familiar brown stripes, the inner surface and the last chamber wall (where the nautilus was attached to its shell) are mother-of-pearl. The nautilus, a cephalopod related to the squid, begins life as a minute creature in a tiny shell and crawls or swims to capture its food in its tentacles.

Let us watch this tiny sea creature for a moment. So small it is nearly invisible, it hunts, it feeds, it grows. It begins to outgrow its tiny shell, and so it secretes nacre to build itself an addition, a new chamber. The spiral begins. Hunt. Feed. Grow.

Pause

Look at us. Even as babies, we hunt for wisdom; long before we can talk, we feed on the small lessons we learn, and thus we grow. Perhaps this process begins while we are still living in the seawater inside our mother's womb.

When I was a child, my first textbook was *Dick and Jane*, which taught me that the whole world was white, Anglo-Saxon, and Protestant, and that boys were active and girls admired them. Try to recall what you first learned about the condition of the world. Our knowledge was limited. The chamber of our earliest wisdom was narrow.

Watch the nautilus, constantly feeding and growing. Look at us. All through our lives we keep learning new things, we keep outgrowing the chamber our limited wisdom once filled. The nautilus builds new nacreous chambers. We build new layers of wisdom. We hold our truest wisdom in our hearts.

Pause

Let us look at our heart-wisdom. Let us become very young and return for a moment to our original wisdom. Here we are—enclosed and limited. We know as much as we can handle. We're curious children, however; we reach out and our intellectual tentacles grasp something. We digest it, and growth happens. It's time to build a new chamber!

In your imagination, build your second mother-of-pearl chamber, and the next, and the next.

Pause

Each chamber both creates and results from a life lesson. Some lessons come from books, some from seminars, some from gurus or shamans, but true wisdom "is the process of living unfolding. It often waits for us where we least expect it."[13]

Carrying our shells with us, we swim through the visible and invisible worlds. Accidents happen and we learn from them, tragedies nearly overcome us, but we find an insight. Our mistakes and failures force us to build new chambers to accommodate our new wisdom. We grow and our shells become larger, smoother, more beautiful. I have learned that Dick and Jane's world is invalid. You have learned what you need to know.

Pause

In your imagination, hold your shell to your ear. When we listen with our physical ears, we hear air currents in the shell that sound like ocean waves. In our imaginations, we can hear the words of the Great Goddess in the sounds of the ocean waves in the shell. Her words are so simple:

> *I love you. I will always protect you. Always say please and thank you. Trust me. Cherish your community. Take time to do your creative work. Live in peace and holiness and know that you are my precious child.*

Priestess Power

In the Goddess religion, it is said, every woman is a priestess, and every man a priest. Let us take as our symbol of priestess power the cauldron. As we know, the cauldron was the "primary female symbol of the pre-Christian world."[14] It represents the womb of the Great Goddess from which all things are born and reborn.

Sit comfortably, close your eyes, and take several deep, easy breaths. My cauldron is cast-iron. It's five inches in diameter and stands three inches high on three little legs. Because I use it a lot, it's a little rusty and there's always a pinch or two of ashes in the bottom. In your imagination, see your own cauldron or one like mine.

Pause

Perhaps you know the story of Cerridwen,[†] the all-knowing Welsh goddess who kept magical herbs simmering in her cauldron for a year and a day. A boy named Gwion watched the simmering pot for her. One day the Goddess went out for more herbs, and some liquid splashed on the boy's hand. He screamed in pain and stuck his hand in his mouth, and "miraculously, he was able to hear everything in the world and to understand the secrets of both the past and the future." Cerridwen pursued the boy through several transformations and finally swallowed him. Nine months later, she gave birth to a baby who grew up to be the great poet Taliesin.[††]

In your imagination, now, look into the cauldron of generation and regeneration, into the cauldron of priestess power, to see what we have simmering and—yecch! What is that garbage?

What's been simmering in our cauldron? Instead of holy wisdom, our cauldron has somehow stewed up five poisons. We need to get that garbage outta there!

Arrogance. Arrogance says, "I know it all. I'm the best ritualist, the best poet, the best drummer or dancer. I'm the highest of all high priestesses. I'm the best-selling of all authors." But there is always more to learn, often in the most unexpected place. Arrogance has no place in true priestess power. Let us throw arrogance away.

Pause

Seduction. Seduction says, "Do you want love? Power over others? Come unto me. Let me love you and teach you spells to attract everything you ever wanted." Seduction lures us with honey-sweet words that promise to manifest our fantasies of lust, wealth, celebrity, or unlimited magical power. We all deserve love and abundance, of

---

[†] Pronounced KARE-ed-wen. In the Celtic languages, C is pronounced K.
[††] Pronounced Tal-ee-ESS-in. Monaghan, *The Book of Goddesses and Heroines*, pp. 72–73.

course, and fame may come to us if the Goddess wills it. If power is to be effective, it must be shared with others. Seduction has no place in true priestess power. Let us throw seduction away.

Pause

Intimidation. Intimidation says, "You're not getting what you want because you're not doing what I tell you. You'd better shape up and do things my way. I'm keeping an eye on you with my great psychic powers. Things can happen to you . . . ." We receive what we need because the Goddess loves us and gives us lessons to learn on earth. It is unethical to use our psychic talents to spy on people. Intimidation has no place in true priestess power. Let us throw intimidation away.

Pause

Manipulation. Manipulation says, "This Tarot reading shows that we have karmic ties through many lives and you were sent to me to pay a karmic debt. This rune says that your power is linked to mine. Your natal chart shows that you have a square to your first house, which makes you weak. My psychic powers can make you strong. Do you want power? You must listen to me and let me teach you." Although the Tarot, the runes, astrology, and psychism have much to give us, any such manipulative reading is unethical. Let us throw manipulation away.

Pause

Control. Control says, "I came into this life to lead and teach. You must do all things my way. My tradition is the only valid tradition, and you may not circle with anyone else." Control craves students and apprentices to feed her ego. *But traditions have something of value,* and the more we get around to see how others do things, the more we'll learn. Let us throw control away.

Pause

But see, now our cauldron is empty. What good is an empty cauldron? The principle of recirculation teaches us that we can't jam more of anything into a space that is already full. To receive, we have to be empty.

We've thrown away the garbage. What do we have to *give away*? One of my friends suggests a give-away every new moon. We can give away just one or two things, and it is best if these are things we have loved but no longer need. We can give to friends or charities. Let's pretend tonight is the new moon. I'll give away some feathers I know someone needs and a book I've already ready six times. What can you give away? In your imagination, select something you once loved and give it away.

Pause

Now we'll pretend the moon is full. What goes around comes back around. It's time to refill the empty cauldron of our priestess power. We'll fill it with our treasures.

1. *Sacred space.* We acknowledge that the cauldron is sacred space and remember that it represents the love of the Great Goddess.

2. *Our security blankets.* We remember that She made our beautiful blankets and that they represent Her protection.

3. *Two bright, shiny pennies.* One for you and one for me, because we are grateful for the loving abundance of the Goddess.

4. *Our wings and flying lessons.* We are learning to trust the Goddess to guide us and hold us up.

5. *A vast starry net.* We have seen our community and know that everyone is part of their own community. We remember that the true center of our community is the Goddess.

6. *A mighty river.* This is the river that represents our creativity. It may begin with only a few drops, but it comes from so many sources that it can flow wherever it must.

7. *A great tree.* We remember how the tree represents our spirituality. It has roots to draw nourishment from deep in the earth, a sturdy trunk, and branches full of miracles.

8. *A chambered nautilus shell.* How tiny our wisdom is at first. Then it feeds on everything it can find and begins to grow. When we remember that our wisdom is centered on the Goddess, it becomes as beautiful as mother-of-pearl.

There. Our cauldron is heaped to overflowing.

Pause

We have enough to share and more than enough. Our cauldron is our sacred store of nourishment. It feeds us now and forever, feeds us both practical wisdom and blessed understanding.

And here lies our priestess power: We share what we know. We share what we receive. We share the blessings of the Great Goddess who is the Divine Creatrix of all the world and all that is in the world.

Endnotes

1. Nancy Blair, *Amulets of the Goddess* (Berkeley, CA: Wingbow Press, 1993), p. 101. For information about the Amulets, see the Resources.

2. Merlin Stone, *When God Was a Woman* (New York: Harcourt Brace Jovanovich, 1976). Monica Sjoo and Barbara Mor, *The Great Cosmic Mother* (New York: Harper and Row, 1987). Marija Gimbutas, *The Civilization of the Goddess* (San Francisco: HarperSanFrancisco, 1991).

3. Monaghan, *The Book of Goddesses and Heroines*, p. 388.

4. My thanks to Jeanine Just, whose seminar on core values helped me find mine. They're included in this list.

5. Itzhak Bentov, *Stalking the Wild Pendulum* (New York: E. P. Dutton, 1977), p. 26.

6. Stewart Edward White, *The Unobstructed Universe* (New York: E. P. Dutton, 1940).

7. My thanks to Holin Badger Kennen, priestess of spinning and drumming, for teaching me what the Goddess does to make a wool blanket.

8. My thanks to my friend Shira Paskin for suggesting this image to me.

9. Quoted in *Bartlett's Familiar Quotations*, 14th edition (New York: Little, Brown and Co., 1968), p. 1010.

10. To help your inner child—or the children in your family—play in sacred space, see Cait Johnson and Maura D. Shaw, *Celebrating the Great Mother* (Rochester, VT: Destiny Books, 1995).

11. From Pauline Campanelli, *Wheel of the Year* (St. Paul: Llewellyn Publications, 1989), p. 51, and Scott Cunningham, *Cunningham's Encyclopedia of Magical Herbs* (St. Paul: Llewellyn Publications, 1988).

12. Quoted in a wonderful book: Cheryl Ann Karas, *The Solstice Evergreen* (Boulder Creek, CA: Aslan Publishing, 1991), p. 49.

13. Anne Wilson Schaef, *Native Wisdom for White Minds* (New York: Ballantine Books, 1995), Jan. 20.

14. Barbara G. Walker, *The Woman's Dictionary of Symbols and Sacred Objects* (New York: Harper and Row, 1983), pp. 124–25.

4
Light Work

Goody Getty

We do light work meditations while the moon is waxing, from the new moon to the full moon. Light Work is the work of planning and planting, of creating and building, of blooming and manifesting the things we want.

Our light work meditations, therefore, are creative meditations.

1. Abundance 1: Ops
2. Abundance 2: Goody Getty
3. Love 1: Aphrodite
4. Love 2: The Graces
5. Compassion: Tara / Kuan Yin / Mary

6. Healing: Coventina
7. Courage and Strength: Wonder Woman
8. Three Wishes: Fairy Goodmother
9. House Blessing: Hestia
10. Celebration: Taillte
11. Beauty and Magic: Freya
12. Soul Walk: Athene or Artemis
13. BodyKnowing: Shakti

Remember that you can do these meditations as "pure" meditations or in rituals. If you do them in rituals, you can use the inductions and return given in chapter 2. You can build an altar to each goddess or do the meditations without altars.

You don't always have to sit with your eyes closed to meditate. The last three meditations in this chapter are moving meditations. In the first, you create a magical necklace, in the second you take a soul walk, and in the third you allow your body to move and to know things it's possible your mind does not know. Enjoy!

Abundance 1: Ops

We get our English words *opulent* and *opulence* from the name of the Roman goddess Ops, whose consort is Saturn in His role as King of the Golden Age. All cultures look back to their Golden Age, a time when the earth overflowed with riches and everyone lived in peace and equality. As the personification of the creative force and earth's riches,[1] Ops was worshipped by rich and poor alike at harvest festivals on August 25 and December 19.

The latter celebration was followed immediately by the Saturnalia,[2] a twelve-day festival celebrating the winter solstice and the beginning of a new year. The most popular of the ancient Roman festivals, the Saturnalia was marked by social chaos, orgies, and carnivals. During this time people visited their friends and exchanged gifts. On the last day of Saturnalia, children were given special gifts. Some of us celebrate the Twelve Days of Christmas, which remind us of the Saturnalia and the powers of Saturn and Ops to touch our lives still today.

Let your imagination rest on the idea of opulence for a minute. My dictionary defines opulence as "having or characterized by great wealth, rich, affluent; abundant, plentiful, luxuriant, profuse, lavish; characterized by fullness and vitality."

Yummy!

In her popular book *The Artist's Way*, Julia Cameron says that artists—that is, all of us—need to recover our "sense of abundance." Abundance, we learn, is more than money, though it does include money. It's also time to be creative, it's supplies to create with, it's doing what we really want to do. It's pampering ourselves because we deserve it, and if we don't pamper ourselves, who will?[3] In several places in the book Cameron asks her readers to stretch their minds and make lists.

Let's try that now. Stop reading and make a list of five things you really want. Let money be no object. Let your imagination soar. What do you really want to have or do?

Now add five more things to your list.

Think awhile: what does luxury mean to you? What will make you feel full and vital? What difference would abundance make in your life? Of what, in addition to money, does great wealth consist?

Imagine how rich you could be, how abundant your life could be. Now begin to make it ten times more abundant.

The Meditation

Holding your list in your hands and watching the visions of solid gold sugarplums dancing in your head, close your eyes and take several deep, easy breaths. In your imagination, find yourself in a great, timeless city crowded with people who live in harmony with each other and with nature. This is a beautiful city, where everyone always has enough to eat and no one goes hungry. Today, everyone is celebrating the mid-winter Festival of Ops, and we're going to the marketplace.

As you follow the road to the Temple of Ops, which is in the center of the marketplace, take note of the laughing and singing people in their elaborate costumes. As you walk along the road, take note of the wealth of this legendary city, the happiness and vitality of all its people, the abundance of food and life's other necessities. As you traverse the marketplace, see its affluence on every side. Notice the booths where food and drink and music and every treasure known to humankind is for sale. This is the place to live!

Pause

The road finally brings you to the center, and you see before you the luxuriant Temple of Ops, the Goddess from Whose hands flow all the riches you have seen along the way. Stop a moment and reflect on how good you feel being in this beautiful city. It is wonderful to stand and walk among such vital people, to gaze at the plenty of this place and know that you can have anything you want. It is wonderful to understand that you will soon meet the Goddess herself and receive Her great blessings. You will receive Her own opulence.

Pause

Hark! The Goddess is coming out of Her temple for Her daily audience with Her people. Petitions and wishes in hand, they gather around Her, and there is no pushing and shoving. These people know they deserve all good things. Join the audience. Know that you, too, deserve all good things.

Just as you are approaching Her, the Goddess stands and raises Her hands. The people become quiet. She speaks:

"My darling people," the Goddess says, "my beloved children, hear what I say to you on this, My festival day." The Goddess extends Her arms as if to embrace the multitude of people standing before Her. Everyone can feel the love of this Goddess of abundance. "My precious citizens," She says, "whatever you desire, that is My gift to you."

Pause

The Goddess sits on Her throne and the people lean forward to hear Her speak. "In future days," She says, "wise men and women will repeat My words to unhappy people, to those who make poverty a virtue. But I say, No! Poverty is no virtue. I say, Yes! Your wishes can come true. You can live in comfort and wealth as you do the work you were meant to do.

"Hear what a wise man will write," the Goddess continues. "Listen to his words and take them into your hearts:

> "Let us reemphasize the Truth, that you can grow, you can improve, you can be prosperous, you can succeed, if you can believe. When you say "Yes!" to the creative flow within you, you begin to experience I-am-positive-I-can attitudes which turn on the power and skills needed to accomplish. When you believe you can do it, the how-to-do-it develops. This is the way the creative process . . . works.[4]

"Take these words into your hearts," the Goddess says again, and Her people murmur and touch their hearts.

Pause

Now it is your turn to approach the Goddess Ops. Bring your ten wishes with you. Speak to this generous Goddess from your heart. Tell Her all the wise and silly things you want to do. Tell Her all the humble and extravagant things you want to have. Hand your list of ten wishes to the Goddess and wait while She reads and considers each wish.

And as you wait for Ops to speak again, notice a new feeling coming into your mind and heart. Notice a new hope, a new knowing. Take note of the new vision in your imagination, the new energy in your hands.

"My friend." The Goddess looks into your eyes and takes your hands in hers. "My friend, you deserve to have the things you want. You deserve to live comfortably. You deserve to become rich while working at your right livelihood. You deserve to travel, to receive gifts, to do wonderful things. My friend, I grant your wishes."

Pause

"But, my friend," She continues, "I do not simply give them to you out of thin air. I give you the know-how and the energy. I give you possibilities and connections. I give you the love and feeling of abundance.

"Now," the Goddess concludes, touching your forehead and heart, "now, my dear, you may go into the world and do your part to bring your deserved abundance into your life. And know that you go with my brightest blessings."

Pause

Thank the Goddess Ops. Let the next person take Her turn with the Goddess and resume your journey through Her marketplace. As you walk, become aware that you are returning to ordinary awareness. Become aware that you have visited a Goddess and She has given abundance to you if only you will recognize it.

Abundance 2: Goody Getty

Because we live in times when issues that were never heard of in ancient days arise, we need new goddesses. Which classical goddess, for example, would you invoke to find a parking place? Who would make your computer more user-friendly? What ancient goddess could help you decide what to take to a potluck?

In these modern times we need Found Goddesses. The concept of Found Goddesses was introduced to the world by Morgan Grey and Julia Penelope, who write that they:

started playing with the idea of creating our own goddesses . . . who not only respond to the specific needs of 20th-century Dykes but whose NAMING calls into being a reality grounded in the will and gynergy of Dyke envisioning. We chortled and guffawed as friends sparked and spun the weird realm of Found Goddesses with us.[5]

I'm quite fond of Found Goddesses. I found Goody Getty, who is dressed in red and white and looks like Mrs. Santa Claus, in a doll store in 1991. All I had to do was sprinkle Her with glitter, make a magic wand for Her (out of a toothpick and gold stars, with red and green threads to show the streaming energy), and add several magical spells to Her little basket of goodies.

One thing about Found Goddesses, though—their names are nearly always puns. There are, accordingly, at least five puns in Goody Getty's name.

While I've been working on this book, I've also been studying *feng shui*, the ancient Chinese art of placement.[6] In feng shui, your living space is divided into eight areas, one of which is devoted to wealth and what Spear calls "fortunate blessings." Figure 2, below, shows the "fortunate blessings" corner of a square home and the rooms in it.

In Chinese philosophy, red is the color of good fortune. Traditional brides wore red, and on special occasions gifts of money were given in red envelopes. I have a store of red Chinese envelopes. They're decorated with cauldrons heaped high with goodies of all kinds.

Before you begin the meditation, write the following affirmation[7] on white or red paper. If you can, use a fountain pen, not with a ballpoint, and real ink so that your energy flows with the ink onto the paper.

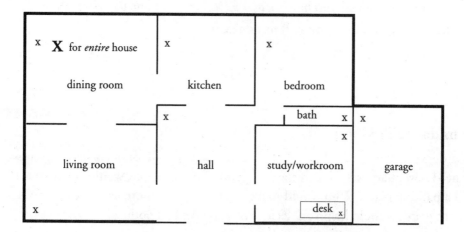

Figure 2. **X Marks Your Fortunate Blessings Area.**

I release my belief that I must sacrifice material wealth in order to follow my spiritual path.

Hold the paper at your solar plexus and breathe on it from your third chakra to empower this affirmation with your will. Fold the paper and put it in a red envelope. If you don't have a genuine Chinese envelope, a red envelope from the stationery store will do quite well.

Let's take Goody Getty and our red envelope into the fortunate blessings area of our room and see what happens. If possible, sit in this corner while you do this meditation.

The Meditation

Sitting in your fortunate blessings corner, hold the red envelope with your affirmation inside it in your left hand. Close your eyes, take a few deep, easy breaths, and allow your body to relax.

Imagine that you are sitting comfortably in a room with red walls and a red door. Soon the door opens and a little old lady enters. Even from across the room, you can see the twinkle in Her eyes. This is Goody Getty. She is the same size as your favorite grandmother and pleasingly plump. She has white hair covered by a red mob cap. The frames of Her glasses are gold and Her cheeks are rosy. She is wearing a red and white polka-dotted dress with a lacy white collar and a glittery white pinafore apron. Even Her old-fashioned shoes glitter. In Her right hand, Goody Getty carries Her magic wand with its golden star and streamers of power. In Her left hand, She holds a basket filled to overflowing with numerous beautifully wrapped gifts and scrolls on which wishes and blessings are written. When you look more closely, you see that stars follow where Goody Getty walks.

Goody Getty smiles at you, tucks Her magic wand into the pocket of Her apron, and reaches out to pat you on the head. Her touch is cool and soothing. When She nods, give Her your red envelope, which She places in the other pocket of Her apron. You can see many red envelopes peeking out of that pocket.

"I take all these red envelopes home with me," She tells you, sitting herself comfortably on a rocking chair that has suddenly appeared behind her. "I place them in my magical cauldron, where they become part of creation itself."

Pause

Goody Getty now leads you through a meditation within a meditation. As you sit with her, a symbol suddenly appears before your eyes. This symbol is something that means abundance to you. What is your symbol of abundance? A four-leaf clover? A shiny silver dollar? What is your symbol?

Pause

You need to run this symbol through your chakras in order to get it firmly into your system. Let it hover above the top of your head and come to rest on your crown chakra. What does it feel like?

Pause

Next, your symbol of abundance moves to your third eye. As it rests in the center of your forehead, focus on how this feels.

Pause

Now the symbol moves to your throat. How does it feel at your throat?

Pause

It moves to your heart. Let your symbol of abundance rest in your heart for a few minutes.

Pause

How does this feel? Next it moves to your solar plexus. What does this feel like?

Pause

Next it moves to your second chakra. How does this feel?

Pause

Finally, the symbol of your abundance moves to your root chakra. Let it rest there.

Pause

Now, breathe deeply and pull it into the base of your spine. Breathe deeply again and pull your abundance up your spine, slowly up, up, up. To your second chakra. To your third chakra. To your heart chakra. To your throat chakra. To your third eye, and back to your crown chakra.

Pull the power and energy of your abundance into your entire chakra system and let your chakras distribute it throughout your body. Sit with this as long as you want to.

Pause

Now it's time for Goody Getty to leave you. She has many people to visit today. But before She goes, She reaches into Her basket and hands you either a small gift or a spell. Thank her, and as She leaves, open your gift or scroll. What did you receive?

Pause

When you return to ordinary awareness, think about your gift from Goody Getty. What goody did you get from this richest of all women?

Love 1: Aphrodite

The earth is filled with sexual beings. From flowers to people, sexual union is part of nature. Sex is survival. It's pleasure and procreation, creation and magic. We yearn to be making love. We hunger to be partnered.

The Fathers of the Medieval Church, of course, abhorred earthly love, especially any pleasure of the body. Theology, writes Uta Ranke-Heinemann, "increasingly became the business of bachelors, [and] sin was more and more placed in the realm of sex." It was Augustine, she continues, "who . . . took the contempt for sex that saturates the work of the Church Fathers, both before him and in his own day, and added a new factor: A personal and theological sexual anxiety."[8] Thus was laid the foundation of the pleasure-hating theology of the standard-brand churches.

That biophobic theology is not ours.

We prefer to believe that the ancient civilizations that honored the Goddess were entirely without puritanism. We fantasize about warm, exotic lands where there are love and sex but neither shame nor disease in them. Our bible is the earth-loving thealogy expressed in the *Charge of the Goddess*, a beautiful "Craft liturgy" written by Doreen Valiente for Gerald Gardner's original coven. Let us reread two excerpts from Starhawk's familiar version of the *Charge*:

> Listen to the words of the Great Mother . . . :
> Sing, feast, dance, make music and love, all in My presence, for Mine is
> the ecstasy of the spirit and Mine also is joy on earth. For My law is love
> unto all beings.

> Hear the words of the Star Goddess . . . :
> Let My worship be in the heart that rejoices, for behold—all acts of
> love and pleasure are My rituals. Let there be beauty and strength, power
> and compassion, honor and humility, mirth and reverence within you.[9]

When I used to read Tarot cards at psychic fairs, ninety percent of my readings focused on romance. Today, when people ask me to create rituals to promote love and sexual partnering, I always beg them to take *every* precaution. I was an AIDS volunteer for several years; I know how it goes.

Great Aphrodite may be the most powerful of all the classical goddesses. Born when the semen of the castrated heaven-god Uranus fell into earth's ocean, She was originally one of the nearly omnipotent mother-goddesses of the Eastern Mediterranean. Aphrodite Anadyomene ("She Who Rises From Waves") is the goddess of all creation, goddess of the impersonal, indiscriminate lust the creatures of the earth require to perpetuate themselves. Janet and Stewart Farrar describe Her as:

> Love itself, the full orchestra—everything from the high strings of enraptured spirit to the percussion-section of engorged genitalia. She was all these things without qualm or apology.[10]

Because Aphrodite's unrelenting sexuality challenged the cerebral Greek philosophers, they reformed Her, making Her into little more than the personification of physical beauty. Her powers to ignite men and women remained so overwhelming, however, that the philosophers sought to reduce Her even further. Plato gave Her two titles. As Urania, She ruled spiritualized (platonic) love. As Aphrodite Pandemos, i.e., Aphrodite of all people, She was the gorgeous Goddess of physical love that we know from 2500 years of art and story. They also called Her Porne ("titillator").[11] Here is the source of our word "pornography"; this Goddess still troubles old men, and now it's the old men who run our governments.

It's good to do this meditation wearing your softest garment. Burn a delicious incense of musk, ambergris, wood aloe, rose petals, and coral. Light scented candles or warm an aromatherapy oil. Anoint yourself with an oil of ambergris, violet, gardenia, and rose.[12] You can even sprinkle rose petals on the floor. Do whatever it takes to make your space for this meditation as sensual as possible.

The Meditation

Sit comfortably, let your eyes close, and breathe deeply as you relax into a fantasy of love. You feel the touch of the zephyr in your hair. It tickles your warm, bare skin. You are floating on an azure sea, bedded in the scallop shell of the Goddess of Love, reclining on silks and swan's down. Feel the luxury of Aphrodite's bed. Gaze upon the decorations, the pearls and precious stones, hear the brushing of the waves against the shell, inhale the fragrances of sea air and perfumes that rise around you. Perhaps you even find something to eat—chocolate or strawberries or apricots. This is a scene of true enchantment. Let it warm you. Let it arouse you.

Pause

Eventually you realize that the scallop is moving. You are being carried across the sea, and soon you feel a bump that tells you the shell has touched the shore. You have come to a tiny beach of golden sand, and only steps away from the sighing water, lush flowers are blooming, hyacinth, jasmine, poppies. Lying on the grass is a chaplet of myrtle leaves tied with shimmering ribbons. Surely someone laid it here just for you. Put it on your head and explore this magical island you've come to.

At first, you hear only the waves and the breeze rustling in the palms and bamboos. Presently you begin to hear soft chanting in the distance.

Pause

Follow these sweet sounds, follow the scent of roses and vanilla that the breezes carry to you. Stroll beneath apple and fig trees and linger a moment beside a pond where the lotus is blooming. Let one hand trail in the water for a moment or two and let the goldfish tickle your fingertips. As the chanting becomes more seductive, you continue along the path through violets and periwinkles and lavender. Excitement begins to stir within you, a longing to know the Goddess pulls you forward.

Pause

Dusk is falling, you approach the clearing, and a full, orange moon is rising through the trees. Beneath the moon and on a small rise sits the Temple of Aphrodite, myrtles and willows arching over it. As you climb this gentle hill, you see that Aphrodite's temple is small and sweet, built of peach-colored alabaster. Graceful caryatids[†] support its domed roof, and its floors are of cinnabar and mother-of-pearl and ebony, inlaid with colorful mosaics that show scenes of love.

Pause

[†] Pronounced carry-AH-tides. These are columns carved as female figures. The most famous caryatids were on the Parthenon until they were stolen by Lord Elgin and taken to England.

Two shadowy figures wait for you inside Aphrodite's temple.

Pause

You are running up the steps when one of the shadowy figures steps out. She stops you on the temple porch. "Welcome to my island," She says, lifting Her veil. "I am Cytherea, whom you also know as Aphrodite." Taking your hand, She leads you to a tripod holding a copper bowl embossed with scenes of love, and there the Goddess washes your hands and feet with perfumed water. "All rituals of love and pleasure are Mine," She tells you, "for love has ever been My province." She caresses your cheek and lays one soft hand on your heart. "You are welcome here. Come to My temple whenever the moon is full, whenever love arises in your heart and in your loins."

Pause

The Goddess leads you inside the temple, and you stop together in the outer room. Directly beneath the golden dome is a sandalwood couch upon which are heaped pillows of satin, pillows striped in lime and rose and apricot, and a counterpane of ivory silk. At Her gesture you recline on this sweet couch, and the Goddess sits beside you and begins to stroke your warm, bare skin. "Sing, feast, dance," She whispers, "make music and make love," She murmurs, and the very air begins to sparkle.

The Goddess gestures toward Her inner room, the holy of holies of Her temple. Humming a melody to charm you, She continues to touch you, stroking and tickling your most tender places. "And know the ecstasy of the spirit and joy on earth," the Goddess murmurs, "for all my law is love."

Pause

You are reaching for the Goddess when She smiles and gestures again. "Wait," She says, "one is here to meet you," She whispers. "Your beloved waits within. Let your worship be in the heart that rejoices, for behold—"

And the Goddess rises and beckons. Someone comes out of the inner room of Aphrodite's temple, moves gracefully across the patterned floor, and joins you on the perfumed couch.

"Make music and love in My presence," the Goddess whispers again, "and let your beloved come unto you."

You may spend as much time as you wish with your beloved in Aphrodite's sweet temple, for all acts of pleasure are truly Hers . . . .

Love 2: The Graces

One May morning, while I was writing the first draft of this book I received a phone call from the husband of my friend and circle sister, Rose. "She's got lung cancer," he said, "and they give her three to six months." But Rose was stronger than they thought. She lived for a year. We talked on the phone every other day and visited as much as she was able. In our very last phone conversation, I said, "Rose, do you remember five years ago tonight, when I was having an asthma attack and you and Louise rushed me to the ER?" She remembered. Then I said, "And, guess what—this afternoon I signed the contract for my meditation book." "Congratulations," she said. "You'll have to come to dinner." That's how Rose was, good friend and gracious to the end. I wrote this meditation for her and read it at her memorial service.

Rulers of love with Aphrodite are the Graces: Thaleia ("abundant, overflowing, flowering one"), Aglaia ("radiance" or "splendor"), and Euphrosyne ("joy and merriment and delight").[†] The embodiment of gentle young love, They are all that is ageless, delightful, and charming. The Greeks called them the Charities, and our English word "charity" means "love."

The Meditation

Sit quietly, close your eyes, and take a deep, easy breath. Feel yourself slipping into a beautiful room, quiet and peaceful. Take another deep, easy breath and make yourself comfortable on a large rose-colored cushion in the center of the room. Inhale the fragrance of violets and vanilla, enjoy the sweet tinkle of windchimes.

Pause

The Graces enter and seat Themselves on cushions so They form a triangle around you. Thaleia is to your right, Aglaia is to your left, and

---

† Monaghan, *The Book of Goddesses and Heroines*, pp. 136–38. The names of the Graces are pronounced THAY-li-a, ah-GLEYE-uh, and you-FRAHZ-uh-nee.

Euphrosyne is behind you. You can feel the abundant grace They bring you, the overflowing lovingkindness that surrounds you. Inhale Their radiance, let joy fill your heart, let the glow of love full all the spaces in your chest.

Pause

Let this glowing love radiate up into your throat and face and head, let it shine out through your third eye and crown. Let shining love flow down your arms and into your hands, let it bring strength and gentleness to your touch, let it shine out through your fingertips and lighten everything you touch.

Let this shimmering love sink down into your belly, let it radiate into your lower chakras, let it flow down each leg and shine through the soles of your feet so that everywhere you walk, you walk lightly upon the earth.

You can see the sparkling light of love as it forms a triangle around you, flowing from Thaleia to Aglaia to Euphrosyne. You are enveloped in shining love, you are enfolded in soft light. Feel the comforting radiance of the presence of the Graces.

"You are a loving person," Thaleia tells you. "You are filled with love. You never hesitate to say a kind word to one in need, you never wait to do a kind deed. You are filled to overflowing with love. This is your first blessing."

Contemplate your first blessing. Recall the kind things you do. Recall how you share your loving spirit with those you meet. Remember gifts you have given, volunteer work you have gladly done.

Pause

"You are beloved," Aglaia tells you. "You are beloved by your family and you have created an extended family with your friends. They come to you when they are in need, they come when you, too, are in need. You are well beloved. This is your second blessing."

Contemplate your second blessing. Remember where you have worked and played and how people always come to you. Remember circles you have belonged to, recall the sharing from heart to heart, the friendships and the fun.

Pause

"You are in love," Euphrosyne tells you. "You live within the ageless love of the Great Goddess Herself, you live in the essence of love. And in Her love, you are complete, you are whole, you are yourself. Your foundation is love, your pillars are love, your crown is love. This is your third blessing."

Contemplate your third blessing. Consider the love that surrounds you as the air surrounds you. Consider the love that lies under your feet as the supporting earth lies under your feet. Consider the strength and the persistence of the love that walks beside you. Consider the love that shelters you in all weathers.

You live in love and you are whole. You are loving, you are beloved, you reside in love itself.

Compassion: Tara / Kuan Yin / Mary

These three Goddesses,[13] who many say are aspects of the same Goddess, are especially known for the quality of compassion. These three are the Gentle Ones Who always come when we call.

The Tibetan Tara (Drolma in Tibetan) is a Boddhisattva who, although She has attained enlightenment, has vowed to remain in a woman's body until all sentient beings have come to safety, liberation, and bliss. Because of Her dark skin, Green Tara is sometimes identified with the Hindu Goddess Kali, another Fierce Gentle One. (In Tibetan, "green" also means "dark.") Iconographically, whereas the most famous Taras are green and white, there are actually twenty-one Taras of several symbolic colors. On the poster that hangs in my bedroom, for example, are Taras whose skin is red, blue, or green; other sources describe her as variously red, white, yellow, and blue. Whatever Her color, Tara dispels evil in all its forms and grants Her petitioner good fortune.

In China, the compassionate Goddess is called Kuan Yin, "she who hears the cries of the world." In Japan, She's called Kwannon. She, too, has vowed to remain in a woman's body until every single living creature reaches the state of enlightenment.

Mary is the Christian church's Mother of God, the Virgin-Mother whom men and women have for a thousand years petitioned to mediate with God the Father and God the Son on their behalf. Queen of Heaven, Mary is our own Blessed Mother, and we all know countless stories of Her appearances from Mexico to Lourdes to Medjugorje, as well as folk tales in which a child or fool appeals to Her and receives a miraculous answer.[14] Like Her Middle Eastern foremothers—Ishtar,

Inanna, and Astarte—Mary is the Queen of Heaven. Here is one stanza of the beautiful Byzantine Akathist Hymn to Mary:

> *Rejoice, O star that go[es] before the Sun.*
> *Rejoice, O womb of the Incarnate God.*
>   *Rejoice, for through you all creation is renewed.*
>   *Rejoice, for through you the Creator became a baby.*
> *Rejoice, O Virgin and Bride!*[15]

Tara, Kuan Yin, Mary—whatever name we use to call Her, we can be sure that She will reply, bringing hope and compassion to Her children.

This may be the most difficult meditation in this book, for we're not meditating to get compassion sprinkled down upon our own bodies and minds. No, we're meditating to bring compassion to someone who has brought tribulation into our life. Here are a few suggestions for who this person can be:

- The lover who has stopped loving
- The friend or family member who knows exactly how to push our buttons . . . and just keeps pushing and pushing and pushing
- The person who made the thoughtless remark or did something that really hurt our feelings . . . and we just can't seem to forget it
- The mindless boss who has harassed us, downsized us, cheated us out of income or opportunity
- The jerk who pulled into the parking place we were waiting (turn signal on) to claim.

A wise man once told me that the divine manifests *in* us, *through* us, and as us. Our task, therefore, is to manifest compassion for someone who hurt us. This is not, however, altogether altruistic, for we all know that "what goes around comes back around." Isn't it better for compassion to be what comes back around?

If you like music with your meditations, a good piece for this one is the Beatles' *Let It Be.* "Let it be" has two meanings. First, it can mean, "just allow something to exist, let it be what it is." Second, it can mean, "leave it alone, don't do anything," as also expressed by the old saying, "let sleeping dogs lie." Ponder both of these meanings as you listen to the song, and prepare to meditate.

The Meditation

Close your eyes, take a few deep, easy breaths, and bring to your mind's eye the image of the person who hurt you. You can visualize what this person really looks like or see a generalized image, but avoid cartoons or stereotypes, for our intention is not ridicule but compassion.

Pause

If that person's hurtful words or actions come with the image, observe them. Observe *from a distance* this time. Don't take it personally anymore. Consciously separate yourself from the hurt and know that its power is puny beside the power of compassion. *Let it be.*

Now visualize the symbol of eternity, a figure 8 on its side. Enlarge the symbol until it's big enough to contain you in one of its loops. Visualize the eternity symbol as pink, then as pink light, then as flowing pink energy. Watch this pink energy for as long as you want to, watch it flowing, twisting, looping, cycling and recycling, flowing around and around you. Feel its warmth. Feel it caressing you as it bathes your body, emotions, mind, and spirit.

Suddenly the person who once hurt you appears in the other loop. See that person standing in the eternity symbol, beside you but separated from you by the cross in the center of the figure 8. What this means is that while you do not have to be close to this person, it's important to understand that he or she is nevertheless just as warmed and loved as you are.

Pause

Know that the person is part of the same compassionate energy you're part of, that he or she is feeling the same love, the same compassion, and the same blessing that you're feeling. Let the energy flow around you both, equally and without judgment or favoritism, for as long as you want to.

Pause

Now another element comes into your vision. There you see Her—balanced on the very point where the two loops cross. There She is—dancing or standing upon the very center of eternity. Tara. Kuan Yin.

Mary. She stands, as She has forever stood, upon the cross of compassionate energy. Soon you can see the source of that flowing energy. It is She, of course. It flows from Her, from Her hands, from Her feet, from Her eyes, from Her heart, from Her womb.

And as you watch, you can finally understand how the compassionate Goddess consciously sends Her loving energy out into a world that surely and sorely needs that love. She has vowed to love us, and Her compassion will come to us whenever we call her. Forever.

Let it be.

Healing: Coventina

The best work we can do on earth is healing work. It's the best work we can do for ourselves. It's the best work we can do for our friends and for people we don't even know. It's the best work we can do for the planet itself.

Healing comes in many ways. When we nurture ourselves we begin to heal ourselves. I feel nurtured when I see my books arranged neatly on their shelves, when I'm spending time or corresponding with my friends. Like me, you probably nurture yourself by walking or gardening, with music or drumming, by making art, by working at your right livelihood.

In Arthur Miller's *Death of a Salesman*, Willy Loman's wife, Linda, defends him, saying, "Attention must be paid. He's not to be allowed to fall into his grave like an old dog." Paying attention is truly listening to someone. It's listening without framing your wisdom-reply while they're still talking. It's responding to what they're saying beneath their words, to both emotions being expressed and body language. Paying attention is healing. It saves lives.

I'm enormously encouraged by the growth of holistic healing in the U.S. Members of the good ol' AMA are actually recognizing the effectiveness of nonstandard modalities like traditional Chinese medicine, Ayurveda, chiropractic, homeopathy, bodywork, guided imagery, nutrition, and herbs. Because, writes William Collinge, of the occurance of new diseases (like AIDS) and the resurgence of old ones (like tuberculosis), and because many disease-producing bacteria (like the common staphylococcus) are now drug-resistant, the "compelling need for a widespread integration of the strengths of all traditions is obvious."[16]

Coventina is one of the Celtic Goddesses who are perceived in wells and flowing rivers. Monaghan describes the relics of Her sacred well in Northumberland. She is an "elegant-looking goddess." One sculpture shows Her "lying on water weeds, pouring the river from an urn she carries." In another sculpture, She holds branches of water plants "while thoughtlessly tipping her bucket." Like Mary at Lourdes, the ancient "watershed goddesses" are also healing goddesses.[17]

Coventina looks to me like the figures on Cards XIV, Temperance, and XVII, The Star, of the Tarot. Temperance, whom I also call "Transmutation," stands on both land and water and pours water (or, says Mary K. Greer, distilled essential oils) from one urn to another. The Star kneels or stands in the water and pours water (or healing scent[19]) on both land and water. Like Coventina, these are watershed goddesses whose water (or essential aroma) may heal the land and its peoples.

The Meditation

Sit comfortably, close your eyes, and take several deep, easy breaths. In your imagination, find yourself standing beside a stream that bubbles up from a cleft in the ground. This is a sacred spring, a holy well, and you know without seeing it that the stream that flows from the well later becomes a great river. Hanging from the branches of the ancient willow that grows beside the well are numberless strips of colored cloth, symbolizing prayers, and offerings of all kinds are heaped around the well and among the willow's roots. Downstream, where the stream broadens, are pools where people can bathe in the clear, cold water and be healed, and if you were to follow the path nearby, you would soon come to the temple complex, where there are areas for bodywork and classrooms, the oracle's cave, and the hypogeum, which is the underground chamber where seekers lie down to dream healing dreams.

Pause

Call into your mind someone who wants to be healed. This can be a friend who has asked for healing or you yourself. Visualize this other person (or yourself) as transparent, with their disease or wound plainly visible. Take as much time as you need for this. Let this person (or your double) be standing beside you.

Pause

Lead the person to the willow. Suddenly you are holding a strip of cloth whose color is the same symbolic color as the disease or wound. With a sincere prayer for the healing that is to come, both of you, together, tie the strip of cloth to the nearest branch of the tree. Now you must give an offering to the Goddess. Reach right into the disease or wound and pull part of it out. It miraculously becomes a token (what does this token look like?), which you lay at the edge of the well in thanks for the healing that is to come.

Pause

Walk hand in hand downstream to the bathing pools. Behold, Coventina herself is on duty today, as She often is. She is fair, with flowing long hair and flowing garments. Standing with one foot on the grass and the other on the water, She is holding a large, red amphora. The Goddess greets you and your friend and directs you both to sit in the water. She next begins to pour pure water from Her red amphora over you and your friend. This water is warm where warmth is needed and cold where cold is beneficial. Feel this water flowing over your body, feel it flowing through the pores of your skin to your bones and organs, feel it flowing to the disease or wound, and feel it saturating the disease or wound. And look!—the water changes color. Whatever color is most healing for this disease or wound, that's the color the water becomes. It becomes green at your heart, red in your blood vessels and muscles, green or purple or indigo or yellow in the disease or wound. Spend as much time as you need to let this healing colored water soak in.

Pause

When you and your friend emerge from the healing pool, Coventina wraps you in colored robes and directs you toward the temple complex. Follow the footpath, along which you see people sitting on benches or lying on couches in the shade. Some people are reading, others are meditating or sleeping, and strolling musicians bring healing music to all.

The glowing temple complex is surprisingly modest, for many of its rooms are below ground. After you announce yourself to the steward, you are directed to a quiet chamber where you and your friend lie on couches to take healing naps. Lamps placed here and there give off soft colored light and project the scents of healing oils—hyssop, clary sage, eucalyptus, and chamomile—through the space. A masseuse also comes to each of you to do her healing work.

Pause

Dusk arrives, and someone comes to take you to the oracle, who is Coventina, or perhaps one of Her priestesses. She invites you and your friend to sit with her. Talk to the Goddess. Tell Her what troubles you, where it hurts, how you came to be sick or wounded. Talk to Her about anything you want to talk about. She really listens to you. She pays attention to you, and you feel Her attention soaking into your disease or wound just as the healing water did. When She speaks to you, Her words are simple. Take as much time as you need to converse with the Goddess.

Pause

At last it is dark, and you and your friend are led to the hypogeum, where beds have been prepared. Here you may sleep in peace and without pain. Here you may dream and find healing in your dreams. Accept the blessing of Coventina or Her priestess and lie down. Sleep and dream.

Pause

When you wake up, you find yourself back in the everyday world. You understand that healing is now taking place. You also understand that healing a dis-ease or wound, whether it is physical, emotional, mental or spiritual, is not the same as curing only physical symptoms. Sometimes the best healing comes with death and the long rest it brings.

Courage and Strength: Wonder Woman

Sometimes we need more courage and strength than we think it's possible to have. Perhaps tragedy has touched our life, perhaps violent crime or abuse. Perhaps the times have just become too hard, and we are trying to deal with downsizing and unemployment, with bankruptcy or homelessness. Perhaps we're facing addiction—our own or that of someone we love. Perhaps we're confronting a troubled spouse, partner, or child and considering extreme measures. I'm not exaggerating here, you know; it happens.

In times like these, Wonder Woman is our hera.[19] This strong, courageous, and compassionate Goddess was born as Princess Diana, Goddess of the Hunt and daughter of Hippolyta, Queen of the Amazons. Thanks to the work of scribe/psychologist

Charles Moulton and All Star Comics #8, She entered Her modern reincarnation in December 1941, and She remains with us to this day, Her works and deeds recorded in D.C. Comics.[20] Like Sherlock Holmes, Wonder Woman is alleged to be fictitious, but we know in our hearts that such as they are real. Who knows—perhaps they're more real than we are.

The Meditation

Take a few deep, easy breaths. In your imagination, see yourself standing in a white room. There is a door behind you and another door in front of you, both closed.

Feel the atmosphere of this white room. It is neutral space, a place for time-out. This is a safe place, a secure, impenetrable refuge where you cannot be reached, disturbed, or abused. You are safe in this room. You are secure in this clean, quiet white room.

Spend a few minutes absorbing what safety and security feel like. Maybe you've forgotten, but now you can remember. Let the power of safety and security radiate to you from the four walls, from the floor, from the ceiling.

This is the ideal room in which to discover the courage and strength you've forgotten you had.

Pause

Here's a scary part now, but don't worry. *Nothing can touch you in this room.* Turn around and face the door behind you. Watch as it becomes transparent. Although you can see through it, that door is as thick and impenetrable as the glass wall that protects a bank vault.

Now you can see what's outside that door: it's everything that has been troubling you. But look—they're all impotent out there. Mouths open and close but no sound reaches you. Envelopes bringing bad news simply puff away before they touch the door. Large, aggressive, discourteous people are diminished until they look like they're in the wrong end of a telescope. Threats are unhearable, overdue bills dissolve into soap bubbles. All the chaos of the neighborhood is powerless to affect you. Anything that has been troubling you is on the other side of that thick door.

Give thanks that you are in a safe and secure space.

Pause

Now turn around again and—surprise!—Wonder Woman is standing beside you. Notice how tall and strong and beautiful She is. See Her red bustier, Her blue-starred shorts, Her red boots. See the gold bracelets on Her wrists and the magical lasso hanging at Her waist. See the tiara on Her black hair. You can be sure that Her invisible airplane is nearby.

Like a dear friend, Wonder Woman takes your hand, or maybe She lays an arm around your shoulders. You are entirely comfortable in the aura of Her friendship.

"You are worthy," Wonder Woman says to you. "You are good and strong and beautiful," She says. "You are brave and wise and fine and fabulous," She tells you.

Believe what She says.

It's all true.

Wonder Woman has more to say to you. She has a private message only for you, a message about your strength and courage. Take a few minutes and listen to Her words.

Pause

As Wonder Women finishes telling you what you need to know, She hugs you. Together, you and Wonder Woman face the door before you. This is the door to your future. There may be interesting adventures beyond that door, but now you know that you can handle whatever comes to you. You are brave. You are strong. You have a Goddess by your side.

Walk to that door and open it. Enter your future.

Three Wishes: Fairy Goodmother

Toss a coin in the fountain and make a wish. Rub the magic lamp. Break the wish-bone with a friend and get the longer piece. Blow out all the candles on your birth-day cake in one breath. Share a double nut or a double cherry with a friend. Wish upon a falling star. "Star light, star bright, first star I see tonight . . . ."

How many ways are there to make a wish? Some people scoff and say it's mere superstition, and although the *Dictionary of Superstitions*[21] calls making wishes "asking favours of the gods," it nevertheless lists thirty-eight ways to ask.

Why not make wishes? When I was very young, my father gave me a piece of good advice. "If it's not worth having," he said, "it's not worth asking for." Tradi-tionally, we can have one wish or three. I say, go for it! My three wishes are for my very own twenty-volume *Oxford English Dictionary*, a one-carat diamond stud for each ear, and royalty checks that pay me huge amounts for all the books I write.

Begin this meditation, therefore, by making your own three wishes. Let them be as extravagant as can be. Let them be serious or silly. Let yourself appear to be self-ish and let them be things for you, not for your friends or family or the whole world. Let yourself believe that you deserve to get what you want. In *The Artist's Way*, Julia Cameron tells us to stop setting limits:

> Most of us never consider how powerful the creator really is. Instead, we draw very limited amounts of the power available to us . . . . We unconsciously set a limit on how much God [sic.] can give us or help us. We are stingy with our-selves. And if we receive a gift beyond our imagining, we often send it back.[22]

Spend a few minutes dreaming. What three things do you, in the heart of your hearts, really, truly wish for? Write them down on red paper for good fortune. Then vow to accept them and work to get them, for as a friend once told me, we must "ask the Goddess and do our homework."

Ask which goddess?

We can ask the Fates or the Norns or any of the eighty-four goddesses of destiny that Monaghan lists. We can ask any of the thirty-two midwife goddesses, who tra-ditionally pronounce the fate of a newborn child. Yes, we can ask. But prophetic goddesses such as these may or may not give us what we ask for. Perhaps we need help from the Land of Faerie.

According to the *Encyclopedia of Fairies*, the familiar fairy "godmothers" of sto-ries like *Cinderella* and *Sleeping Beauty* would be "entirely out of place" at a Christ-ian baptism or in a Christian home. This is because by the nineteenth century, when fairy tales were written down and published by the Grimm Brothers and other scholars, Europe had long been Christianized and our supernatural patrons had become saints and guardian angels. "But there is a deep-rooted foundation for their appearance at a heathen [sic.] name-giving. It was on such occasions, indeed, that the norns, the parcae and the fortunae . . . made their appearance."[23]

Now is the time we need a Fairy Goodmother. Notice the word: *Good*mother. Because this is not a book of superstition but a book of goddess meditations, I call her Fairy Goodmother. After all, She brings good into our lives. And what does She look like? I like the old-fashioned Disney fairies: Cinderella's smiling fat lady, Pinocchio's Blue Fairy. You can visualize one of these great ladies or call upon someone you know better or even encounter someone no one has ever seen before.

The Meditation

Holding your three wishes written on red paper in your hand, relax, close your eyes, and take several deep, easy breaths. In your imagination, fly away to an enchanted land and find yourself standing at the drawbridge of a beautiful castle. You're on your way to find your Fairy Goodmother. Before you go, turn and look at the beautiful castle, with its turreted towers and flying banners. This is civilization. To find your Fairy Goodmother, you must go out to the heath.

Walk under the portcullis and across the drawbridge and follow the road down the hill. As you walk, notice how green and fresh the countryside is. Perhaps there are knights in shining armor riding by, perhaps there's a dragon hovering in the distance. Remember that dragons are not our enemies. They are guardians of wisdom and treasure.

Soon you come to the tall hedge that divides one realm from another. As you find the opening in the hedge, you hear a sound. Someone is clearing her throat. It's an ugly, smelly old hag, dressed in rags and sleeping under the hedge. "My child," she croaks, "will you feed a starving old lady?" In the Land of Fairy, you realize, such a being may not be a panhandler. She could be a Witch, a Fay, an Enchanted Princess. Don't take any chances. Look in the drawstring purse hanging from your belt and pull out the most valuable thing you find in it. What is this valuable thing? No matter how much you prize it, give it without hesitation to the hag.

Aha! We knew it. She stands a little taller, waves Her hand mysteriously in the air, and says, "For your generosity you will be rewarded. You'll see me again." And—poof!—She disappears into the hedge.

Pause

Pass through the hedge and keep walking. Now the road enters a dark forest where the trees loom over you. Keep walking. Soon you come to the place where three roads meet. And there, sitting smack in the middle, is a lady. "I am your Fairy Goodmother," She announces. What does She look like? She pats the ground. "Come sit beside me for a minute." At such a time, you are compelled to do what She says.

"Because you were generous to a poor old soul," She says, looking into your eyes, "I will grant you a wish. What is your wish?"

Tell Her your first wish.

Pause

Your Fairy Goodmother pulls Her long star-tipped magic wand out of Her little purse (how did She do that?) and waves it above your head, showering stars into your hair. "Granted," She says. "But," She says, "you must be alert, for things don't always happen as we plan, and things often come in disguise."

She waves Her wand again, more stars falling from it, and gets up and walks down one of the roads. "You'll see me again," She calls over Her shoulder.

Choose which road you want to follow, get up, and continue your journey. The forest seems thicker, if that is possible, but eventually you come to an opening. It's a circle marked by ancient trees and standing stones. You have come to a fairy ring. Magic rules here. Approach with care.

"Aha!" You hear a familiar voice. "It's a sign of wisdom to pause before a fairy ring. What gift have you brought?"

Search your drawstring purse again and pull out something that you value above all else. Without regrets, lay this precious thing before the standing stone closest to you.

"Enter the ring." There She is, hovering in the center, your Fairy Goodmother. She beckons, you walk to her, and She touches your forehead with Her star-tipped wand. "For your wisdom, you are granted another wish. What is your second wish?"

Tell Her your second wish.

Pause

"Granted," She says, "but remember, things often come when we least expect them, and they seldom appear as they truly are."

And, as you watch, She sinks slowly to the ground and continues sinking down into the ground. "You'll see me again."

Leave the fairy ring where you came in. See that your gift has been accepted and that you are free to continue your journey. The road takes a sharp turn and before long the forest dwindles into a bright green meadow that is punctuated by small hills.

Follow the road, which twists and turns through this meadow and among the hills. Soon you find yourself standing before a hill just a bit taller than you are, and the side of the hill facing you is littered with stones. It's a fairy barrow, of course.

"Well, here we are again," a familiar voice says. "What gift have you brought this time?"

Search your drawstring purse a third time and pull out a gift as valuable as your life. Without fear, lay it among the stones.

"Very good." Your Fairy Goodmother comes out of the barrow. "What is your third wish?" She is carrying a large covered basket.

Tell Her your third wish.

Pause

"Granted," She says, "but remember, the Goddess has given you the power to make your own wishes come true. Remember, also, that She has a sense of humor." Your Fairy Goodmother reaches into Her basket and hands something to you. It shines as bright as a star and its true shape is known only to you. "Go now," says your Fairy Goodmother. "Return to your mundane world," She says, going back into the barrow. "But," She calls back to you, "always remember me and trust the Goddess and trust the power She has given you."

As you stand before the barrow, your Fairy Goodmother's words echoing in your mind, the barrow and the land begin to shimmer. A haze surrounds you, you hear sounds as gentle as owls' wings, and soon you find yourself back in the ordinary world. When you're ready, open your eyes.

House Blessing: Hestia

In dreams and often in "real" life, our home is us. Clare Cooper Marcus conducted interviews with more than sixty people to prove it. "A home fulfills many needs," she writes:

> [It is] a place of self-expression, a vessel of memories, a refuge from the outside world, a cocoon where we can feel nurtured and let down our guard. A person without a fixed abode is viewed with suspicion in our society, labeled "vagrant," "hobo," "street person." . . . Those of us lucky enough to have a home may rarely reflect on our good fortune.[24]

I've learned to reflect on my own good fortune. I once lived for six months in the spare bedroom of someone I had thought was my friend. Forty boxes of my books were in another friend's garage, along with all my dishes and the precious *tchotchkes* I keep in my hutch in the dining room. Another dozen boxes of books went to yet another friend's home, and my plants and garden goodies went somewhere else. During that time I had no real home. The stress of living where I was unwelcome made me physically ill.

When I moved into my own home, therefore, I was overjoyed. I got all my stuff back! I retrieved my surviving plants from my friend's garden and bought new ones. I cleared out old energy and drummed new energy into my new home,[25] got out my feng shui books and put things in their proper places, and established the healing energy I needed. I became productive again. (I guess I should confess that as a double Cancer I'm a compulsive and enthusiastic nest-builder.)

I'm also a firm believer in the efficacy of house blessing.

Hestia is one of the eldest Goddesses, first daughter of Rhea. Robert Graves says that it is Her "glory" that "alone of the great Olympians, she never takes part in wars or disputes." She is so holy that She was seldom portrayed as anything more than a flame:

> The archaic white aniconic image of the Great Goddess [Graves continues], in use throughout the Eastern Mediterranean, seems to have represented a heap of glowing charcoal, kept alive by a covering of white ash, which was the most cosy and economical means of heating in ancient times; it gave out neither smoke nor flame, and formed the natural centre of family or clan gatherings.[26]

Even today, Hestia is the heart of the home, its literal or metaphorical hearthfire. She is the source of family unity, the source of our "homefulness."

For your meditation, use a real candle to represent Hestia. Get a fat red candle and set it in a black saucer or candleholder and make sure it won't burn the house down while you're meditating. Light the candle and get the image of the flame fixed firmly in your mind before you close your eyes.

The Meditation

Sit quietly with your fat red Hestia candle and close your eyes. Take several deep, easy breaths (but don't blow out the candle) and visualize Hestia's flame rising painlessly and magically from the palm of your stronger hand.

In your imagination, raise your hand or extend it in front of your heart and let the magical flame rise higher. Let its light create a sphere that fills the room you're sitting in, that overflows into the next room, into the next, until it fills your entire home. Let the light spill out into your porch or balcony or patio. Let it suffuse your yard, touching your trees and bushes and potted plants. Let it touch your mailbox and your garbage can. Let it extend to your garage or parking place, and let it fill your car, too.

Feel the energy of that radiant light. What qualities does it bring you? Look for cheer, for peace, for security in this new light that fills your home.

Pause

With your breath or imagination, reach down into your spiritual center and call up the qualities you cherish most—creativity and wisdom, privacy or openness, good fortune and healing. Call these qualities up from yourself and project them in Hestia's magical light into every nook and cranny of your home. Open all the doors, all the cabinets and drawers in the kitchen and bathroom, all the closets and drawers in your bedroom. Project Hestia's light into every possible space, among your socks, among your spoons, among your computer disks.

And now—somehow—in this beautiful, magical light you glimpse an eye. A hand raised in benison. The curve of a shoulder or back. Hestia is present in your home. Pray that She will take up residence, for She participates in no disputes, Her essence is cozy and economical.

Pause

Know that the Goddess is with you and within you, Her essence circulating in your blood and breath. Even if you are currently rootless or not ordinarily very attached to the idea of "home," Hestia is now teaching you how important it is to have a center, a metaphorical hearth to which you may return for comfort, nourishment, and self-expression. Listen to the important lessons of this elder Goddess.

Vow to remember Hestia's lessons and ask Her to bless your home always and in all ways. When She has done so (and, be sure of it, She will), project Her light farther out until it fills your community.

When you return to ordinary consciousness, you may want to place Hestia's red candle as near to the center of your home as possible. You may also want to clean house.

Celebration: Taillte

What a lot we have to celebrate! At a minimum, the sun comes up every morning. Even if life is pretty crummy right now, we get another day to hope and work for change.

What's to celebrate? Consider our life events and blood mysteries. You felt the baby kick today. A child is born and named. A child learns to read. A little girl has her first bleeding. A teenager gets her first job and first paycheck. A young adult graduates from high school or college. You get married or establish a home with a life partner. There are career successes. A woman completes menopause. There are post-retirement beginnings. You die and begin a new kind of existence.

Celebrate it all. Celebrate whenever you need a lift. It's possible that every day holds a reason to celebrate.

The Irish earth Goddess Taillte[†] was said to be the foster mother of the light, embodied in Lugh, a fire and grain god sacrificed every year to be reborn again. Taillte lived upon the great Hill of Tara, magical center of the island. Irish maps still show where Her palace stood at Teltown, near Kells. Taillte educated Her Foster Son, instructing Him in government and polite learning, and in gratitude Lugh instituted the Tailltean Games, which resembled the Olympic Games.[27] For generation upon generation, the Irish gathered to honor their Goddess, celebrating Her first harvest with the Games, bonfires, horse races, and a great fair where, it is said, all Ireland met. The sacrifice/harvest celebration lasted for the whole month of August. Modern Neo-Pagans call the sabbat that falls on August 1 Lughnasadh[28] after Taillte's Foster Son.

[†] Pronounced approximately TELL-teh. Her foster-son's name is pronounced LOO.

The Meditation

Harvest or new beginning or success—select your reason to celebrate today. Sit quietly, close your eyes, and take several deep, easy breaths. Recall your reason to celebrate and let all the feelings of joy and pride and cheer flood your mind and body.

Perhaps it's your birthday, perhaps it's another day of sobriety, perhaps you just got a new job or completed a whiz-bang project—whatever it is, *you deserve a celebration.*

Let's visit the Goddess Taillte in Her enchanted palace.

You find yourself sitting at a table in the great hall, sitting in the place of honor beside the Goddess herself. The chiefs of the tribes are gathered here in your honor. Strangely enough, for imaginary reality anything can happen, your present-day friends are also present. Everyone is celebrating with you, acclaiming you as the best-beloved child of the Goddess. On the table in front of you sits the magical cake, upon which your name is written in sparkling letters. Under your name it says WHOOPEE. It's an enormous cake, a titanic cake, your favorite flavor, the best cake ever baked. At your nod, the Taillte's pages cut and serve pieces of cake to everyone present. This is such a wonderful cake that there's enough for everyone to have seconds or even thirds. If anyone wants ice cream, ice cream magically appears on Taillte's great table.

Pause

Next on the agenda of this great celebration is the presentation of your Certificate of Achievement. Taillte's Foster-Son Lugh, God of Light and Land, raises His hand for attention. Your Certificate is so grand that it takes two pages to hold the scroll. As they unroll it, trumpets and trombones play a majestic fanfare and drums roll. Lugh reads your Certificate:

BY THE GRACE OF THE GODDESS HERSELF AND ALL THE NOBLES PRESENT HERE—

WE CELEBRATE THE MARVELOUS ACCOMPLISHMENTS OF THIS ROYAL PERSON.   *Your name*   HAS DONE GREAT THINGS AND IS TO BE REMEMBERED AND COMMENDED FOREVER AND EVER. FOR ALL DAYS AND NIGHTS TO COME, POETS AND BARDS WILL CELEBRATE THESE GREAT

THINGS. LEGENDS WILL BE WRITTEN. MYTHS WILL BE TOLD. THIS EVENT WILL ENTER HISTORY AS A GREAT DAY.

IN COMMEMORATION WHEREOF, WE ESTABLISH MAGICAL GAMES AND FESTIVITIES TO BE CELEBRATED IN PERPETUITY IN THIS MAGICAL PLACE. SO SHALL IT BE!

The applause is as loud as thunder, and people line up to hug you and pat you on the back. The pages parade your Certificate around the grand hall, and Taillte graciously directs them to set it upon Her throne for all to admire.

You are the cynosure of the realm, divinity for a day, honored throughout the land for your accomplishment.

Pause

Taillte takes you by the hand and leads you to the courtyard, where jugglers are juggling, tumblers are tumbling, bards are reciting, musicians are playing, and dancers are dancing. "Dear friend," the Goddess says to you, "look around. This great celebration is in your honor. You have done well, my friend," She says, "but remember, even when you have done less well, you are still worthy. Even when you believe you have no reason to celebrate, you are a great person. Never hesitate to believe in yourself. Never hesitate to come to my magical palace to celebrate." And She kisses you on each cheek.

As you bask in the sunshine and the applause of your friends and the love of the Goddess, reflect that yes, indeed, you are worthy of honor. Yes, indeed, you are a great and accomplished person. Yes, indeed, you deserve a celebration.

The Games are beginning. Take your place in the royal box with Taillte and Lugh. Spend as much time as you want to watching contests and sporting events and drama and dancing.

Today is your day to celebrate. And you can return to this magical celebration anytime you want to. Enjoy!

Beauty and Magic: Brisingamen—Freya's Magical Necklace

Not all meditation is sitting still with your eyes closed, breathing, and maybe seeing things. Sometimes we can do a working meditation, which is a purposeful activity performed in an enhanced state of consciousness. In this working meditation, you will create something beautiful and magical: a necklace.

Like the ring, the necklace partakes of the symbolism of the circle: it's one of the primary feminine symbols, both never-ending and protective, and all parts of a circle are equal (and nonhierarchical). Famous circles include the chakras, Stonehenge, King Arthur's Round Table, and the Ourobouros (the world serpent holding its tail in its mouth).

Brisingamen ("shining fire") is the magical golden or amber necklace belonging to the Norse Goddess Freya. This necklace is "not just an ornament," says Ralph Metzner, "but an instrument of magical transformation" created by four dwarves, which suggests that it incorporates the four elements.[29] Brisingamen may represent the rising sun or the aurora borealis. It is so beautiful and powerful that Loki the trouble-maker tries time after time to steal it.[30]

Freya (sometimes identified with Odin's consort, Frigg) is most often equated with Venus. Actually, Her name means "Lady," and She is one of the Vanir, the gods of the farmers and fishermen of Old Europe, whose invaders were Odin and the Aesir, or sky gods. The Valkyries were originally Freya's priestesses and the Volvas were seeresses devoted to her. Freya also owns a robe of falcon plumes that allows its wearer to fly through the air. She's a Goddess of love, magic, fertility, and death, a swan Goddess, and a sow Goddess, and She rides through the sky in a chariot drawn by cats or by a huge boar.[31]

To empower the necklace you create, do this working meditation under a new or full moon. In a class I teach from time to time, we collect ceramic, glass, wood, bone, and other kinds of beads, plus shells, sequins, *milagros* and other charms, and our personal treasures. We string our necklaces on yard-lengths of silk or rayon cord, whose color can be symbolic of the energy desired. We wear our magical necklaces to rituals and other special events and bear their beauty and magic with us. We add to them, take things off, and after a time we may even take them apart and make something entirely new out of the components. It's another example of the eternal cycle of creation/destruction/re-creation.

The Meditation

Gather your beads, charms, and cord. Light candles and burn incense if these will help inspire you. Hold these treasures in your cupped hands, and close your eyes. Take several deep, easy breaths.

In your imagination, find yourself at night on a bleak northern plain, an empty plain peopled only by boulders and standing stones and by evergreens and barren oaks, and scoured by the ferocious north wind. The only light is the light of the full moon. As you stand in this wilderness, still holding your treasures, search the heavens until at last you glimpse a dark speck high in the sky. The speck comes closer, growing larger, and soon you can see that it's a large golden chariot pulled through the air by two giant black cats. A minute later, you can see the Goddess standing in the chariot. Freya is coming to visit and inspire you. As She comes closer, you can see Her feather robe, and soon the gleaming necklace, Brisingamen, is visible around Her neck.

Freya reins in the cats as the chariot comes to a stop near where you're standing, then She steps to the ground.

This is your opportunity to talk with this powerful and beautiful Goddess of life-death-fertility. Tell Her that your intention is to create a magical necklace that will echo the beauty and power of Hers. Tell Her what kind of energy you want to invest in it. Ask Freya for Her blessings. Ask also for divine guidance and design advice. Listen to (or feel) Her words. Receive Her ideas, with or without words, knowing that you will retain what you need to know.

Pause

At the proper time, thank Her and *as gently as possible* open your eyes. So that you can maintain your alpha consciousness, be sure to move gently, making no abrupt gestures. Unless you are speaking to the Goddess, do not speak aloud.

Now begin to create your magical necklace. You may find yourself abandoning a pattern you might have had in mind before you began this meditation. That is not unusual. As you work, notice the smoothness of your cord as it moves between your fingers. Notice the power of its color, and recall the symbolic meaning of its color and what that color will bring to you.[32] As you work, pay attention to your beads and other treasures. Notice how the lights works in and around them. Notice their shapes, their textures, their colors and designs. Recall the magic each of these treasures will bring to your life. *Accept the magical beauty you are receiving from your necklace even while you are creating it.*

When your necklace feels complete (for the time being), tie the ends of the cord together. Because you are also using knot magic, you can recite a little charm, something like, *May this never-ending circle of beauty and power bring the never-ending magical energy of* _____ *into my life. As I will it, so must it be.* Tie the knot and hold the entire necklace in your hands, reciting your charm three times for the magic to work.

Now close your eyes again and gently lay your necklace around your neck. With a yard-long cord, the centerpiece should hang near your heart. Ask Freya to endow your new necklace with Her magical powers of creation, destruction, and re-creation, of love and beauty. She lays Her hand on the center of the necklace, above your heart, and pronounces Her blessing. Then She nods, steps back into Her chariot, and flies away.

Open your eyes, return to normal consciousness, and examine what you've created.

As I said before, you may be surprised. We may go into this working meditation with a plan, but we often come out with an unexpected work of art. It is sometimes a challenge to learn to accept such intuitive inspiration.

You may want to wear your magical necklace to rituals or while you do goddess meditations.

Soul Walk: Athene or Artemis

Here is another goddess meditation where you don't have to sit with your eyes closed. It's a walking meditation. As those who have studied Tai Chi, Zen, or yoga know, moving meditations are both interesting and powerful. Anodea Judith and Selene Vega include movement as part of the practice of using the chakra system to "work on ourselves." Movement is important, they say:

> [It] has been used in many settings, both ancient and modern, to enhance self-awareness, group bonding, and connection with the sacred. Without our conscious attention, the ways we move and hold ourselves in day-to-day life express [our] feelings and attitudes . . . . When we pay attention to this process, we can access many things that have been hidden from the conscious mind.[33]

Besides, the physical exercise you get in a walking meditation is good for your cardiovascular and respiratory systems.

Vietnamese mystic Thich Nhat Hanh writes that walking is also good for your soul. He gives the following instruction on how to do a walking meditation, which is, however, less purposeful than my version.

> When you practice walking meditation, you go for a stroll. You have no purpose or direction in space or time. The purpose . . . is walking meditation itself. Going is important, not arriving. Walking meditation is not a means to an end; it is an end. Each step is life; each step is peace and joy . . . . We seem to move forward, but we don't go anywhere . . . . Thus we smile while we are walking.[34]

In *The Vein of Gold*, Cameron makes walking a major tool for spiritual and creative renewal. Both Druids and Wiccans, she says, "quest by walking," and so do Tibetans and Native Americans. "Walk prayfully daily," Cameron urges, and while you're walking "consciously, vocally, enumerate your blessings."[35] Likewise, in her popular *Simple Abundance*, Sarah Ban Breathnach advises walking as meditation. "One step at a time," she writes, "I have found peace" and "I have found there is no wrong way to do a walking meditation."[36]

When I first wrote the following meditation, I had the good fortune to live downtown in a city full of interesting people and wonderful Art Deco architecture. Almost anywhere I wanted to go, therefore, I walked. And I discovered other benefits of walking. My clothes fit better. I started a new book and wrote several magazine articles I'd been postponing. I redecorated my home (I ended up with 120 glow-in-the-dark stars on my bedroom walls) and completed three lingering art projects. You may have a similar burst of creativity when you practice your walking meditation.

Before you set out, invoke the appropriate goddess. If, like me, you're an urban Witch who admires the great outdoors but don't want to get it on you, the goddess for your walking meditation may be Athene. She's an urban Goddess, founder of a major city, and in Her martial aspect She rules defensive warfare—She protects Her people and Her place.

If, on the other hand, you live where the trees and plants grow in the ground instead of clay pots and the wild things are bigger than roaches and rats and feral cats, then you want an authentic outdoor goddess. In a rural setting, the goddess for your moving meditation is Artemis, the mistress of wild beasts and the moon. Artemis can be more than a Goddess of wild places, however; it seems to me that She also guards domesticated rural areas like farms and even the parks in our cities.

The Meditation

Before you go out, follow these preliminary steps.

1. Set your intention, both practically and spiritually. That is, know that while you're going to the post office or grocery store, you're also doing important inner work. You may have a nagging problem to solve, a decision to make, a question to answer. The solution, of course, will come from your inner (or higher) self, and during the walking meditation you allow that inner self to work while your outer eyes are watching where you're going. The principle is the same as sleeping on a problem and waking up with the solution.

2. Invoke the appropriate goddess. You can light a candle and recite a ritual invocation or simply ask Her to be with you as you walk.

3. Visualize the presence of the goddess. Before you leave home, see Her beside you and see yourself wrapped in Her grace and power. As you walk, see Athene's face in the faces of the streetpeople, see Her hand on the traffic lights, see Her feet on the sidewalk. Know that Athene is watching over the city. As you walk, see the face of Artemis in nature, see Her hand on the trees, see Her feet upon your path. Know that Artemis still bathes in the streams, know that She still stands with Her bow and arrows to protect Her wild ones.

Don't drive. Don't take the bus. Don't run or jog. Walk. Walk purposefully and see what there is to see, hear what there is to hear, feel what there is to feel. Although you may be looking at the Walk/Don't Walk signs or scanning the ground for molted crow feathers, keep the Goddess somewhere in your consciousness. Be aware that She is indeed walking with you.

Look for small miracles. I've seen hummingbirds in the downtown alleys and been greeted with sincere courtesy by strangers. Pay attention to where you're going (unless you enjoy getting lost) and pay attention to the Goddess at the same time. Sing aloud if you want to. In the country no one will hear you; in the city it won't matter if anyone hears you.

When you come back home, take a few moments to give thanks to the Goddess who walks beside you . . . whether you ask Her to or not.

Note: Friends have told me that this meditation is also a useful preparation if you must walk alone at night (because your car broke down, for example). Invoke the goddesses and keep your eyes open.

BodyKnowing: Shakti

As anyone who knows me can tell you, I live mostly in my head. Yes, I love to drum, and I drum every week to ground myself, but I'm just not a mover or a dancer. I've taken three beginning dance classes from my friend, Judith Kali Evador, a priestess, dancer, and actress, and still—I just don't get it. The theory of movement, per se, I do get, and Kali Evador's technique of BodyKnowing makes a great deal of sense, even to me. In fact, it's especially useful for us cerebral types.

What is BodyKnowing? When I interviewed Kali Evador for help in writing this meditation, she told me that it is:

> attunement with the body's language that gives a direct experience of Spirit. The body speaks through subtle sensation, breath, sound, movement, and e-motion. This conscious awareness of subtle body energetics awakens our Deep Memory Cellular Be-ing and enables us to experience the ancient transforming power of women's mysteries.[37]

People get "gut feelings" all the time. We experience strong or subtle physical reactions to people we meet, places we go, things we do. But we don't always pay attention to these purely physical reactions. Consider your own body language. In a difficult situation, do you unconsciously assume a protected posture? Does your heart ever "skip a beat" or beat faster or slower? Do you find yourself leaning away from an unpleasant person? What does your body do when you are eager or joyful? What feelings do you get in the pit of your stomach, how does your breathing change? Have you learned to recognize your body's signals, its unique language?

Our body, Kali Evador says, "is an oracle. It's an oracle as reliable as Tarot cards, if only we will listen to it." The purpose of this meditation is to teach us to pay attention to our body oracle.

The Goddess of BodyKnowing is Shakti. Just as the yoni surrounds the lingam, so does Goddess energy surround and activate the energy of a god. Thus, every Hindu god—and, by extension, perhaps the gods of other cultures—needs a Shakti. Every god needs the Goddess' activating, empowering energy. Each of the three gods of the Hindu trinity, for example, is associated with a Goddess who embodies empowering female energy: Brahma's Shakti is Maya or Sarasvati, the Shakti of Vishnu is Lakshmi, and Shiva's Shakti is Parvati or Kali.[38]

Activating, invigorating, and empowering, the divine energy of Shakti can awaken us all to the true energy of the universe. And because the body has its own intelligence, we know that Shakti lives in each of us.

Kali Evador suggests that we do this BodyKnowing meditation every day for a week, and check in two or three times a day to build up a sense of awareness of what our body knows.

Before you begin, choose an issue about which you want clarity. Should you move? To this city or neighborhood or another one? Should you move in with a roommate? What about that job interview? How do you really feel about a new or potential relationship? What decision do you have to make? You may be thinking in your mind about one thing, but your body knows what's really going on with you.

The Meditation

Sit comfortably and close your eyes. Take several deep, easy breaths and begin to focus on your breathing, tracing its path through your body. When you're relaxed, do a body scan. Locate your usual aches. Find out where you feel tense, where you feel good. Become aware of *how your body is*. Become aware of the presence of Shakti, of your Goddess power. Become aware of the Goddess standing near you. Become aware of the site of Her power within you.

When you're ready, release the issue to your body. Ask your body the question you chose. Let your body react. Let your body move. (Open your eyes if you need to so you don't bump into the furniture.) Move and be aware of how your body is moving and feel what happens.

You may experience a physical shift like a sigh or a release or a flow of warmth. These generally indicate a YES answer. You may feel a change in your breath, like a gasp, or you may find yourself holding your breath. You may feel a tightness in your chest. These generally indicate a NO answer. Focus primarily on your trunk as you move and meditate and notice what your body says and how it says it. What gestures do you find yourself making? What steps or leaps are you taking? Are you spinning or galloping? Do you sit or lie down? Do you crouch or crawl?

When you're ready, sit down again and listen to your body. What is it telling you? What is Shakti telling you? Try not to use words to describe what is happening. Tune into your body and listen to its wordless intelligence. Focus on the activating energy of the Goddess and feel Her support.

Know that the power of Shakti moves in your body. Know that Her energy is your energy, that it is the Goddess who activates and empowers you. Know that She is always with you and within you.

Endnotes

1. *Larousse Encyclopedia of Mythology*, pp. 219–21.

2. J. C. Cooper, *The Aquarian Dictionary of Festivals* (London: Aquarian Press, 1990), pp. 191–92.

3. Julia Cameron, *The Artist's Way: A Spiritual Path to Higher Creativity* (New York: Tarcher/Putnam, 1992), Week 6.

4. Eric Butterworth, *Spiritual Economics: The Prosperity Process* (Unity Village, MO: Unity School of Christianity, 1983), p. 73.

5. Morgan Grey and Julia Penelope, *Found Goddesses: Asphalta to Viscera* (Norwich, VT: New Victoria Publishers, 1988), p. 4. Another hilarious collection of Found Goddesses is Sally Swain's *Oh My Goddess* (New York: Penguin Books, 1994).

6. Pronounced FUNG SCHWAY. Though there are many books on the subject, my favorite is William Spear's *Feng Shui Made Easy: Designing Your Life with the Ancient Art of Placement* (San Francisco: HarperSan-Francisco, 1995). Spear teaches "intuitive feng shui," which is not bound by Chinese custom and decorative style.

7. This affirmation and the meditation within the meditation were given to me by my feng shui consultant, Frances Daws. My meditation is loosely based on a meditation we did together. Frances advised me to do it every day for 27 days. On the 27th day I burned my affirmation and red envelope to release it. You can do the same.

8. Uta Ranke-Heinemann, *Eunuchs for the Kingdom of Heaven*, trans. Peter Heinegg (New York: Doubleday, 1990), pp. 59, 76.

9. Starhawk, *The Spiral Dance*, 10th Anniversary edition (New York: Harper and Row, 1989), pp. 229, 90–91.

10. Farrar, *Witches' Goddess*, p. 112.

11. Monaghan, *The Book of Goddesses and Heroines*, pp. 28–30.

12. These are the recipes for Venus incense and oil created by Scott Cunningham and given in *The Magic of Incense, Oils and Brews* (St. Paul: Llewellyn Publications, 1988), pp. 67 and 91.

13. One of my favorite books is China Galland's *Longing for Darkness: Tara and the Black Madonna, a Ten-Year Journey* (New York: Viking, 1990).

14. See Michael S. Durham, *Miracles of Mary: Apparitions, Legends, and Miraculous Works of the Blessed Virgin Mary* (San Francisco: HarperSanFrancisco, 1995).

15. *Dictionary of Mary*, p. 13.

16. William Collinge, Ph.D., *The American Holistic Health Association Complete Guide to Alternative Medicine* (New York: Warner Books, 1996), pp. 317, 319. Because I have friends coping with cancer, I also recommend Kathy LaTour, *The Breast Cancer Companion* (New York: Avon, 1994). Every woman should have this book on her shelf.

17. Monaghan, *The Book of Goddesses and Heroines*, p. 83.

18. See Mary K. Greer, *The Essence of Magic* (North Hollywood, CA: Newcastle Publishing, 1993), pp. 42–43.

19. "Hera," like "ovular" and "thealogy" (to replace "hero," "seminal," and "theology") are words used in the writings of feminist spirituality to bring a feminine dimension into our largely masculine language.

20. My thanks to comic book expert Paul Cummins for this history. See also Gloria Steinem, ed., *Wonder Woman* (New York: Holt, Rinehart and Winston, 1972), for the comics themselves, plus commentary.

21. Iona Opie and Moira Tatem, eds., *A Dictionary of Superstitions* (Oxford: Oxford University Press, 1989), p. 493.

22. Cameron, p. 91.

23. Katharine Briggs, *An Encyclopedia of Fairies* (New York: Pantheon Books, 1976), p. 147.

24. Clare Cooper Marcus, *House as a Mirror of Self* (Berkeley, CA: Conari Press, 1995), p. 4.

25. Among other things, I followed suggestions in Denise Linn's *Sacred Space* (New York: Ballantine Books, 1995).

26. Robert Graves, *The Greek Myths* (New York: George Braziller, 1957), pp. 74–76.

27. Lawrence Durdin-Robertson, *The Year of the Goddess* (London: Aquarian Press, 1990), p. 144.

28. Pronounced approximately LOO-nus-uh.

29. Ralph Metzner, *The Well of Remembrance* (Boston: Shambhala, 1994), pp. 155–56.

30. For a modern take on this legend, see Diana Paxon's novel *Brisingamen* (New York: Berkeley Books, 1984), which is set in San Francisco.

31. Farrars, *Witches' Goddess*, p. 222; Metzner, *Well of Remembrance*, pp. 71–72.

32. There are many books on color symbolism. Two I like are Manly P. Hall, *The Symbolism of Light and Color* (Los Angeles: Philosophical Research Association, 1976), and Scott Cunningham, *Cunningham's Encyclopedia of Crystal, Gem and Metal Magic* (St. Paul: Llewellyn, 1987), chapter 4.

33. Anodea Judith and Selene Vega, *The Sevenfold Journey* (Freedom, CA: Crossing Press, 1993), p. 24, emphasis added.

34. Thich Nhat Hanh, *A Guide to Walking Meditation* (Philadelphia: Fellowship Publications, 1985), p. 4.

35. Cameron, *The Vein of Gold* (New York: Tarcher/Putnam, 1996), pp. 25–31, 306.

36. Sarah Ban Breathnach, *Simple Abundance* (New York: Warner Books, 1995), April 16.

37. From Judith Kali Evador's brochure for the *Woman Mysteries of the Ancient Future Sisterhood*. Founder and Elder Priestess of this women's mystery school, Kali Evador lives in Los Angeles. Other information used in this meditation came from my interview with her on June 8, 1996. For information on how to reach Woman Mysteries, see the list of Resources.

38. Monaghan, *The Book of Goddesses and Heroines*, pp. 314–15.

5
Dark Work

Grandmother Spider

Dark work is cleansing, letting go, destroying one thing so another can be born, laying to rest. We do dark work while the moon is waning, from two or three days after full until the night before the new moon.

It's important to remember that work done during the waning moon can be as "positive" as work during the waxing moon and that for every birth there is a death and for every death there is a birth.

Our dark work meditations, therefore, recognize and use the cycles of creation, destruction, and re-creation to make necessary changes in our lives.

1. Cutting Ties: The Fates
2. Letting Go: Cloacina
3. Dumping Old Toxic Tapes: General Terminatrix and Her Cosmic HazMat Crew
4. Setting Limits: Themis and Nemesis
5. Meeting Your Shadow: Hel
6. The Path Into the Underworld: Hecate and Persephone
7. Grief: Rookha
8. Germination: Tellus Mater and Ceres
9. Rebirth: Madder-Akka and Her Daughters
10. Learning From Your Mistakes and Failures: White Buffalo Woman
11. Changing the Energy in Your Home or Workspace: Poza-Mama
12. Divination: Postvorta and Antevorta
13. The Widdershins Spiral: Grandmother Spider

Cutting Ties: The Fates

Sometimes it happens. Even the most spiritual people can be painfully "honest," both tactless and tacky. We manage to offend someone, or to be offended, and a friendship ends.

Actually, I don't think this is such a bad thing. If we don't manage to, as they say, "rattle a few cages" during our lifetimes, maybe we should take a closer look at issues of codependency. Or maybe we're just dull people and nobody's even noticed that we're here. (Which could be a fate worse than death.)

So words have been spoken in anger, unthinkable deeds cannot be undone, apologies are of no use, and it's over. Someone has been hurt, and while we really don't want to cause any more damage, we want to cut the ties that have bound us.

It's time to move on.

Clotho[†] ("the Spinner"), Lachesis ("the Measurer"), and Atropos ("She who cannot be turned or avoided") are the white-robed daughters of Nyx (Night) or Necessity. Clotho spins the thread of our life on Her spindle, Lachesis measures this thread against Her rod, and Atropos snips it with Her shears. These three are among the most ancient pre-Hellenic goddesses, and it was said that even the mighty Zeus—who foolishly dared to call Himself "Leader of Fates"—could not overrule Them.[1]

Can we change our fate?

If you still hate the person with whom you quarreled, your first task is to shed the hatred. Though it may take several sessions of meditation to do this hard work, it must be done. Do the "Compassion" meditation in chapter 4 (page 73) or visualize your hatred as blazing hot white energy and let it drain into the earth, where it will

---

[†] The names of the Fates are pronounced CLOE-tho, la-KEE-sis, and AT-ro-pos.

be absorbed and recycled as useful thermal energy. W
calm while thinking of the other person, do the foll

Please be aware that because cutting ties is ser
take a fair amount of time. Give yourself at least h
a thorough job.

The Medit

Sit quietly, close your eyes, and take sever
now standing on the porch of the temple of the Fates. ᴵᴼᵤ
with Their kind permission and within Their sight. Bow before the
Fates and acknowledge Their invincible power.

Visualize the person to whom you have been bound and from whom
you want to be free. Without emotion, examine this person, seeing him
or her as living out a fate planned long ago. Know that this person is as
free as you are to live and love and work and play.

Pause

Now take a mental step back so you can see yourself. Examine yourself carefully, taking as long as necessary, until you have found all ties
linking you to this person.[2] Most will be attached to your chakras, or
near them, which chakra depending upon your relationship with this
person and the issues of the relationship. These ties were spun on the
spindle of Clotho. They have been part of your fate.

Pause

If the quarrel was especially vicious, it is possible you will also find
metaphorical weapons—knives in your back, swords in your gut. If you
find knives, swords, hatchets, or other weapons, pull them out gently and
easily. See them for what they truly are: thoughtforms. Wrap each one in
"Goddess goo"[3] and bury them all in the earth. The goo will dull them
and render them harmless. Know that these weapons have no power over
you. Not now. Not in the past. Not in the future. Declare to yourself that
these weapons can hurt no one. Ponder the truth of your declaration.

Pause

e yourself again. Are you bleeding from any of those
dest cuts"? If you are, lay your hands over the wounds and be
ed. Visualize healing light coming out of the chakras in the palms
f your hands or treat yourself with more Goddess goo. All your
wounds are soon healed, from bottom to top, from deep to surface, and
without scars. Know that you are whole again.

Pause

Now trace the ties that still connect you to the other person. Identify
each one again. They may look like wires or hoses or shafts of light.
They may look like umbilical cords or tree trunks with hard, deep
roots. They may be thick or thin, and they will probably be variously
colored. Identify what each tie means. One can, for example, symbolize
the love you once shared. Another can symbolize work you did
together. Another tie can symbolize a book or a play or music you both
loved. A tie can symbolize a vacation you once took together. Other ties
can symbolize organizations you both belong (or belonged) to, places
where you used to meet, things you used to do together. Measure each
tie with the rod of Lachesis. Take its true measure, and understand
what it signifies both to you and the other person. That is, what are the
issues here? Take as much time as you need to take the measure of these
ties to be cut.

Pause

It is possible that many of these ties will trigger bittersweet memories. If you truly want to be free from this person, you must first
acknowledge the memories and then remember that all ties between
you must be cut and rooted out. This can be hard to do, but know that
you can do it. Know that you *must* do it.

Now look once more and see where the ties are attached. Mind to
mind? Heart to heart? Mind to heart? Gut to gut? Heart to gut? Heart
to sex? Sex to sex? *Find all the ties.* Take as long as necessary to trace
each one from your mental or emotional body to the other person's. If
it helps, you, attach little tags to the ties, as electricians tag hot wires.
You will know to handle these emotional hot wires with respect.

Pause

With the silver shears of Atropos, cut every tie between you and the other person. *Get every one of them.* Again, take as long as necessary to do this work, for you must be thorough. As you cut each tie, let it wither and drop out of your body as an umbilical cord dries and falls away. Know that you are freeing yourself, that you are being reborn free from all of these ties, past, present, and future. You will be free to follow your fate, and the other person will likewise be free.

When all the ties have been cut, see them on the floor at your feet, tangled in a heap like dead, dark wires.

Your next task is to eradicate the roots left in your body. In your imagination, find a powerful magnifying glass nearby and search each of your wounds. Find the roots and rootlets and dissolve them in a powerful cleanser. Find every bit of residue left by the roots and wash it away, too. Finally, shine a full-spectrum light on each wound to cauterize it.

Pause

Find a basket nearby and gather all these severed ties into it. Present the basket to the Fates. If They accept the basket, know that you are free. If They do not, or if They pull one or two ties out of the basket and hand them back to you, you must understand that you will, alas, have future business with the other person. You must accept this, for we cannot disobey the Fates.

Know, however, that we create our reactions to reality. Know that if you can carry out your unfinished business without hatred or rancor, then you are truly free. Know that it sometimes happens that we can learn the necessary lessons from other people than the one whose ties we just cut.

Bow down before the all-powerful Fates and return to ordinary consciousness.

Letting Go: Cloacina

Sometimes you just gotta let go. You have to get rid of the stinking, sticky stuff that's clogging up your life, eliminate that awful stuff that's got you all blocked up. During the waning or dark moon, invoke Cloacina, the Roman goddess of sewers. She's one of the most practical and least appreciated goddesses in the world.

If we didn't get rid of our old stuff, where would we put our new stuff? It's as true in our minds, closets, and bookshelves as it is in our digestive systems.

The Meditation

Visualize yourself sitting on the toilet. This toilet, however, is *magnificent*. It's a magical throne, with armrests inlaid with alabaster, a tall, supportive back with pillars of ivory, amber, and jet, a crown-embossed cloth-of-gold canopy above, and a jewel-studded golden bowl below.

Consider all the stuff inside you—blocks to your happiness, blocks to relationships and love, blocks to creativity, blocks to abundance of all kinds. What's got you all blocked up? Try these: fear, anxiety, jealousy, dysfunctional relationships, anger, self-pity, despair, addiction. These have been on my list from time to time. Add to them and make your own list.

Pause

It's time to dump all this awful stuff out of your life. Or at least to make a start on getting rid of it, since what took a long time to build up is seldom released overnight. You're bloated with all your stuff, flatulent with it. The stinking, sticky stuff you're carrying around inside is poisoning your entire personal environment. People can smell—or at least sense—it, and your toxic waste keeps them away from you.

Let it go. Dump it! Flush it away!

Pause

This is the highest of colonics, one that unblocks and clears out your soul, your mind, and your heart.

Begin elimination in the usual way, the same way you do it every morning (or whenever). Since this is a magic toilet, however, your stuff flows into warm, sudsy water. Then it flows down through shining silver pipes into a series of filters deep in the earth beneath your golden throne. Watch it go. The filters break your stuff up into smaller and smaller pieces and remove all toxins. Watch it happening.

Notice that Cloacina is standing near those filters, wearing Her divine hip boots, holding Her silver shovel and Her rainbow broom. She shovels your stuff from filter to filter until it's broken down into crumbs and dried by the cleansing east wind of new beginnings. Soon Cloacina sweeps all the crumbs of your old stuff into the cosmic compost heap. Now your stuff is good, clean, fertile manure that can be recycled and used to fertilize other people's gardens, where beautiful, nourishing things will grow. With your help!

Pause

Know that there is nothing inside you, mind or body, that is so nasty, noxious, or poisonous that it will not be understood, accepted, transformed, and recycled by the Great Goddess.

Pull off a streamer of your healing green toilet paper, wipe yourself, and flush. Realize how good you feel now, how clean and smooth you feel inside after this healthy dump. Send thanks to Cloacina for Her valuable help, open your eyes, and do some productive work today.

Dumping Old Toxic Tapes:
General Terminatrix and Her Cosmic HazMat Crew

Have you ever heard yourself channeling your mother? Saying things to your children or your friends that you swore you'd never, *ever* say? Do you find yourself reacting inappropriately? Conflicted? Doing really dumb things? Unable to *sincerely believe* the affirmations you sincerely repeat every day?

It could be those old toxic tapes still playing in your mind. You know them—the mindless rules and threats you kept hearing over and over when you were a defenseless kid. You heard them so often, in fact, that you internalized them:

- The dumb tapes, like this one that still stops you from eating salad: "green food will make your mouth all green."
- The good ol' basic tapes, like "girls are only good for one thing" and "women can never be executives because their hormones screw up their minds."

- The tapes of ignorance, like "don't ever let a boy think you're smarter than he is" and "it's all right, you've still got such a *nice personality*."
- The really stupid ones, like "nice girls never do that" and "the only way you'll ever get rich is to marry a millionaire" and "take education in college so you'll have something to fall back on if you don't get your MRS. degree."
- The life-searing tapes, like "I wish you'd never been born" and "you're worthless, just like your father/mother" and "why don't you just get out of my way—forever."

If you're not running those particular tapes in your head, you're surely listening to others just as toxic. We carry a lot of heavy mental baggage around, don't we? It's all hazardous materials. The dumb old beliefs and the cliches confuse and clutter up our minds, the ignorant and life-searing tapes threaten our mental health as well as our relationships, our career, and our spiritual growth.

It's time to dump those old tapes. Let's turn them over to an efficient team of Found Goddesses: General Terminatrix and Her Cosmic HazMat Crew.

General Terminatrix is an Amazon, a take-charge, no-nonsense warrior queen who knows how to get the job done. The members of the Cosmic HazMat Crew work with terrifying efficiency. Borea, Master Sergeant of the North Winds, will blow the power out of your debilitating beliefs. Salamandra, Master Sergeant of Fire, will reduce your toxic tapes to ashes. Maelstromia, Master Sergeant of Water, will drown them. And, finally, Terra Firma, Master Sergeant of Earth, will bury the remains in the cosmic garbage pit.

To begin, of course, you must identify the tapes to be dumped. Give yourself a private, quiet hour (or longer) with your journal or a notebook. It's better not to do this task on a computer. It seems to me that when we hold a pen or pencil in our hand and actually *write*, our emotions flow more readily. The legibility of your handwriting and how much you scratch out and rewrite can also provide useful clues about the level of your emotions as you do this task.

Ask your inner self to recite those old toxic tapes aloud. Write them down as you hear them. Play as many tapes as you want to deal with right now. (You can save some old tapes for future meditations.) Let yourself be angry. You can put that energy to good use.

The Meditation

Holding your toxic list, close your eyes and take several deep, easy breaths. When you're ready, see yourself standing outside a chainlink fence. You are holding a cardboard box full of old toxic tapes. When you look through the fence, what you see is a dump, a deep garbage pit whose sides are corroded and charred. Heaped randomly around the pit are centuries of unrecognizable wrecks, the shells of beliefs beyond salvaging. The Cosmic HazMat Crew is working industriously, and as you stand there you are witnessing destruction in action.

One of the members of the Crew finally notices you and points toward the gate. Carrying your box, which may be very heavy, walk along the fence to the gate and tell the guard, a strong woman in a camouflage uniform, who you are. Tell her, "I have an appointment to meet General Terminatrix and dump some toxic thought-patterns into the pit." The guard nods, checks the list on her ebony clipboard, and lets you in.

Still carrying your box of toxic tapes, walk to the command center, a square black building with windows on all four sides. The windows are shielded slits and the door is iron. Knock on the door. Knock firmly so that you will be heard.

General Terminatrix Herself comes out of the command center and greets you. "You've made a wise decision," She tells you. "Dump that stuff and dump it now. Get that poison out of your life today."

"Yes, ma'am," you reply. You've already figured out that General Terminatrix takes no prisoners and you're mighty glad She's on your side. Walk with Her to the first destruction post.

Here you meet Master Sergeant Borea. She takes your box and sets it in Her wind tunnel. "My cold north winds are blowing the power out of that hazardous waste," She tells you. "My winds are sharper than the sharpest words, stronger than the strongest prejudice." Watch as your old toxic tapes are blown out of the box and through keen-edged filters. The shreds of your tapes are collected in a brass box. Master Sergeant Borea hands this box to you. It's much heavier than you expected it to be.

Pause

Now General Terminatrix leads you to Master Sergeant Salamandra's station. "My fires will incinerate your old toxic tapes," She tells you, putting them into Her brazen furnace. "My fires are hotter than the hottest temper. They blaze higher than any high-flying, false belief can reach." Watch the shreds of your old tapes as they burn. The ashes are collected in a marble bowl. Master Sergeant Salamandra hands this bowl to you.

Pause

General Terminatrix leads you to the third destruction station, where Master Sergeant Maelstromia is waiting. She takes the ashes of the shreds of your tapes and pours them into Her titanic whirlpool. "My waters flood away all obstacles to truth," She tells you. "They wash away the darkest errors and the grossest lies." Watch as the ashes are washed and flushed into a small white coffer, which Master Sergeant Maelstromia hands to you. It's noticeably lighter than the bowl was.

Pause

General Terminatrix leads you to the last station. Here you meet Master Sergeant Terra Firma and hand Her the small white coffer. "What is freely given to me," She says, "I bury. I bury hazardous mental wastes in the black earth and in eternal silence." Master Sergeant Terra Firma picks up a small crate filled with black earth, empties the white coffer into it, and turns the soil with Her iron fork to bury the wastes from your old toxic tapes. She hands the crate to you. You're amazed at how light it is.

Pause

Follow General Terminatrix now to the garbage pit in the center of the compound. "Are you ready to give up the last remains of your old toxic tapes?" She asks you. If you are ready, tell Her yes and hand Her the crate. Watch Her hurl it into the pit, which pulses and heaves and flashes. This pit, you suddenly realize, is really a cosmic a black hole. Watch the crate filled with the remains of your old toxic tapes shrink and disappear.

If, however, after all you've done and seen, you still want to hang on to some of those toxic old tapes, thank the General for Her efforts and take your crate and go home.

It's your decision.

Setting Limits: Themis and Nemesis

How hard is it to say NO? Because girls are so often socialized to be agreeable and not make waves, saying NO—and meaning it and making it stick—can be a major issue. Some of us become workaholics because we can't refuse an assignment. Some of us have troubled and troublesome children because we can't set and maintain limits for them. We're taken advantage of by friends who negate our priorities and insidiously persuade us to do what they want. We're overcome by pushy sales clerks and repairmen because we can't say NO. We overspend on our credit cards and our energy because we ignore our limits.

Sometimes the inability to set limits becomes life-threatening. If we can't say NO, if we have nowhere safe to go after we've said NO, we may become victims of emotional or physical abuse—rape, incest, battery, stalking. When this happens, *it's time to get help.* Call the police. Go to a shelter. Find a trustworthy psychotherapist. The following meditation is not a substitute for legal or therapeutic assistance, but it may help you make a positive decision.[4]

One of the first daughters of Eurynome, Goddess of All Things, Themis[†] is a titaness and the ruler (with the titan Eurymedon) of the planet Jupiter. The Seasons and the Fates are Her daughters. Ruler of prophecy and goddess of order, Themis divided the year into thirteen months and two seasons marked by the summer and winter solstices. Monaghan says that *themis* was also a common Greek noun "indicating the power of convention, of whatever is fixed in society as steadfastly as the earth beneath us."[5]

Nemesis, "due enactment or divine vengeance," is a daughter of Night and Erebus ("the pit"), a nymph-goddess whom the Greeks transformed into a philosophical concept and who sometimes transformed Herself into an ash tree. Worshipped beside Themis in Attic Rhamnus before the Olympians conquered Greece, Nemesis "tormented those who broke the social rules that Themis represented."[6]

Setting limits is thus both a personal and a social issue. We are often urged to "think globally and act locally." If we can learn from these two goddesses how to find and set our limits and stick with them, we can act locally in transforming ourselves, though we may still have to deal with people who persist in trying to violate our limits. I believe that if enough of us find, set, and stick with our limits, we can

† Rhymes with GEM-iss.

also act globally and transform society. With the help of Themis and Nemesis, we can bring order back to our so-called civilization, an order created by partnership, cooperation, and shared power.

The Meditation

Sit quietly, close your eyes, take a few deep, easy breaths, and contemplate your life. Identify several situations in the past when you wish you had set limits, either in your own behavior or to guide someone else's behavior. Such situations can involve children, partners, coworkers, or others. Gently and without guilt, let yourself understand how troublesome a lack of limits has been for you. Remember the inconvenience, the guilt, the danger. See what you look like when you are thus troubled.

Pause

Let a current situation come into your mind. Is this a new situation or another episode of an old, old story? Again, this can involve children, partners, or other people.

Pause

Visualize this current situation as clearly as you can. Who is involved? What are they doing (or not doing)? What are you doing or not doing? What are your needs and wishes in this situation? What specific limit do you need to set? What do you need to tell these people who are pressuring you?

Pause

Understand that just as your failure to set limits in the past makes it harder to set limits today, so your failure to set limits today will make your future more troublesome.

Call on the Goddesses. Ask Them to help you.

Themis appears first. Explain your dilemma to Her. Because today's practice makes tomorrow's behavior easier, ask Her to help you set just one limit. What *one thing* can you do today to set a limit? Where and to whom can you say NO? *Listen to the answer you get. Resolve to remember it. Resolve to act on it.*

Pause

Themis gives you not only a sample limit but also a token to help you remember it. This token can be a fence (white pickets, chainlink, barbed wire), a wall (concrete, glass, bricks, stones), a hedge or a row of trees, a firebreak, a border-crossing with a gate (the kind you see in movies set in wartime Europe), a barricade like the one the students in *Les Misérables* erected in the street. Whatever image ignites your imagination, that's the one to keep and take back to the everyday world.

Visualize yourself in the current situation where you need to set a limit. Say, "This far and no further." Say, "This is my limit." Say, "I set this limit and it must be honored." Say, "This limit is impassable." Where your limit is, plant your token there. Anchor it deep into the ground if you need to, with rebar. Glue it down with epoxy. Just make sure it will stay where you put it.

Pause

Still visualizing the current situation, watch the other people encounter your new limit. How do they react? With anger? Do they try to ignore your limit? Do they test it and push as far as they can? Do they try to slide underneath or slink around? Do they try to distract you? How? Thrust your limit away?

Pause

Call on Nemesis. Call the white-robed avenger, and She appears. Let Her show you how to handle these poisonous people who keep ignoring your limits. She can stand as firm as the Ring-Pass-Not. She can chase the people away. She can rough them up. She can bring in other authorities and permit them to take action. Watch Nemesis torment those who wish to violate your limits. Resolve to take Her lessons back to your everyday world.

Pause

When you have a plan of action firmly in mind, thank these two Goddesses and return to your normal awareness. Now you know what to do. If your plan involves taking a self-defense class, for example, go out and sign up today.

Meeting Your Shadow: Hel

Ages upon ages before Sigmund Freud gave birth to the id monster and thrust it into an innocent world, the wise ones knew that we have shadows. There is, and always has been, a wild thing lurking somewhere in our unconscious, a dark creature of whose roaring we may be unaware.

Psychologists have tended to view the unconscious as a dark closet, a cluttered and dirty basement full of repressed emotions, negative archetypes, suppressed memories, and fears. Occasionally, Jekyll drinks the potion and becomes Hyde, and things rise up: shock and horror, psychosis, deviancy, psychological projection. The shadow self seems to spring forth without control. Fearing any chaos or lack of control, mainstream metaphysicians immediately pour their all-purpose white light into any dark crack and eliminate all shadows altogether.

Eventually, though, we figure it out. We see that the darkness provides balance to the light. Why would we want to live eternally in the light and see only what is obvious? Shadows give depth to our vision, dimension to our understanding. The dance of light and shadow makes the world more interesting.

The dance of our bright and shadow selves makes us more interesting, too. Not nicer, perhaps, not docile, not obedient, not always polite, seldom politic. When we pry beneath our social masks, we discover how complex we are as human beings. Sometimes we find talents and strengths we didn't know we had.[7]

To meet your shadow, you can go to Hel. But Hel is not a place. Hel is the Scandinavian goddess whose name was appropriated by the standard-brand churches for their imaginary pit where sinners are gleefully tortured through all eternity by the lieutenants of their angry god.

The goddess Hel, whose name means "One who hides" or "One who covers up," rules a nine-circled realm under the roots of the World Tree itself where people who die of disease or old age come to hide or be covered up. It's nothing like the Elysian Fields, however, for Hel's palace is named Sleet-Cold, Her servants are named Senility and Dotage, and Her gate is guarded by the hellhound, Garm. Those who come to Her travel on a road named Helveg ("Troublesome Road"), which is guarded by a maiden named Modgud. As Monaghan concludes, "Hel is more ancient than the heroic myth of Valhalla, the hall of dead heroes—old, perhaps, as the grave itself."[8]

Prepare yourself for a shadowy journey through deep, dark caverns and terrible underground places.

The Meditation

Sit quietly, close your eyes, and take several deep, easy breaths. In your imagination, find yourself wrapped in a warm cloak. Travel to the northern desert and find a winter village that is older than the ice itself. The hovels here are built of sticks through which the wind whistles, and the hearthfires here can spare little warmth as they falter before that wind. Look up and see the Northern Lights flaring in bursts of violent greens and purples. You can just barely see the moon, which has reached its palest waning crescent. Tomorrow night, when the moon is dark, you will sleep in Hel's bedchamber.

A dozen small huts encircle an open space. Select one to visit, go to it, and knock on the door, which shakes beneath your knuckles. A crone, blind and as old as her village, answers your knocking. Say to her, "I come in pilgrimage to meet my shadow."

Toothless as well as blind, the crone grins and nods. "I've been expecting you. Well, then, let's get going." Locking the door with an enormous iron key, which she tucks under her ragged blue doeskin cloak, she leads you to a well that is even older than the ancient village around it. This well is covered by a thick wooden lid upon which are engraved five red runes—Thurisaz ("gateway"), Raido ("journey"), Tiwaz ("warrior"), Berkana ("growth"), and Mannaz ("self").[9]

Thurisaz   Raido   Tiwaz   Berkana   Mannaz

Pointing to the first rune, Thurisaz, the crone mutters something about gateways in your ear. Listen carefully, for her message is different for everyone who comes here.

Pause

She next points to Raido and talks to you about your journey to come. Again, her message is different for each person who comes to her.

Pause

Next, the crone speaks of Tiwaz, the warrior, and asks you what it it takes to make a warrior of you.

Pause

Fourth, she points to Berkana. How are you growing? How will you grow if you survive this journey?

Pause

Last, she points to Mannaz. Listen carefully to her words. Who will your *self* be after your journey to Hel's palace in the Underworld?

Pause

And now the crone lifts that heavy well cover, pushes it aside, and points down into the well's dark center. Holding her great iron key in her hand again and nodding for you to follow her, she steps into the well and disappears. What are you afraid of? Follow her. Take that step into empty space. Step into the well. Feel how cold it is.

You're falling. There is a faint light—from what source can it come?—and you observe that the brickwork becomes more primitive as you fall. It changes to worked stones, changes to stones piled together without mortar, changes to hard-packed earth, changes to carved volcanic stone, changes to—how can this be?—changes to the roots of an enormous tree.

Pause

You have arrived at the roots of Yggdrasil, the World Tree, the *axis mundi*, the great ash tree that supports all nine realms of existence.[10] You have entered the great darkness. You are standing in the great frozen caverns under the world.

But where is the crone? Look around. No one is here. Nothing. You are absolutely alone. Where are you to go? Who will give you direction? You find yourself standing at the edge of a precipice and far below, so far below that it looks like a twisted white thread, is the River Gjoll.

Suddenly you feel the warmth of someone standing beside you. The crone is gone, and here is a maiden, but she is dressed in the same ragged blue doeskin cloak, she is holding the same enormous iron key. The maiden nods. "I am Modgud. I guard this path." Where Modgud points you see that the abyss is spanned by a swaying golden bridge. "There lies your path. Take no false steps or you will fall and die forever."

"Where is the crone?" you ask, but Modgud says only, "Go that way," and points again at the swaying bridge. This is outrageous! How dare she? How dare the crone desert you? What if the bridge breaks? You don't want to die forever. Are you angry enough to strike Modgud?

Modgud nods again, turns her back on you, and walks away. Will you stand there or go on? What can you do except cross the bridge? You've come this far, why turn back? How would you get back? "Troublesome Road," indeed. Just cross the bridge. If you look down, who knows what you may see. What kinds of monsters lie down here in such dark and cold? Look down. What do you see in that deep abyss? What could rise up to attack you?

Pause

It's a hard crossing. The gold pavement makes the bridge slippery. The hand rails are flimsy. You can hear the river roaring below, the cold wind pushes you this way and that, and the far end is veiled in shadows. Take one step at a time. Cross the bridge. If anything comes up, deal with it.

There. You made it. But how dare they make you do this alone? Who do they think they are? And now—sound where before there was dead silence. Groaning and wailing. Moaning and crying. There is nowhere to go but forward. Where is this groaning and crying coming from? You might as well go on.

Soon you see the gate, Hel's gate, and it's guarded by the black hound, Garm. Did anyone warn you about this? The hound is as tall as you are. It probably outweighs you, and its sharp fangs are longer than your fingers. When the hound sees you it begins to bark, the bristles on its back stand up. It's up to you to deal with this hellhound, and you have no weapons. Do whatever you must do to get past the hound and reach the gate.

Pause

At last the gate opens, you slip in, and the growling, barking dog is shut out behind you. An old man turns to you. "I am Senility," he says, "and you must come with me." The way he leads is the only way there is to go. Though this path is covered with sharp rocks and blocked by wild bushes with sharp thorns, there is no other path. Follow the old man to Hel's palace, Sleet-Cold, and knock at the door.

Another old man answers your knock. "I am Dotage," he mumbles. "You must pay to enter here." And without warning, he snatches your warm cloak from your shoulders, and then he takes the rest of your clothes as well. You are now defenseless.

Hel's great hall is crowded with ragged people. Many are pacing, stalking prey only they can see, others stand and sway and hold themselves, others sit on threadbare couches or lie and roll on the greasy floor. Everyone is complaining, moaning, wailing, crying, weeping. The awful noise of this bedlam seems to crawl right into your head. Suddenly one sees you, then another. As a mob they rush toward you.

You're surrounded. They're shouting their names at you. Jealousy. Greed. Covetousness. Arrogance and Self-Pity. Insensitivity. Seduction, Intimidation, and Manipulation. Addiction and Rage. Control. Violence and Cruelty. Every name they shout at you strikes you like a physical blow, every name pierces your skin, every name draws blood.

"We have named you," one shouts. "Name yourself!" someone else shouts. "As you are us, so we are you!" a third shouts.

What is your name? Who are you when you stand in Hel's dank palace under the dark earth?

Pause

You see a tall stone arch at the far end of this great hall. Perhaps you can find refuge there. But how will you get there? How can you pass through this mob? Do whatever you can to cross the great hall, to pass among these mad, ragged people who grab at you and scratch you with their filthy nail.

Suddenly you see that all those shouting people look like you. Can you pacify them? Tame them? At the cost of your life, you must do so. You must meet these mad, awful people. You must recognize them, acknowledge them, befriend them. Take as much time as you need in Hel's crowded hall.

A piebald old woman, black and white, suddenly appears beneath the arch. Ignoring the noise of the mob, She walks toward you and meets you in the center. Soon you see that She wears a shabby white gown, a faded black mantle, and a tarnished crown. "Yes," She says, taking your hand, "yes, I am Hel and I rule here." She leads you across the now-silent hall, under the arch, and into a room where you find a bed draped with curtains of red damask. You also become aware of the scent of roses.

"You have met your shadow," says Hel. "You have encountered your fears and survived. Sleep here in My warm bed this night and reflect on what you have seen and done. Dream of what you may do. Tomorrow, when the moon is new, you may return to your own world."

Once more, consider the runes you saw at the beginning of your journey to meet your shadow. Remember what the runes meant before your underground journey and ponder what they now mean to you: Thurisaz ("gateway"). Raido ("journey"). Tiwaz ("warrior"). Berkana ("growth"). Mannaz ("self"). After you return to daytime consciousness, write about these runes in your journal.

And consider this, too: Did you really meet monsters, or was this merely a bad dream? It often happens that what we project is far worse than what really is.

The Path Into the Underworld: Hecate and Persephone

Death is all around us, not only in nature every autumn but also stalking our friends and families. In the age of AIDS and cancer, in a time when children seem to take guns to school as often as they take their homework, in a time when random violence can find us on the freeway, at an ATM, in the grocery store—this is the time to begin to make friends with death.

For as a friend once told me, "Death is only the little part at the end."

When I was an AIDS emotional support volunteer, I helped three "buddies" (two men and a woman) prepare to die. When I first wrote this meditation, my beloved friend Rebecca lay in her bed two thousand miles away. We'd been friends for nearly twenty years. We raised our sons together and we did wise and foolish things together. (I still remember the night we went into an Albertson's bakery and ordered two of everything.) She was a wonderful artist, and I'm proud that I once arranged a one-woman show for her.

One bright August day she phoned me: "I have stomach cancer." A week later, the doctors removed her stomach, sewed her esophagus to her small intestine, and sent her home. It took her three months to die. As I learned at Hallows, nearly a year later, my beloved friend is now resting in a beautiful blue place.

You, too, have friends who will die. If you want to—*and only if you have their permission to do so*—you can help them. Begin with the "Love" meditation to the Graces in chapter 4 (page 71). When the time comes, here's a meditation to the great goddesses Hecate and Persephone, Crone and Queen of the Underworld.

Hecate was originally a pre-Olympian triple goddess of the underworld and magic. Magic was thought to be especially successful if done at night where three roads meet. This setting was called *trivia* (tri-via, or three roads); now it's just trivial. How diminished this Goddess is today! She came from Thrace, the northern wilderness where the Greeks said all the witches lived. Graves says She has three heads, lion, dog, and horse, which refer to a three-season year. The dog head, and also the three heads of Her dog, Cerberus, refer to the dog-star, Sirius. Cerberus is the Greek counterpart to the Egyptian Anubis and to the northern European Hounds of Annwm.[11]

We all know the story of the "rape of Persephone," wherein the young daughter of Demeter, the Grain Mother, is kidnapped by Hades to become His queen. In the pre-Hellenic story, by contrast, She goes voluntarily to the shades of the dead to initiate them into their new existence. Touching each dead one with pomegranate juice, She says "You have waxed into the fullness of life/ And waned into darkness;/ May you be renewed in tranquility and wisdom."[12] Graves says that Hecate and Persephone represent the "pre-Hellenic hope of regeneration," whereas Hades symbolizes "the ineluctability of death." "Gracious and merciful" Queen Persephone is faithful to Hades but has no children by Him and prefers the company of Hecate to His. The Farrars say that as Hecate is the "dark link" between earth and the Underworld, Persephone is the "bright link."[13]

If it's appropriate to do so, sit with your friend and read this meditation aloud. As I learned from my AIDS buddies, a person who seems to be unconscious can still hear our words and feel our concern and love.

Light a candle, too. I like the "guardian angel" candle, its glass jar wrapped in the sentimental Victorian print of the beautiful angel guarding two children as they cross a bridge. How appropriate this candle is for this final crossing.

The Meditation

We are going to take a journey together, you and I. We're going to visit the Underworld, the realm of shadows guarded by fierce Hecate and Her three-headed dog and ruled by gentle Persephone. Let me be your soul's guide, your psychopomp. You'll find much to ponder as we travel, but there is nothing to fear.

In your imagination, arise from your bed. Notice that you are vitally healthy again. There are no drugs, no IV tubes, no bandages, no catheters, no machines. You are strong and whole and beautiful, just as you were . . . before. Arise and come with me. Take my hand and we'll fly magically to the edge of the world, beyond the moon, and back again, and we'll find an earthly meadow filled with green grass and flowers. Near the center of this meadow is the entrance to the Underworld, surrounded by flowering almond and globe amaranth for hope and immortality, by daisies and eglantine for innocence and simplicity, and by sage for wisdom. In the midst of these flowers, and more, beneath the sheltering yew and cypress trees is the door. Let us go in together. We will come to three rooms.

Just inside we encounter three-headed Cerberus, Hecate's dog of the crossroads. Cerberus demands gifts before he will let us pass. Choose three things from your life you will gladly give up. An unforgotten quarrel. A lie never owned. Hurtful words spoken too loudly. Give these things to the dog and let him bury them as they deserve to be buried.

Pause

The first room is small and dark, lit only by a few coals in a brazier, which also gives off scant warmth. Hecate waits here, She who called the Crone, the ancient Queen of the Night who rules thresholds.

Bow down before this awe-ful Crone. She is as old as time, Her face plowed through with life and death, Her back bent with courage and suffering. The Crone is the survivor. She has survived all things, and from Her we may learn that we too will survive all things.

Hecate also demands a gift before we may pass. Give Her some small thing from your old life . . . a faded memory, a habit long outlived, a worn-out prejudice, worthless words. Useless to you, this thing is useful to Hecate, for she'll add it to Her dungheap to be recycled.

And perhaps Hecate will give you something in return, a story or a lesson. We'll sit in silence before Her for a while and see what She has to tell us.

Pause

Now we must move on, and the next room is the three-sided Chamber of the Judges, Minos, Aeacus, and Rhadamanthys.[†] They are the Three Lords of the Dark Sun, the three wise Lords of Endings and Beginnings, and no smile touches Their lips, no compassion lights Their eyes, no rancor stirs Their hands. They tower above us, They stand as still as granite statues. We know that They represent justice, judgment, and balance. See the dark sun shining through the roof of Their chamber, the jet black walls, notice the maze in the floor, jet inlaid in ebony.

Are we strong enough, brave enough to face the Judges? Let us pause here and take stock of our lives, recalling both the good and bad, recalling both successes and failures.

Pause

The Judges also require gifts. When in your life were you unjust? Give that injustice to Minos. When did you make a faulty judgment? Give it to Aeacus. What part of your life was out of balance? Give it to Rhadamanthys.

Pause

As Inanna did when She descended to visit Her sister queen in the Sumerian Underworld, you have now made seven sacrifices. You have given up seven things that were once important to you, seven secrets, seven things that perhaps held you back.

Let us now go to meet Persephone.

Her chamber is large and well lighted. It is a high place, golden and warm. But the room has no shape, no shape we have ever seen on earth. It is neither round nor square, and we realize that the room is shape-shifting, the walls are forming all the geometrical shapes. This is the throne room of Persephone, and it is also a galaxy of scents, tender rose, pulsing violet, singing jasmine, also sandalwood and pine.

† Pronounced MEE-nos, EE-ah-cuss, and rad-uh-MAN-theez.

As we stand and wait, the room becomes still, and now we see the golden beeswax candles, the beautiful tapestries upon the walls, the mosaic floor, the archways beyond which we glimpse gardens and strolling men and women and children.

Pause

"My precious friend." This is the voice of Persephone Herself, and She speaks from Her throne. "I welcome you to My palace. I welcome you and beg you to stay here with Me and let Me entertain you. I beg you to be My friend and to know that here you are loved."

Persephone stands before us, an imposing queen in starry black robes, with Her pale face and silvery eyes, and Her onyx crown upon Her head, Her ruby scepter in Her right hand.

"I welcome you and bid you know that here you find peace. Here you find rest and entertainment and love."

Tell Persephone whether you will stay or not. This is your choice and no one else's. If you wish to stay, She will gather you into Her healing arms. Friends and loved ones who have come here before you will greet you with their customary affection, and you may rest and learn until you choose to enter a new life.

Yes, tell Persephone whether you will stay or not. No one will force you to stay or return. You may choose when to return.

Pause

If you choose to stay, bright blessings.

Pause

If you choose to return to our life on earth for a while, thank Her courteously and know that you may return to Her when you are ready.

If you choose to return to life on earth, let us now go back. We find an arched door on one side of Persephone's throne room and go through it. We pass through a garden full of blooming apple trees, we pass a pond blooming in water lilies. We can see light as we move forward, but if we dare to look back, there is only a dark maze. Look forward.

Pause

Ah, we've come back to ordinary life. Slip into your body and rest and know that you are loved. Rest awhile and remember your journey and know that you may go there alone when you want to go.

Grief: Rookha

It's surprising (and sad) how many occasions we find in our lives for grief. There are all the little things we grieve for, things that probably seem insignificant to most people—the disappearance of your mother's cameo or a small gift you received from your very first lover, yet another rejection slip from a dumb little magazine that pays its poets in copies instead of cash, the closing of an old favorite theater or store, a phone call that doesn't come, a petty quarrel with a friend. You grieve, and someone says, "Oh, you're just too *sensitive*," as if such things don't matter. But they do matter, and we must grieve, if only for a little while.

More socially respectable are the major losses. The death of a spouse, a parent, a child, or a dear friend can nearly destroy us. Divorce, "downsizing" and consequent job loss, and moving from a beloved old home also need to be properly grieved. When such things happen and we cry, people say they understand. They give us permission to grieve, but only within strict bounds. We're supposed to keep a "stiff upper lip" and hide the wildness of our grief. We're supposed to keep it from becoming "messy." We're not supposed to embarrass other people with our grieving.

Malidoma Patrice Somé, who comes from the Dagara culture of West Africa, looks at our stiff Anglo culture in the United States and is shocked at such an attitude. "If death disturbs the living," he writes:

> it offers a unique opporunity to unleash one of the strongest emotional powers humans have: the power to grieve. People who do not know how to weep together are people who cannot laugh together. People who know not the power of shedding their tears together are like a time bomb, dangerous to themselves and to the world around them.[14]

Let's not be time bombs. Let's give ourselves permission to feel those terrible, messy feelings and express them. Let's give ourselves permission to grieve, to wail and deny and bargain, to be angry. Let's give ourselves permission to live and die and come and go and survive and remember.

Rookha is an Aramaic word that means both "wind" and "spirit."[15] Because this is the word used in Acts 2:2—"suddenly there came a sound from heaven as of *a rushing mighty wind* and it filled all the house where [the apostles of Jesus] were sitting"—in the original Aramaic manuscript, *rookha* also means intelligence and

Holy Spirit. The Holy Spirit traditionally is our Comforter—the Paraclete, from the Greek *Parakletos*, "advocate."

Although the biblical patriarchs and scholars might object to my use of this Aramaic word to describe a goddess, it seems to me that we need a Found Goddess named Rookha. Ancient and new at the same time, She will be our Holy Spirit, our Inspiration, our Comforter.

Before you begin this meditation, clarify what it is you are grieving for. It can be a big thing or it can be something anyone else would consider quite minor. What is important is how this issue affects you. It's significant to you. It might be useful to write a few paragraphs about this issue in your journal; better yet, write out your feelings on a sheet of beautiful paper that you can burn at the end of the meditation.

The Meditation

Holding your writing, close your eyes and take several deep, easy breaths. Spend a few minutes remembering what this person or issue you are grieving for means to you. Say aloud, "I deserve to grieve over *name your loss*." Say aloud, "I now give myself permission to grieve," and hear what you're saying.

Now sit quietly with your grief. Pay attention to where it is in your body. A churning in your stomach. An ache in your chest. A tightening of your throat. Weakness in the muscles of your arms and legs. Tears. If you need to cry, that's OK. Cry as gently or violently as you want to. Take as long as you need to express feelings you may not have had permission to express until now.

Pause

Sit quietly, again, in your grief. Remember. Go through the "it might have beens" and the "if onlies" again, and let yourself have your regrets. Let yourself also have your memories of better times.

Pause

She comes quietly to you. She comes as softly as the fog in Carl Sandburg's poem, on little cat feet. Roohka comes as sweetly as a spring breeze, as gently as a caress, and you may not even feel Her at first. Let Her come. Let Roohka be with you.

It is beautiful to sit with grief in a holy place. It is beautiful to have company who is entirely undemanding. Rookha does not demand your attention. She neither tells you to cry nor not to cry. She will not come too close or hug you without your permission. She simply bears witness to your grieving.

Let yourself begin to feel Rookha's presence in the room. She is not a mighty rushing wind today, but only the softest breeze. Her presence is a sign that you will be comforted.

Pause

Let Her speak to you. "You will not forget," She whispers, "you will not be forgotten," She murmurs. "You have suffered a grievous loss. But," She says, "but I am always with you. I am with you in glad days and sad ones. I am with you on the mountains of your emotions and in the swamps. Like the shepherd, I walk beside you through the valley of the shadow of death, and I am also with you in the flowering gardens and upon the green hills."

Pause

Let the presence of Rookha comfort you. Perhaps you see Her as a guardian angel, as a madonna, as a beloved friend. Perhaps She holds you in Her arms or on Her lap. Perhaps she takes a corner of her veil and wipes your tears away.

"And know," Rookha says to you, "know that eventually you will let go of this grief. It may never go away, but it will diminish and you will be happy again. Know that this is true, for all cycles turn, even the cycle of joy and grief."

Allow Rookha to bring comfort to you. Allow Her to return to you whenever you need comfort.

Pause

When you return to ordinary consciousness, light a white candle, burn the paper on which you wrote about your grief, and scatter the ashes in the wind. Let your grief go with Rookha, the wind.

Germination: Tellus Mater and Ceres

I wonder how many of us have learned by experience that if you plant seeds and then pull 'em up and look, nothing's gonna grow. It's not just kids who dig the seeds up and look for roots, is it? (For anyone who's as gardening-challenged as I am, here's a suggestion. Plant cat grass. It sprouts fast. Because you cover the seeds with only a quarter-inch of soil you can see both roots and stems.)

The need for germination time is true both literally and metaphorically. Whether you're planting corn or marigolds or cat grass, you have to let the seeds germinate. Whether you've sent out a resume, done a spell, or have a project to accomplish, you have to give it time to work.

For example, I carried the idea for this book in my mind for over a year, although I wrote two or three of the meditations for friends or to submit to magazines during that time. That year was its period of germination. When I actually sat down to write, I finished the book in a little over two months.

But when I write, I'm continually planting new seeds. I'll look at my list and say to myself, for example, *What kind of meditation can I write about germination and rebirth?* I'll do my research. Then I'll comb the cats, read paperback mysteries, watch sitcoms on TV, go shopping. And all the while, some part of my mind is visualizing goddesses, creating images, and rehearsing the words and sentences that flow through my fingers into my computer. Even after I print a meditation out, further germination is required before I can edit and rewrite it.

Germination, from the Latin *germinare*, "to sprout," and means "to begin to grow." A related concept is incubation, from the Latin *incubare*, which means "to lie down upon."

Whether we're planting seeds or hatching eggs, we have to let them lie in the darkness and get ready to grow.

Tellus Mater is the Roman Earth Mother (that's what Her name means); Her constant companion is Ceres, the Grain Mother. These two Goddesses supervise both vegetative and human reproduction. I have this fanciful image of Them strolling arm in arm under the land, telling the grain when it's time to grow, pulling on a carrot, tapping an acorn to wake it up, reminding the roses that they need to start climbing the trellis, and urging the sunflowers to grow as tall as the sky.

As a reproductive goddess, Tellus Mater was invoked at marriage, and the dead were given back into Her care. She was also the Goddess upon whose name oaths were sworn, it being understood that "the earth, witnessing all doings on Her surface, would see that an oath taker kept his promise."[16]

What's your project? Do you have software to write, a PR campaign to plan, your master's thesis to complete? Is it time for spring housecleaning or preparing your tax returns? Are you writing a book or painting a mural? Have you made a promise to your company or yourself that you intend to complete this thing under budget and ahead of the deadline?

Maybe it's time to get down to serious work.

The Meditation

Sit quietly, close your eyes, and take several deep, easy breaths. In your imagination, you suddenly find yourself in a dark underground maze that extends for miles in all directions. The illumination is so faint you can hardly see, but you see all too clearly the mountain directly in front of you. It's tall and sharp, with false paths and outcroppings of rock and stunted vegetation. On the earthen floor at your feet is a little red wagon full of papers and equipment.

This underground mountain is your project. In the wagon is all the stuff you need to complete your project.

Try to tidy up the load. Try to push and pull the wagon up the mountain. Just as the summit is only steps away, however, the wagon tips and rolls back down, spilling parts of its load along the way. You have to pick everything up, try to neaten it up, and pull the wagon up to the top again. Again, it rolls back down.

Pause

Like Sisyphus with his rock, you realize you'll never get this job done. That cunning old Greek king had tried to outwit death and was punished for his hubris by being sentenced to roll a huge rock up a mountain every day; every night it fell down again. Forever.

Maybe you can escape from your Sisyphean task. Call upon Tellus Mater and Ceres.

Tellus Mater and Ceres arrive, arm in arm, and examine your mountain. Shaking Their heads, the Goddesses poke here, prod and push there, dislodge a few things that come tumbling down, prop up a shaky spot or two. "Do you truly mean to complete this project?" Tellus Mater asks you.

Promise Tellus Mater—and yourself—that you'll get organized. *Really.* This time you *will* get organized.

Stop! Realize that you have just taken an oath upon the sacred Earth Herself. You are committed, for Tellus Mater will enforce that oath. She will also help you.

When the Goddesses ask, tell Them how long this mountain has been down here. Explain (honestly) why it's been down here so long. With

Their help, separate the important parts of the mountain from the trash. Tellus Mater calls upon Her benevolent army of earthworms, beetles, and ants to cart the trash away and shore up the remaining bits of your project.

Pause

"Your seedtime has ended," Ceres tells you. "Germination is complete. See? There are sprouts all up and down your mountain."

It's true. Your project is coming to life. Take some time to identify each stem and leaf in practical terms—steps to be taken, costs, equipment to be used, milestones, input required from other people, feedback, meetings, etc.

Pause

Now you hear a rumbling. A crew of dwarves in a covered wagon is approaching from another part of the Underworld. Under the supervision of the goddesses, you and the dwarves disassemble your mountain and load it into the covered wagon. Tellus Mater and Ceres lay Their hands on each part of the load to bless it. Tellus Mater and Ghob, the dwarf-king, confer for a moment, then She sketches a rough map on the floor.

The dwarves make a place for you in the wagon. Climb in. It begins to move. You can feel the energy of your project, its warmth, and you know that it will soon emerge from the earth and grow into its proper form.

Tellus Mater will be keeping Her eye on you.

Rebirth: Madder-Akka and Her Daughters

Sometimes it's not a project but we ourselves who need germination time. Maybe we've been through physical trauma, like illness, surgery, or an accident. We know from our own experience, or that of our friends, how healing sleep is needed in such times. The trauma can also be emotional, like divorce, a workplace crisis, completion of an academic degree. My friends who have completed MBAs or law degrees tell me they want to sleep for months before going back to work. I also have a friend who went through both divorce and major surgery within six painful months. She sleeps as much as possible. She is healing. She will be reborn to ordinary life soon.

Madder-Akka, the Saami birth goddess, lives under the earth with Her daughters, Sar-Akka, Juks-Akka, and Uks-Akka. Sar-Akka, the first daughter, is the creator of the physical body that houses the soul. Her tool is the forked stick that separates a child from its mother at birth. Juks-Akka, the second daughter, receives the baby into the light and carries a bow to protect children from harm. Uks-Akka, the third daughter, changes girls to boys in the womb and blesses anyone leaving the womb/home.[17]

It's good if you fall asleep during this meditation.

The Meditation

Turn the lights down low, and curl up comfortably on your bed or sofa, with a pillow under your head and a warm blanket to cover you. Close your eyes and take several deep, easy breaths.

In your imagination you soon find yourself in a cozy room far below your house. You are there as the guest of Madder-Akka and Her three daughters. They give you a warm welcome. Under their mother's supervision, one daughter helps you settle yourself on their chaise lounge. The second brings you a cup of hot herb tea. The third brings you toast with honey. Madder-Akka is stirring hot, nourishing soup in Her cauldron over the fire.

You can see through the window that the sun is setting, and now in this magical time the Goddesses gather around you to bless you. With a little circle dance, They bring flowering almond (for hope), lily of the valley (for return to happiness), jasmine (for grace and elegance), mint (for virtue), sage (for esteem), and arbor vitae (for unchanging friendship). You can feel the weaving lines of energy in Their dance, the weaving of affection and healing around you. Perhaps They also sing a little song to you.

Watch Their dancing, inhale the scent of the flowers, sip your tea, eat a bite of your toast and honey. This is the best place you've ever been. Someone brings you a bowl of healing soup. There is no possibility of pain here, no possibility of wounding.

Pause

The goddesses touch your forehead and cheeks and hands, and then, in silence, take Their posts around you. Madder-Akka stands in the north beside Her cauldron. Sar-Akka stands in the east with Her forked stick. Holding Her bow, Juks-Akka stands in the south, and Uks-Akka stands by the western door.

Relax. Stretch out your legs under the magical quilt the Goddesses have covered you with and idly trace its appliqued stars and pine tree design (for rebirth) with your fingers. Let the tea and the soup warm your whole body. Let the wisdom of the flowers heal your soul. Rest, and know that as the egg will hatch in its proper time and the seed will sprout at its proper time, so will you be nurtured and reborn. Rest and dream.

Pause

And, yes, at last your proper time has come. Madder-Akka awakens you. Sar-Akka hands you a tiny glass of a magical elixir and touches you with Her forked stick. Drink, and know that your body is whole again.

Pause

Juks-Akka brings a tiny bowl of porridge and holds Her bow above your head. Eat, and know that you face success in your new life.

Pause

Finally, Uks-Akka takes your hand, helps you up, and leads you to the eastern door. As She opens the door, you feel the warmth of the rising sun and the light of new wisdom. "Go forth," the Goddesses tell you, "go forth into your new day and life, and go with Our blessings."

Learning From Your Mistakes and Failures: White Buffalo Woman

In *Native Wisdom for White Minds* there is a splendid quotation from a Mohican writer named Don Coyhis. It's good to make mistakes and fail, he says:

> The Creator designed us to learn by trial and error. The path of life we walk is very wide. Everything on the path is sacred—what we do right is sacred—but our mistakes are also sacred. This is the Creator's way of teaching spiritual people. To criticize ourselves when we make mistakes is not the Indian way. To learn from our mistakes is the Indian way. The definition of a spiritual person is someone who makes 30–50 mistakes each day and talks to the Creator after each one to see what to do next time.[18]

So. What mistakes have you made lately? What mistakes have I made lately? In addition to multitudinous finger errors at my keyboard, what else am I doing wrong? What phone calls have I neglected to return? Where did I make a wrong turn and get lost? How did my emotions get out of control? What did I eat that wasn't good for me? Who did I unknowingly insult? What did I buy that I don't need? Which "fashion don't" am I wearing and how much time have I wasted today?

My list of mistakes and failures could run on forever. Yours probably could, too.

The popular self-help books admonish us not to flog ourselves with guilt, and many of them discuss the concept of sin, which actually, they tell us, means "missing the mark." When you make a mistake, they say, when you try to do something and fail, it's basically because you have bad aim. You can practice, improve your aim, and do better next time.

I accept that good advice. I keep trying to improve my aim. How about you?

Long ago, when the Lakota people still lived in forests in the Midwest, White Buffalo Woman came to them. She first appeared to two young warriors, one of whom said, "That is a sacred woman. Throw all bad thoughts away." The other young man, however, was overcome with lust for Her. She embraced him, a white cloud covered them, and when She opened Her arms, the first young man saw his companion's skeleton at Her feet. White Buffalo Woman told the survivor her name and sent him back to his village with instructions to build Her a sacred lodge.

When She arrived, the people greeted Her with reverence. She walked around the sacred fire seven times, then gave teachings to the people. She sang:

> With visible breath I am walking.
> A voice I am sending as I walk.
> In a sacred manner I am walking.
> With visible tracks I am walking.
> In a sacred manner I walk.

She gave them the sacred pipe with a bison calf carved on the bowl to represent the earth and twelve eagle feathers hanging from the stem to represent the sky.[19] She also showed them important ceremonies. Finally, reminding them of their duties to Mother Earth and saying they would see Her again, She disappeared in the shape of a white buffalo.

Small wonder that the Native American nations celebrated when a white buffalo calf was born in August 1994. Her name is Miracle.

Before you begin this meditation, take the time to list some of your recent mistakes and failures. It might be helpful to ask around; if your friends are like mine, they'll be pleased to tell you, very kindly and for your own good, of course, what you've been doing wrong.[20]

The Meditation

Sit quietly with your list of mistakes and failures and close your eyes. Take several deep, easy breaths and see yourself standing in an open space in an ancient forest. There is a large opening among the trees, and at one side of it is a white lodge decorated with figures painted in black, white, red, and yellow dancing around its circumference. Beside the entrance hangs a shield decorated with sacred symbols.

Where you are standing, the earth has been swept clean and smooth. Soon White Buffalo Woman comes out of Her lodge. She is carrying Her sacred pipe and a small white bag, out of which She takes tiny crystals. First, She uses Her finger to draw a medicine circle in the dirt, then She lays the tiny crystals in a the shape of an equal-armed cross inside the circle. "This is sacred space," She tells you. "The circles of the earth and sky are sacred, and this small circle mirrors those larger circles. This cross shows us the four directions and it also shows the path that you walk. Now, my friend, sit with me."

White Buffalo Woman raises Her pipe to the four directions and prays.[21]

Great Spirit, you have been always, and before you no one has been. There is no other one to pray to but you. The star nations all over the universe you have finished. The four quarters of the earth you have finished. Everything you have finished. Mother Earth, the only Mother, you have shown mercy to your children. Hear me, four quarters of the world—a relative I am! Give me the strength to walk the soft earth as a relative to all that is. Give me the eyes to see and the strength to understand, that I may be like you. With your power only can I face the winds.

This is my prayer. Hear me!

In your imagination, now, let yourself become very small, tiny enough to walk the four paths White Buffalo Woman created with Her tiny crystals, which are now as big as boulders beside you. You will walk each path.

Begin walking from the center along the eastern path. As you walk, you find yourself tripping over White Buffalo Woman's tiny crystals, which are now as large as boulders. Repeatedly, you stub your toes, repeatedly you bruise your ankles and bump your knees. You have to walk around the crystals, and sometimes you even forget which way you're going. Walk each path of the wheel, walk around every obstacle in the path. Again and again, you fall down. Again and again, you pick yourself up. You become angry at your clumsiness. You become frustrated that it's so hard to do something that seemed so easy. You become furious with yourself for being so stupid and awkward. Perhaps you lose your temper.

Pause

Walk the four paths. In this sacred space, walk east, walk south, walk west, walk north.

Pause

Don't give up. Keep walking. Find your way back each time. Even though you keep tripping and stumbling, walk around the circle and then, as always, return to the center.

Pause

At last you hear White Buffalo Woman clap Her hands. Suddenly you are your normal size again, sitting across the circle again. At the same time, you can look down and see this tiny you-person still walking among the tiny crystals, still tripping and getting confused and angry.

"My friend," says White Buffalo Woman, "you see yourself walking the four paths upon the earth. You see yourself enclosed in sacred space, and still you become awkward and confused and lost. My friend, what are you learning from this experience of watching yourself?"

Sit with White Buffalo Woman and speak heart to heart with Her. Contemplate your path. Look at how you walk. Talk about your mistakes and failures. Be as specific as you want to; cite the mistakes and failures on your list.

Pause

"My friend," White Buffalo Woman says again, "What are you learning from your mistakes and failures? What corrections can you make?"

Speak heart to heart with Her again. Tell Her what you're learning. Listen to the teachings She may give you.

Pause

When you return to normal awareness, know that the space in your heart is sacred space, and know that whenever you make a mistake or fail at something you may return to White Buffalo Woman to discuss what you're learning from your mistakes and failures.

Changing the Energy in Your Home or Workspace: Poza-Mama

It sometimes happens that though we're growing and changing, something isn't keeping up with us. For a while we think it's our friends, then maybe it's our family. Finally we figure it out: *our environment* is what isn't keeping up with us.

Denise Linn explains that our homes are composed of "overlapping energy fields" that make up the spirit of the place:

> Your home has consciousness. Homes as well as people are nourished by how we hold them in our heart. They have a living spirit that is sustained through the reverence and love that we hold for them. Without that care they become inanimate and lifeless: the spirit recedes and they become merely physical structures that can neither sustain nor nurture us . . . . Your home is an evolving creative being . . . . It has cycles just as you and all of nature has [*sic.*] cycles.[22]

We grow spiritually and get brand-new stuff in our souls, but we still have the same old stuff in our homes. This stuff can be physical, like the second hand furniture or the familiar art on the walls or the jewelry we never wear but still hang on to, or it can be invisible stuff, like the residue of outgrown ideas and prejudices, childish feelings, and superseded information. It's like having ghosts in the house.

Bit by bit, we've become uncomfortable where we're living. We think we need to move. We blame it on the neighborhood, on the lack of parking, on a roommate or relationship that "hasn't worked out," on any number of tangible or intangible things. The issue really is that we've changed, but the energy, or spirit, of our place hasn't.

The same thing can happen where we work. Our workspace is more temperamental, of course, than our home. We can't choose the people who are there. Sometimes we can't decorate our cubicle more than just minimally. Office politics can create horrendous vibes. Supervisors and managers seldom have our best interests at heart or in mind. "Sick building syndrome" attacks. We realize how bored we are with our job and how overqualified we are. We feel that what we are doing in this office is not our right livelihood.

Since it's usually inconvenient or just plain impossible to move or get a new job, making friends with the spirit of your place and changing its energy are workable solutions.

Poza-Mama is one of several Siberian home goddesses. Like Hestia and Vesta, She lives in the hearthfire and provides a locus of home and kinship. A fire goddess, She also provides light in the home, and at least one tribe believes that Her bright light shows them the way to the afterlife. Shamans begin their work with prayers to this great goddess.[23]

Ask Poza-Mama, therefore, to warm and enlighten your home or office. Ask Her to help you get in touch with and adjust the attitude of your home and workplace spirits.

The meditation is about home, but you can adapt it to your workplace. Begin with your own desk, cubicle, or office. After your initial success, you may want to do the meditation again and expand your magical work to a wider area. Could you do the entire building? It might be worth a try, but keep in mind that a building spirit is probably larger and more entrenched than a cubicle or office spirit.

The Meditation

Sit quietly and close your eyes. Take several deep easy breaths and in your imagination come into your home through the front door. Pretend you've come to buy the home and tour all the rooms. Notice the good features, like gorgeous built-in cabinets in the kitchen, and the bad ones, like the tile coming unglued around the shower. Tour the home without judgment. All you want to do is *see what it looks like.*

Pause

Next find two magical chairs. These can be chairs you already own. Perhaps fantasy chairs will come to you, gilded rocking chairs, wooden chairs stenciled with red flowers, Victorian parlor chairs, plain Shaker chairs.

Carrying these chairs, find the center of the home. Since you're working in your imagination, you can go into the middle of a wall or under the kitchen stove if that's where the center is. Set the two chairs down, a few feet apart and facing each other. Sit in one chair and wait.

Pause

While you're waiting here in the center, send out all your little psychic feelers. Locate the spirit of the place. Perhaps it's big and already in your face. Perhaps it's feeling rejected and shrunken and is hiding under the bathroom sink. Wherever the spirit is, ask it to come and talk to you.

Invite the spirit of the place to sit in the chair opposite you and tell you how it feels. See the spirit. What does it look like? Does it look like a person or an animal? Is it energy that has assumed a shape? Hear its voice. *Really listen to what the spirit of the place has to tell you.*

Pause

Let your conversation be as long as necessary. Sometime during this conversation, you will become aware of the presence of Poza-Mama. She is a tall woman with braided hair and a friendly face, and She wears a long shawl covered with magnificent embroidery: stylized flames, trees, birds, cooking pots, stars, dancing people, frame drums, horses, reindeer. She stands between the chairs, facing you sometimes, facing the spirit at other times. She coaches you and helps the spirit of the place express itself more clearly.

Pause

Your purpose in this conversation is to make friends again with this spirit, to nurture it so that it will nurture you. Tell the spirit how beneficial mutual aid can be. Promise to do your part by building an altar, bringing flowers, doing a good housecleaning, rearranging the furniture, painting the walls. Promise to buy a good book on feng shui and make some rearrangements; another name, after all, for the spirit of the place is *chi*, and your purpose is to encourage favorable chi and redirect unfavorable chi, which is called *sha*.

Pause

When the conversation is complete, Poza-Mama asks you and the spirit to stand up. Do so. Now She leads you on another tour through your home, room by room, and with Her wonderful embroidered shawl, the Goddess scoops up negativity and waves it away. She flaps it out the windows, just like a housewife shaking the rugs out. Walk beside the spirit of the place, follow the goddess as She cleans your home, and soon you find that you have spiraled back into the center.

Pause

Poza-Mama asks the spirit of the place to sit in its chair again, and She gives the spirit a wonderful gift: Her embroidered magical shawl. The spirit wraps itself in Her shawl. The spirit of your place is now enthroned with beauty and light and love.

When you return to everyday awareness, remember your promises to the spirit. Do your part to fill your home or workspace with beauty and light and love.

Divination: Postvorta and Antevorta

Although we can read cards or runes or bones and do numerological or astrological charts any time, day or night, any day of the month, divination is properly a dark moon kind of work. This is because when we divine truly, we work in a trancelike state where we are using "a deeply intuitive sense that puts [us] in touch with the source of creation and enables [us] to foresee the possible outcome of future events."[24] We are reaching into the realms of mystery and otherness "beyond the veil" and pulling back shadowed images and intimations upon which we shed light for our querent.

Although I've been a successful Tarot reader for over twenty years and do a few other psychic things as well, I'm suspicious of psychics in general. Some of them are just too weird. When I go for a reading, I want groundedness and common sense. I want a psychic to be in touch with this reality along with that other one. The psychic readers I respect, respect the darkness into which they travel during divination, and it's interesting how many of them turn off the electric lights and then set a lighted candle on the table both to symbolize their journey to mystery and light their way home again.

Think about which divinatory tools you use and how you use them. Think about where you use them and where they take you. Think about your responsibility to your querent and your understanding that prophecy doesn't come *from* you but *through* you. Whose blessing do you ask before you shuffle the cards or cast the coins? Whom do you invoke for truth before you pick up your pendulum or gaze into the dark mirror?

Postvorta and Antevorta are Greek goddesses of prophecy and inventors of the alphabet. Their names come from three Latin words: *post*, "after," *ante*, "before," and *vertere*, "to turn." They are also alternate names (or, as I like to think, daughters) of the calendar and door-hinge goddess, Cardea, She who stands upon the hinge of the year and looks both backward and forward.

When Julius Caesar created his calendar in 45 B.C.E., he moved the hinge of the year and assigned it to the two-headed Roman god Janus (whence January). But, as Peter Bogdanovich explains, Janus had "appropriated" the attribute of looking in both directions from Cardea. Cardea was originally an oak goddess, and in the lunar tree-calendar Her symbolic place was between Oak and Holly. The oak is not only the central tree of the "year and a day" calendar system but also the tree of more deities than any other. The month of Oak runs from June 10 to July 7; midway through is the summer solstice.[25] Postvorta and Antevorta thus stand in the year's brightest light. Postvorta looks back to the past winter's darkness, and Antevorta looks forward to the coming winter's darkness.

The Meditation

Sit quietly and close your eyes. As you take several deep, easy breaths, imagine yourself standing in a hazy valley before a steep, round tor. It's a moonless night, and though you can hardly see, you must climb the tor. Soon you can discern its crest. There stands the midsummer lighthouse, whose two bright lights shine out in opposite directions into the darkness around the tor. Continue climbing until you reach the lighthouse. As you walk around this mysterious structure, you notice that it is octagonal. When you come to the door, a voice invites you to enter.

Inside, the lighthouse is illuminated by candles of all colors and sizes. They surround a round oak table and two chairs. It's the perfect setting for divination.

Displayed on shelves around the eight sides of the midsummer lighthouse are all kinds of divination systems: shamanic tools, bones, runes, shells and sticks, sacred stones, Tarot and quasi-Tarot decks, a crystal ball, a dark mirror, tea leaves in a cup, a palm reader's hand, the Ifa, the Mah Jongg game, the I Ching, dice, knotted cords, a Ouija board, pendulums and dowsing rods, even a personal computer with astrological and numerological software. A voice directs you to select a divinatory tool. Make your selection and carry it to the oak table and sit down.

Pause

Just as you are preparing to begin reading and wondering who you will read for, your querent arrives. It's a person wearing a floor-length black veil. Without a word, your querent sits in the chair across from you.

Now Postvorta enters through a hidden door across the room from you, a door under one of the bright lights. She is carrying a black candle on a white disk. "I see the past," She says. "I see what has been and look to see how it foreshadows what is now and what is to come." She sets Her candle on the table to your left and stands beside you.

Antevorta enters through a hidden door behind you, the door under the other bright light. She is carrying a white candle on a black disk. "I see the future," She says. "I see what will be and how it has grown from what is and what has been." She sets Her candle on the table to your right and stands beside you.

What does the querent need to know? Listen with your inner ears until you sense the true question. If you ask your querent to confirm it, the only reply is a nod or shake of the head. Be sure you have the true question, the question from the heart.

Pause

As you begin the reading, you find yourself moving into your familiar altered state of consciousness. Suddenly all the candles go out. Darkness fills the room and you feel as if you, too, are veiled in black. You feel winds, you hear whispering voices, and you know that hands are manipulating the stones or shells, that eyes are gazing into the mirror or crystal ball. Not quite your hands. Not quite your eyes. You sense the Goddesses to your right and left, you sense other movement, you feel Their guiding touch. You sense danger, you sense calm, you know there are other presences in the room. Has the floor disappeared from beneath your feet? Has the top of the midsummer lighthouse blown away? The Goddesses have woven a web of safety around you, but it is also a web of mystery.

Pause

At last the candles flicker to life again, and you can see once more. Your querent reaches up to remove the veils and you realize that this person is, of course, yourself. Your reading has also been unveiled. The Goddesses still stand at the table. Ask them to help you see what has been revealed. Ask them to help you interpret truly what you see in this divination in the midsummer lighthouse.

The Widdershins Spiral: Grandmother Spider

When Witches and ceremonial magicians and others who honor the Goddess or follow the Old Religion create magical circles, movement is customarily done in a sunwise direction, or deosil.[26] We move sunwise to cast the circle and seem to believe that (except at Samhain) sunwise is the only good, right, and proper direction. It's the famous "right-hand path." Moonwise, or widdershins, movement is the infamous "left-hand path," which is evil, wrong, and improper, to be avoided at all costs.

Not so. If we believe that we can move in only one direction, we've fallen for someone else's propaganda.

As Timothy Roderick explains, it's the *double spiral*, which moves both sunwise and moonwise, that more accurately describes our lives and works. The double spiral, he writes, is:

> the power cycle that coils you back to the center of your being, to touch the sacred source of Witch power, and arouse inward movement and illumination . . . .
>
> The energies of the widdershins spiral are like the twin brothers and sisters of air, fire, water, and earth. They are born from the same four elements, and as many brothers and sisters do, they create tensions. Widdershins powers create an opposite or reverse polarity to that of their brother and sister energies in the deosil spiral. This polar tension is the source behind all movement in magic.[27]

The double spiral is the combination of inner-directed and outer-directed polar energies, the former fueling the latter, that creates true magical power. We begin in the center and dance outward, moving toward the right, sunwise, from pure unmanifest energy into physical manifestation. Then we dance back to the left, moonwise, moving back into the center for rest and meditation. We find our true power when we move in both directions, for while some magic is inner-directed and some is outer-directed, the most successful magic happens when we work on ourselves as well as in the world.

I want to add a third movement to the double spiral. After we've returned to the center, we need to dance back out into the world. We need to dance sunwise again and carry back to our blessed earth the lessons we learned during the first two parts of what has now become a *triple spiral.*

It is mandatory that we dance the widdershins spiral. We must dance under the moon as well as under the sun. It's that middle part of the eternal triple-spiral dance that we must never forget.

Grandmother Spider is the grandmother of the sun and the wind and the corn—and perhaps of all creation—to the Cherokee, Keres, and Dine people. As Paula Gunn Allen describes Her, She is the "power of creative (magically empowered) thought." Her medicine power is so vast we humans cannot even imagine it:

"She thinks, therefore we are." "But Her intelligence," Allen writes, "goes beyond human beings; it permeates the land—the mountains and clouds, the rains and lightning, the corn and deer."[28]

Embodied in one of earth's smallest creatures, the spider, this Great Goddess is also humble. She lives everywhere and blesses our home with Her elegant webs, at the same time keeping us free from insect pests. One of Her modern incarnations is E. B. White's cheerful and maternal Charlotte.

She who weaves will also ravel Her work in order to weave a newer pattern. She who creates inevitably destroys in order to create anew.

The Meditation

Close your eyes and take several deep, easy breaths. In your imagination, you are standing in a place where the whole world and everything in it is. Where you are, there the sun and the moon and the stars and comets are. Where you are, mountains and crystals and waterfalls and glittering jewels are. Where you are, sequoias and green grass and corn and violets are. Where you are, whales and lions and hummingbirds and lizards are. Where you are, black and red and white and yellow people are. All the peoples of the earth are there where you are.

Where you are, Grandmother Spider is. She is sitting with Her power. She is singing Her power. She is weaving Her web which touches all that is.

Pause

And now it begins, the dance of the widdershins spiral. Take your place in the line, join hands with the person to your right and the one to your left, and step to the right. Dance the widdershins spiral, very slowly at first. Hear the music of the moon and the beating of the drums under the moon. Take a step and another step, dancing ever toward the right.

Dance, and one day you reach the first station, the western corner of the widdershins spiral, and here we all must pause. There is silence, there is rest, and the only sound is the beating of your heart under the moon.

Time comes, and the dance continues. But look—all the people are gone. Perhaps they have gone off to their own dancing. Oh, well. Take your place with the owl and the turtle, join hands with the dolphin and the wolf, and dance again. Dance under the moon, dance the widdershins spiral. The dance is faster now, and you begin to do some fancy steps.

Dance, and one day you reach the second station, the southern corner of the widdershins spiral, and here we all must pause. Here is silence, here is rest, and the only sound is the beating of your heart under the moon.

Pause

Time comes, and the dance continues. But look—all the animals are gone, all the mammals and reptiles and birds and fishes and insects. Perhaps they have gone off to their own dancing. Oh, well. Take your place with the pine and the hollyhock, join hands with the cattail and the tomato. Dance again. Dance the widdershins spiral, and the dance is faster, and now you're leaping and turning.

Dance, and one day you reach the third station, the eastern corner of the widdershins spiral, and here we all must pause. Here is silence, here is rest, and the only sound is the beating of your heart under the moon.

Pause

Time comes, and the dance continues. But look—all the plants are gone, all the trees and herbs and flowers and fruits and vegetables. Perhaps they have gone off to their own dancing. Oh, well. Take your place with the agate and the granite, join hands with the lava and the shale. Dance the widdershins spiral, and the dance is even faster. You're spinning and flying.

Dance, and one day you reach the fourth station, the northern corner of the widdershins spiral, and here we all must pause. Here is silence, here is rest, and the only sound is the beating of your heart under the moon.

Pause

Time comes, and the dance continues. But look—all the minerals are gone, all the gems and geological formations, the mountains and the mud. Perhaps they have gone off to their own dancing. Oh, well. Take your place with the sun and the moon, join hands with asteroids and comets. Dance the widdershins spiral, and the dance is so fast now that you seldom touch the ground.

Dance, and one day you come again to the first station, the western corner of the widdershins spiral. But this is not a circle. This is a spiral, and a spiral never returns to the same station. You have reached a different level. Here you must pause. Here is silence, here is rest, and the only sound is the beating of your heart under the moon.

Pause

Time comes, and the dance continues. But look—the sun and moon and stars have gone. Perhaps they have gone off to their own dancing. Oh, well. You can dance alone. Dance the widdershins spiral and dance as only you can dance.

Dance, and one day you reach the center of the widdershins spiral, and here you must stop dancing. Here is only Grandmother Spider, and here She is singing and weaving. Here there is no light or dark, no warm or cold. Here is only the power of Grandmother Spider, and Her power is pure. It is like the powers of our dreams and visions, but Her power is purer and clearer. Her power has no shape, it has no movement. It is. It is the power that creates all that is, and "it is the power of all that is."[29]

Pause

You have danced the widdershins spiral and come to the Mystery. You have danced the widdershins spiral, and in the center you meet the Goddess face to face. You may rest here.

And one day you may dance again. When you dance again, you will dance sunwise, and you will dance back to the earth.

Endnotes

1. Graves, *Greek Myths*, pp. 48–49.

2. My friend Judy Dienst, a Reiki Master/Teacher, uses the term "cording" to refer to the process of cutting ties. When she gives someone a Reiki treatment, she uses a magnet to remove the roots and residue of the cords.

3. "Goddess goo" is an all-purpose, magical, healing balm. There must be 10,000 recipes. Here's mine. To a handful of starstuff, a handful of rich black earth, and a moon's length of spiders' webs, add the scent of a summer night. Moisten with honey, spit, and blood. Stir with the energy of a cat. Store in an alabaster jar in the cabinet of your mind. Will keep forever.

4. This topic was suggested by my friend, Karima Seabourne, who said, "Sometimes you have to find out where your NO button is."

5. Graves, *Greek Myths*, pp. 27, 54; Monaghan, *The Book of Goddesses and Heroines*, p. 339.

6. Graves, *Greek Myths*, pp. 401, 126; Monaghan, *The Book of Goddesses and Heroines*, p. 251.

7. For more information on meeting and working with the shadow, see two books by Demetra George, *Mysteries of the Dark Moon* (San Francisco: HarperSanFrancisco, 1992), and *Finding Our Way Through the Dark* (San Diego: ACS Publications, 1994); see also Roderick, *Dark Moon Mysteries* (St. Paul: Llewellyn, 1996).

8. Monaghan, *The Book of Goddesses and Heroines*, pp. 150-51, 240.

9. My thanks to Sandra Lange for helping me choose these five runes.

10. Pronounced IG-druh-sil. See Ralph Metzner, *The Well of Remembrance* (Boston: Shambhala Publications, 1994), pp. 199–211.

11. Graves, *Greek Myths*, pp. 124–25.

12. Charlene Spretnak, *Lost Goddesses of Early Greece* (Boston: Beacon Press, 1978), pp. 105–18.

13. Graves, *Greek Myths*, p. 122–23; Farrar, *Witches' Goddess*, p. 125.

14. Malidoma Patrice Somé, *Ritual* (New York: Viking/Arkana, 1993), pp. 96–97.

15. Pronounced ROO-khah (it's that Scottish or Yiddish KH that sticks in your throat). George M. Lamsa, *Gospel Light* (Philadelphia: A.J. Holman, 1967), p. 19. Other information about *rookha* from notes taken in classes taught by Dr. Rocco A. Errico.

16. Monaghan, *The Book of Goddesses and Heroines*, p. 336.

17. Monaghan, *The Book of Goddesses and Heroines*, pp. 184, 215, 305, 349.

18. Schaef, *Native Wisdom for White Minds*, March 27.

19. This is adapted from John G. Neihardt, *Black Elk Speaks* (Lincoln: University of Nebraska Press, 1961), pp. 3–5.

20. My thanks to Valerie Meyer (Eagle Heart) for her teachings and friendship. She inspired this meditation.

21. Her prayer is adapted from Black Elk's prayer in Neihardt, pp. 5–6. Note: this meditation is not intended to replicate Native American ceremony. It's only a meditation.

22. Linn, *Sacred Space*, p. 9.

23. Monaghan, *The Book of Goddesses and Heroines*, pp. 285-86.

24. John Matthews, ed., *The World Atlas of Divination* (New York: Little, Brown and Co., 1992), p. 6.

25. Peter Bogdanovich, ed., *A Year and a Day Engagement Calendar*, 1993 (New York: Overlook Press, 1993), pp.8–9, 111–12. The calendar was first published in 1990 and continues to be published every year. It's a learned, exquisite book.

26. Pronounced JESH-l, according to traditional English Witch, Rhiannon Ryall, *West Country Wicca* (Custer, WA: Phoenix Publishing, 1989), p. 40.

27. Roderick, *Dark Moon Mysteries*, chs. 5–9, *passim.*, p. 79.

28. Paula Gunn Allen, *Grandmothers of the Light* (Boston: Beacon Press, 1991), pp. 33–37. Because Grandmother Spider is also mother of the corn, see also Marilou Awiakta, *Selu* (Golden, CO: Fulcrum Publishing, 1993).

29. This paragraph paraphrases Allen's description of Spider's power in *Grandmothers of the Light*, p. 34.

6
Chakra Goddesses

Sophia

From ancient times, we have recognized that our physical body is not all we are. Behind, above, or all around us is a usually invisible[1] body, which is, some say, the real being that is currently going by our name. It's our connection to the "higher life force" (i.e., the Universe, the Cosmos, Goddess, God, Christ Consciousness). The usually invisible body has been given several names, including "light body" and "subtle body."

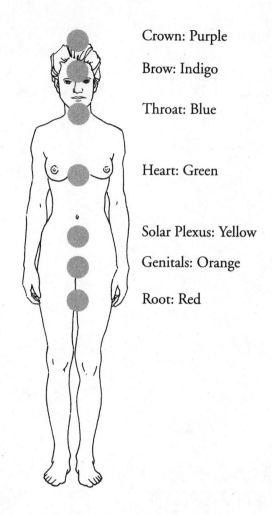

Crown: Purple

Brow: Indigo

Throat: Blue

Heart: Green

Solar Plexus: Yellow

Genitals: Orange

Root: Red

Figure 3. **The Chakra System.**

In the light body are seven energy centers that we call the chakra system (see Figure 3, above). The word *chakra*, which is Sanskrit, is commonly translated as "wheel" or "disk," though the chakras themselves are more often depicted as stylized flowers. Anodea Judith says the chakras are "centers of activity for reception, assimilation and transmission of life energies."[2] This is the best definition I've seen.

The earliest descriptions of the chakras seem to come from Hindu (Vedic) writings, specifically from some of the later Upanishads, which were written between 700 and 300 B.C.E. and the *Yoga Sutras of Patanjali*, which was written in the seventh century C.E.[3] Buddhist descriptions of the chakras seem to have originated in Tantric Buddhism (known in Tibet as Vajrayana Buddhism), which evolved during the seventh and eighth centuries.

We in the West first learned of the chakra system late in the nineteenth century through writings of the Theosophical Society and especially in books by C. W.

Leadbeater published in the 1920s. In *The Serpent Power*, which is his translation of the Upanishads and which was also published in the 1920s, Arthur Avalon gave further information.

While both Hindu and Buddhist descriptions of the chakra system identify seven major chakras (root, genital, solar plexus, heart, throat, third eye, and crown), their names for and descriptions of the chakras differ, which may explain why present-day "experts" so often contradict each other.

Hindu, Buddhist, Theosophical, and New Age scholars and mystics have discovered and invented innumerable correspondences to these mystical spinning wheels of but not in our bodies: elements, colors, directions, deities, saints, angels, sounds, mystical letters, numbers of petals (or spokes or rays), poisons, scents, gemstones, flowers and herbs, animals (including birds and fish), schools of yoga, archetypes, functions, *Sephiroth,* verbs, planets, Tarot suits, emotions, and so on. The chakras are also metaphysically connected with six sets of nerve ganglia and seven endocrine glands in the physical body.

To these already copious correspondences, I am adding goddesses for meditation. It seems appropriate. The "higher life force" to which our light body connects us is the Goddess, and it is the life energy She gives us that we must receive and assimilate and then transmit into our environment. This is, in fact, what we've been doing all along in our goddess meditations.

It has long seemed to me that it would be beneficial to have a goddess assigned specifically to each of the seven major chakras. We can meditate on a chakra goddess to strengthen, unblock, or balance a chakra. We can learn to understand the essential energies that direct our lives by meditating on chakra goddesses. We can work on ourselves using the energy of each of the seven chakra goddesses as that energy manifests in or through her chakra.

Judith and Vega use the term "energy currents" to describe the workings of the chakra system. Because, they say, we're upright creatures, one current flows from the crown chakra down to the root chakra in "the path of manifestation." That is, thoughtforms that come into our minds work their way down until they manifest in physical reality. "At each level," they write, "the thoughtform becomes more specific and more dense [and] we take something abstract and bring it into the concrete."[4] For example, ideas for Goddess meditations enter my consciousness and I process them through my chakras: I see visions and images, I talk about them with trusted friends to check them out and turn them into language, I love what I'm doing, I have enough will power to keep sitting at my computer, and (at last!) the visions and images are grounded on the paper that spirals through my printer. Thus a book becomes a concrete reality, and thus magic starts in our mind and manifests on earth.

Conversely, the other energy current rises from the root chakra to the crown chakra along the "path of liberation." "That which is bound to a form," Judith and

Vega write, "is gradually freed from the form to encompass greater scope and abstraction. Energy stored within matter is released."[5] In magic, again, we sometimes write wishes or spells on paper and then burn the paper, releasing the energy to the universe. In our goddess meditations, we've taken specific, concrete images and transformed them into mental energy (which, hopefully, will move back down again into physical manifestation).

From time to time, I meet perfectly nice New Thinkers who opine that the three lower chakras, and especially the root chakra—which is "down there"—are base, impure, dirty, and always to be ignored. It seems to me that such people wish the lower chakras would just go away, though they won't, of course. Such people want to live Light-headed, to exist only in their "pure," intellectual upper chakras. I once knew a woman, for example, who consistently ignored pentacles whenever they came up in Tarot spreads.

Though this attitude is fairly common in Theosophical and New Age literature, it's really quite foolish. We live on earth. We live in physical bodies. We use our whole body every day. We eat and drink and shit and fuck and sleep. None of these activities is nasty.

When we're in touch with our lower chakras, and in touch with the *entire chakra system*, then we're in touch with the real business of our lives.

We're in balance. Our "higher" and "lower" worlds are in balance. Our spiritual/intellectual and physical selves are in balance. Remember—the spiritual does not manifest through the physical; it manifests *as the physical.*

Table 2, page 151, lists my chakra goddesses. The chakra goddess meditations that follow are somewhat related to the Goddess Pillar Meditation in the next chapter: they bring us around again in the spiral dance we're doing with ourselves. In these chakra goddess meditations, we will pull goddess energy into our bodies and ourselves and use that energy to do a bit of chakra choreography to work on our issues. In the Goddess Pillar Meditation, we will pull goddess energy into parts of our body that approximate the chakra locations and then project that energy out into the world.

The seven major chakras are not, of course, the only chakras, and following the meditations with the major chakra goddesses is information about the other chakras and suggestions for goddesses that might rule them. I invite you to create your own meditations, however, for these additional chakra goddesses.

Chakra	Location	Issues[6]	Goddess/Her Origin
crown	top of head	knowing understanding connecting	Sophia/Gnostic
brow	forehead third eye	imagination intuition psychic perception	Cumaean Sybil/ Greco-Roman
throat	throat	clear communication self-expression creativity	Sarasvati/Hindu
heart	heart	compassion self-acceptance balance in relationships	Kuan Yin/Chinese
solar plexus	solar plexus	strength of will sense of purpose vitality	Oya/Afro-Brazilian
genital	genitals	pleasure sexuality emotions social issues	Hathor/Egyptian
root	base of spine	physical health right livelihood prosperity grounding survival	Baba Yaga/Slavic

Table 2. **Chakra Goddesses.**

Root Chakra: Baba Yaga

The fundamental issue is living on the earth. This is where we live in our physical bodies, where we interact in mental, emotional, intellectual, and spiritual ways with other people and with our other kin on earth—animal, vegetable, mineral, and transcendent. It's where we interact with the Earth Herself.

The root chakra issues are *physical health, right livelihood, prosperity, grounding,* and *survival.* Like the needs at the bottom of psychologist Abraham Maslow's famous pyramid—physiological needs like air, water, food, and shelter, plus safety and security needs[7]—the root chakra issues are fundamental to life. That is, unless we pay attention to these issues and take care of them, we cannot live any kind of meaningful life.

Let me use an extreme, negative example to make my point. We've all seen street people, the unfortunate, homeless ones who are living in doorways and crawlspaces and under hedges. It's pretty easy to see that these people are not healthy. They don't get enough to eat and have no place to go to attend to personal hygiene. They lack meaningful work, and if they work at all, they probably earn less than minimum wage. They just barely survive.

No matter how "highly evolved" or "intellectual" or "spiritual" we are, we have to work on our root chakra issues. This work won't, by itself, keep us away from disaster or homelessness, of course, but it will help us live meaningfully on the earth. When our root chakra is balanced and flowing with its proper energy, we can be truly present in our bodies and on the planet.

The logical choice of a goddess for the root chakra might be an earth goddess, like Gaia or one of the Great Mothers. If you feel a strong need to relate to an earth goddess while you're working on your root chakra issues, create a meditation, build an altar, and do what you feel guided to do.

I chose a Crone, however, as the root chakra goddess for this book. Who can be more concerned with survival than Baba Yaga, a goddess of life, death, and regeneration?

Baba Yaga is a Slavic Crone. She comes from Mother Russia and is known to the many tribes of Eastern Europe, from the Baltic nations in the north down to the Balkans in the south. She comes, in fact, from the very area that Marija Gimbutas has named Old Europe. This is where the "civilization of the Goddess" flourished peacefully for thousands of years.

Baba Yaga is *old.*

She's usually shown as the cliché wicked old witch—gruesome and nasty. She hides in the forest and scares travelers. She eats children. She flies around in a mortar, using the pestle as Her oar. She lives in a little house with birds' feet under it and a picket fence topped with human skulls around it. Just think of any of those awful fairy tale witches that lived out in the forest, like the one that tried to eat Hansel and Gretel. That's Baba Yaga.

No. Not really. She's a harvest goddess. She harvests not only grain but also people. She plants us, raises us, cuts us down, stores us through the dark winter's night, and then replants us again.

And that is the essential issue of life, the concern underlying all other issues of survival: living, dying, and being reborn. Physically and emotionally. Literally and metaphorically.

The Meditation

Select something red to sit on. A throw rug or a cushion, a towel or a scarf, even a fabric remnant will do. Red is the color of blood, which carries oxygen throughout our bodies and helps keep us alive. It's also the color associated with the root chakra. Your sit-upon is your symbolic blood.

Sit comfortably and let the base of your spine relax into your red sit-upon. Breathe deeply and easily as your body becomes more and more relaxed.

Pause

Feel yourself settling into the red. Feel the slow, steady vibrating energy of the red, feel its pulsing heat at the base of your spine. This pulsing of your root chakra goes on and on; it continues, steady and faithful, throughout this meditation, as steadily and faithfully as your heartbeat, as powerfully as a shaman's drumbeat. Let the pulse of your root chakra flow with your blood throughout your body, touching and blessing every cell, feeding every cell, from your toes to the top of your head. Relax in this grounding red energy for a while. Let it support and nourish you. Let it carry you into the other world of your imagination.

Pause

When you're ready, open the eyes of your imagination and look around. You're in a dark forest. You're on a path, but it's so faint and narrow that you feel lost. You may, in fact, begin to be afraid of what can happen to anyone who strays into the dark forest. You remember what happens to unlucky people in the old grandmothers' tales.

All you can see around you are the ancient trees—oaks and pines and elders so tall and thick and dark they nearly block out the sky. This forest is so old it seems to be as old as creation itself. Indeed, standing there, you might be present at the childhood of the earth.

Look around again. What do you hear? What do you smell? What kind of life can possibly dwell here in such an ancient forest?

Pause

Though the shadows are so deep you can hardly see the path, walk on through the forest. For a while you hear the singing of birds and the occasional growl or snort of an unseen animal, but soon you become aware that all has become silent. The only sound is the sound of your feet in the dry leaves that cover the path. Ah, now you begin to feel something, an intuitive something that grazes your skin and your soul. Just past the next turning of the narrow path, here it is—a little green cottage with its thatched roof and birds' feet. Here is the fence around the cottage, and, look, there is a grinning skull on every stake. Where else can you go? You can only walk on. Walk along the path toward that little green house.

Pause

Suddenly Baba Yaga comes out of the house. You know She's been watching you. You know She was aware of your presence in Her forest as soon as you walked under the first old trees. You know that She is the fiercely protective mother of this forest, the Oldest One who has ever lived here.

Though Her black eyes glitter, Her face is gray and wrinkled and caved in. She's lost most of Her flesh and nearly all of Her teeth. She's bony and bent over by age, and She wears dark, raggedy old clothes. In Her right hand She carries a stick that's as long as Her arm. It's really just an old tree limb, and there's a shining skull nailed to the end.

This stick must be Her magic wand. She's going to point it at you and ask you three questions. Beware. When you face Baba Yaga, you dare not lie or equivocate. Answer each question She asks without thinking about your answer. That is, let the mind of your root chakra speak for you. Let your creative soul reply before your social, parental left brain can formulate a socially approved answer.

She shakes the stick at you, then steps closer and thrusts the skull right into your face. You feel the freezing-burning touch of the skull all the way through your forehead, and its power reverberates through your head. She shouts Her first question at you:

"WHAT MUST YOU DO TO IMPROVE YOUR PHYSICAL HEALTH?"

Answer the Crone.

Listen to your answer. What did you say?

Pause

Baba Yaga cackles and nods, then She thrusts Her awful wand at you a second time. You feel its freezing-burning touch in your heart, you feel it all the way to your spine. Its power throbs through your lungs and muscles. Again, answer Her question *before you think about it:*

"WHAT IS PROSPERITY AND HOW CAN YOU GAIN IT?"

Answer from your heart.

Pay attention to your answer.

Pause

The old Witch nods and cackles again and for the third time thrusts Her awful wand at you. You feel its freezing-burning touch in your gut, you feel it all the way to the soles of your feet. Its power shocks your root chakra. Baba Yaga whispers:

"WHAT IS YOUR RIGHT LIVELIHOOD?"

Again, speak before you think.

Answer from your gut and listen to your answer. What did you say?

Pause

Baba Yaga nods. She is apparently satisfied. But you cannot back away from Her. Suddenly you can't move at all. She stares at you for a long moment, and then She begins to make some sort of wobbly movement, back and forth, in front of you. After a few minutes you realize what She's doing. The Crone is dancing a spiral dance around you. You can hear the faint sound of an invisible drum. It's the entrancing beat the shaman travels on to other worlds.

Sunwise the Crone goes, bobbing, weaving, stepping forward and back, dipping, jumping, waving Her hands. She takes a sharp turn, and now she's moving moonwise around you, up and down, leaping, waving Her hands. Unable to join Her dance, you can only watch this ugly, ungainly hag. Suddenly—there's a radiant queen dancing where the Crone just was. She's graceful, this queen is, and Her steps might be a minuet, a gavotte. Still, you cannot move. Now there's a dark, tiny Old One dancing around you, stomping, nearly flying. Now She's a fat, naked baby, and you realize She's moving sunwise again. Watch Her, watch how She dances Her primal dance around you . . . and you glimpse faces you might remember, forms you might recall . . . and after a long time, the dancer becomes a gentle virgin, and Her dance is so shy, so modest you know She must be innocence embodied. You long to dance with her. But look, the Crone returns, still dancing, still cackling and waving that awful wand with the skull on the end at you.

Suddenly you are released. Dance with the Crone. Dance with Baba Yaga through all Her incarnations, dance sunwise and moonwise and sunwise again. Dance through all your own incarnations. Dance with the Crone until you're so weary you think you'll never dance again. You must keep dancing. Dance round and round and round.

Pause

You're dancing your root chakra issues, dancing your root chakra into balance. Dance until you feel you must sink into the earth. Dance yourself into health, prosperity, right livelihood, grounding, survival.

At last She stops. At last you may stop. Finally She faces you, Her wrinkled old face just inches away from yours, and She stares into your eyes again. What does all this mean? Take a few minutes to contemplate what's happening to you.

Pause

Baba Yaga steps back. She nods and lifts one hand in benediction, then turns without a word and goes back into Her little green house.

You can still feel the vibrations where Baba Yaga's wand touched you in your head, your heart, your gut. You still feel the pulsing of your own blood, the vibrating energy of your own root chakra. You still feel the throbbing of Her spiral dance around you, the web She wove with Her spiral dance still holds you in its enchantment.

And as you watch, wondering where you really are, Baba Yaga's little house stands up on its birds' feet and runs away. It disappears deep in the dark forest. The fence sinks into the ground under the ancient trees, and now you see that all the skulls have become seeds, and they are sinking into the rich, black soil.

You're still feeling the rhythm of the Crone's spiral dance. You're feeling the power of your own dance, and now you realize that its source is the energy of your root chakra.

When you return to ordinary awareness, sit still and consider what you've felt and seen. Know that you will retain what you need in your normal conscious state and that you will receive "messages" and opportunities to act on what you have told Baba Yaga about your health, your prosperity, and your right livelihood.

Know that it's up to you to take action.

Genital Chakra: Hathor

In a society founded, and in many ways still ruled, by Puritans, where guns and violence make for good, wholesome fun but the nude body is obscene, people like to snigger that all the genital chakra is about is *S-E-X*. As I explained in the Aphrodite meditation in chapter 4, this horror of the natural functions of the body is largely the fault of the biophobic old fathers of the standard-brand churches, and if those Light-headed people I mentioned earlier shudder to think about what's "down there" at the first chakra, they shudder twice as much at any mention of "that part of the body" at the second chakra.

The genital chakra issues are *pleasure, sexuality, the emotions,* and *social issues.*

When you get out of your pantyhose and silk dress, or out of your suit and tie, what do you do for pleasure? Stop reading for a few minutes and make a list of ten pleasurable things. To get you started, here are the first five I thought of:

1. Using vanilla-scented hand and body lotion.
2. Petting purring cats.
3. Eating real whipped cream.
4. Drumming, especially when the group gets "in the groove."
5. Visiting a greenhouse when they're watering the plants.

Now make your list of ten things.

Done? Add ten more.

I hope you listed things that appeal to all five of your senses—to smell, taste, sight, hearing, and touch. I hope you're not just living in your head. Four of the five sensors are located in our heads, of course, and one of the pop clichés is that the brain is the most powerful sexual organ. It's likewise popular to believe that our pleasure center is in our brain, for when we feel pleasure—or any emotion—"they"[8] tell us, "It's all in your head."

But is it? Diane Ackerman writes that the latest findings in physiology suggest that "mind" is not synonymous with "brain." Mind "travels the whole body on caravans of hormone and enzyme, busily making sense of the compound wonders we catalogue as touch, taste, smell, hearing, vision."[9]

The point of our second chakra meditation will be to use our imaginations to get out of our heads for a while. *Really doing* those twenty pleasurable things you wrote on your list can be a second chakra moving meditation. Sex can, too. Anyone who has ever had an orgasm surely knows the volcanic power the genital chakra is capable of transmitting. (Do your own research.)

The emotions, which are "the result of *consciousness meeting the body,*"[10] are another second chakra issue. We saw consciousness meeting the body—felt it, really—in the BodyKnowing meditation in chapter 4. In our Puritan-born society, emotions are often considered to be "childish." That is, if we cry too much or laugh too loud, we're not acting like adults. I'd like to make the pejorative into a positive: I believe our emotions are "childlike," and the more I think about it, the more I wonder if our "inner children" live in our lower chakras. The part of us that plays and feels, that explores all sorts of ways of feeling pleasure, that really digs sex— that's our inner child, and perhaps She lives in the genital chakra.

Perfumed Hathor, cow-eared goddess of ancient Egypt, is a goddess of the sun.[11] She is the divinity of pleasure whom the Greeks identified with Aphrodite. As shown in temple friezes, she's the Goddess with the frame drum and the sistrum that banish evil spirits. She's the Goddess of art and music and dance and touch and cosmetics, Goddess of all the pleasures of the body. Jean Houston quotes a sensuous Hymn to Hathor:

> It is the Golden one! Lady of drunkenness,
> music, dance,
>   of frankincense and the crown, of women and
> men
>   who acclaim her because they love her.
> Heaven makes merry, the temples fill with
>   song, and the Earth rejoices.[12]

The Farrars say that Hathor was "undoubtedly" the Golden Calf wrought by the wandering Israelites out of the golden earrings of their wives and daughters:

> And they rose up early on the morrow, and offered burnt offerings, and brought peace offerings; and the people sat down to eat and drink, and rose up to play.[13]

This sounds second chakra to me—people Moses calls "stiffnecked" indulging in social pleasures around their altar to the smiling goddess of the lush land they had left behind when the stiffnecked prophet ordered them to follow him across the desert.

Let's go with our inner child to visit Hathor. Let's get ourselves aboard those hormonal caravans and get our senses back in our bodies.

The Meditation

Select something orange to sit on. Bright and sunny, orange is the color of the genital chakra. Sit quietly, close your eyes, and take several deep, easy breaths. Feel the warmth of your orange sit-upon rising up into your body. Let the energy of orange touch your genitals and warm them, allow this pleasure to fill your lower body and dance inside you. Let it rise through your chest and let yourself smile.

Pause

In your imagination now, find yourself in a warm land beside a dark river. You have come to Egypt, to the marketplace in the city of Dendera, and before you is a caravan headed toward the temple complex where Hathor is worshipped beside Her consort, Horus the Elder. It's dawn, and the breezes warm your skin. You can see the light just rising across the Nile and hear priests and priestesses of Hathor singing throughout the city to welcome another day's rebirth of the sun. Here in the marketplace you can smell the fresh produce being set out for sale. Someone hands you a piece of fresh melon. Eat, and enjoy its sweetness.

Your guide is a smiling young woman dressed in white, with a wide beaded collar around her neck and—is it possible? Are those cow's ears peeking out from her long black hair? She smiles and directs you to a wagon pulled by a donkey. Climb into the wagon and sit among the bright orange pillows you find there. There are other passengers in the caravan. Who are these people? Why are they traveling with you to Hathor's temple?

Pause

Now the caravan begins its short journey out of the city. The animals, bedecked with ribbons and garlands of flowers, are led by a number of young women who play frame drums and shake sistrums as they walk. Listen to the mingled complex rhythms of the drums, to the jingling of the metal rattles. All evil spirits have indeed been banished from this place.

You have arrived at Hathor's temple. Look up. See how the capital of each column has been sculpted in the form of a sistrum, how the figures sculpted on the columns and on the temple walls are engaged in rites of pleasure. Many of them, like the young women with your caravan, play frame drums and sistrums. Planted in even rows around the temple is a forest of sycamores, for Hathor is also known as Lady of the Sycamore. She sits in the tree and offers bread, fruit, and water to the newly dead, then guides them into the Underworld.

Follow the road through the trees to the porch of the temple. There—do you see it? Sculpted on the wall opposite the columns and painted in bright colors is the great Celestial Cow whose legs mark the ends of the earth and whose milk rains down upon Her children. Golden Hathor is also a mother goddess, and a thousand of Her daughters live here in Her temple.

Pause

One of those priestesses, a young girl, comes forward now and hands you a cup of milk, Hathor's sacred beverage. Thank her and drink the milk. How nourishing it is. How wonderful it would be to live always in the shelter of the goddess.

This young girl also hands you one of Hathor's sacred hand mirrors, in which the glass is the sun disk between the goddess' horns. When you look into this mirror, therefore, your own face becomes the sun. Look at yourself in Hathor's magical mirror. Look more closely at the young priestess. Can you see? Mirrors know and show everything. Can you see how closely this young priestess resembles you as a child? The mirror shows that she is shy and sensitive, though her sparkling eyes reveal a mischievous and daring temperament. You are facing your inner child, and she is beautiful beyond words.

"Today is New Year's Day," the child-priestess says. "It's Hathor's Birthday, and on this festival day we are encouraged to pleasure ourselves. What will you do for pleasure?"

Think back to your list. Today you may do three of the things you wrote down. And because you are in a magical place, you may do things no ancient Egyptian ever did.

Pause

Hathor's priestess leads you through the mysterious corridors of Hathor's temple to an inner chamber, where it is dim and warm and the floor is paved with orange tiles. "Here is a place of magic and power," she says. "Here you may do whatever brings pleasure to you. She walks once around the chamber, shaking her sistrum to banish any negativity that may have crept in, then smiles and leaves you alone. Do one thing that pleasures you. If you need props or other people, they are present. If you wish to travel, leave from this chamber and return to it. Take as much time as you need.

Pause

When you're ready, the child-priestess comes back into the chamber. Smiling, she asks, "Are you happy here?" Tell her what has made you happy today.

Pause

Now she leads you out of the temple through a side door and along a shady path to a private place among the sycamores. This is a small terraced garden with a shallow pool where you can see orange fish swimming among the roots of the blooming lotuses. At the boundaries of this pocket paradise innumerable orange flowers are in blossom. "Here is another place of magic and power," the child-priestess tells you. "Here you may do your second pleasurable thing." She comes forward and hugs you. "Please enjoy yourself," she whispers, then she runs back into the temple. What will you do now? Whatever you need is again provided. Spend as much time as you wish doing the second pleasurable thing from your list.

Pause

When you're ready the child-priestess comes to you once more. "Have you found joy here?" she asks. Tell her what joy you have found in Hathor's temple today.

Pause

The priestess asks you to follow her again, and now she leads you along a winding path through the trees, and it seems that you are going around the temple. Sure enough, you re-enter the temple under a high arched door at the end of two rows of sculpted columns. There are open windows and magical mirrors high in the walls, and the floor is paved in sunlight. "Here is a third place of magic and power," the priestess tells you. "Here you may do your third pleasurable thing."

After kissing you gently on the lips, she departs. Again, whatever you need is magically provided. Take as much time as you need for the third thing from your list.

Pause

When you're ready, the child-priestess comes for you again. "What pleasure have you found today?" she asks. Answer her question.

Pause

"We are expected," she says, leading you through the maze of mysterious corridors again. Just as you are feeling thoroughly lost, she steps aside and allows you to precede her into the central chamber of Hathor's temple.

This is the Hall of Appearances, the sanctuary of the Goddess. Someone is sitting on a basalt throne against the far wall, Someone wearing the *menat*, which is the miraculous healing necklace, and the headdress of cow's horns with the red-orange solar disk suspended between them. Yes, you are in the presence of the Goddess, and She is smiling at you. Gradually you realize that you are not alone. Your friends are here. Your community has come to this holy place with you to share your happiness. You may greet your friends and tell them what you've been doing today. They are pleased that you've been doing interesting, playful things.

Pause

But hush now. The Goddess wishes to speak to you of the pleasures of the world. "You may have works of art," She says, "you may have music and dance and good food. You may luxuriate in life. You may ache fiercely with love, lust, loyalty, and passion. You may burn with the gorgeous fever that is consciousness."[14] The Goddess smiles at you and stretches out Her hand to caress your cheek. "I call upon your soul to arise and come unto me. For I am the soul of nature that gives life to the universe. For behold, all acts of love and pleasure are my rituals. And behold, I have been with you from the beginning, and I am that which is attained at the end of desire."[15]

Sit for as long as you want to among your friends in the joyous presence of this golden Goddess.

When you return to your everyday awareness and have to go back to your everyday life, remember the Temple of Hathor. Remember the words of the Goddess and know that they are true. The world is overflowing with pleasure and *you are allowed to play in it.*

Solar Plexus Chakra: Oya

The third chakra issues are *strength of will, sense of purpose,* and *vitality.* Starhawk writes that will "is very much akin to what Victorian schoolmasters called 'character': honesty, self-discipline, commitment, and conviction." Judith and Vega define will as "the conscious direction of our life energy toward a manifest goal," which suggests how we may use our honesty, self-discipline, commitment, and conviction. Will is, they continue, "what guides, contains and harnesses that energy. To have strong will we need . . . to *know* what our goals are."[16]

I'm tempted to ask, what is your goal in life? Do you have a sense of purpose for being on the planet this time? But these questions are too big; most people never even ask them, much less find answers. Let's set them aside, therefore, and consider smaller questions: What is your goal for this year? What is your goal this month? This week? Today? Right now? The last question is the easiest to answer: your goal—and mine—right now is *mindfulness,* which, we remember, is "being fully awake and present." Mindfulness is, in fact, our true goal for all of our right nows.

So think of an achievable goal. Perhaps you want to upgrade your skill with a spreadsheet program. Perhaps you want to adopt a cat. Perhaps you want to do a reversing spell to direct harmful energy back at the person who has invaded your psychic space and made you sick.

The process of setting and meeting goals is outlined in the Witches' Pyramid, an occult teaching of apparently unknown genesis that sets forth four steps on the path to wisdom: To Know, To Will, To Dare, and To Be Silent. As we reach the solar plexus chakra, therefore, we begin to deal (1) with what we truly know, (2) with the power of our will, (3) with what we dare to do, and (4) with understanding when to speak and when not to speak.

These four steps work on two levels. On the mundane level, you're learning Excel, seducing a stray cat with fancy food, visualizing yourself inside a mirrored sphere that will shoot bad vibes back at their sender. On the cosmic level, you're doing what the alchemists call the Great Work, which is getting the lead out of your golden soul. I see knowing, willing, daring, and being silent in terms of two cards of the Major Arcana in the Tarot. Card I, the Magician, is the person who manipulates the four elements to create things on earth. Card III, the Empress, is the person who works in subtle and magical ways to create a new reality. In the office you're the Magician guided by the Empress. In your magical group, you're the Empress guiding the Magician.

First, you need to know what you want to do. You have to have a sense of purpose. Next, you have to focus your energy. You need the will to get up off the couch and get to work. Then you must have the daring to stop fantasizing and really get out there. Actually *doing something,* of course, comes with all the usual risks of making mistakes and failing; another risk is *learning.* Finally, you need to understand when it's wise to speak and when it's wiser to be silent. Because talking can dissipate magical energy, it's sometimes better not to talk about what you're doing. It's also possible that someone who hears you babbling about your ideas around the office will steal them and take credit for them.

The founder of the Re-formed Congregation of the Goddess, Jade, has adapted the four steps to wisdom for her thought-provoking *Affirmation of Women's Spirituality.* Here is a much abbreviated version:

> There is one circle of . . . energy and I am part of this energy and it is mine to direct. I wish to direct this energy . . . .
> To Know:
>> —That I can create my own reality and that sending out a positive expectation will bring a positive result
>> —That every situation is an opportunity to practice and develop my craft
> To Will:
>> —That I shall grow in wisdom, strength, knowledge, and understanding
>> —That I shall, as much as I am aware, act in honesty to myself and to others
> To Dare:
>> —To be myself
>> —To take responsibility for myself and my actions . . . .
>
> And to understand when to speak and when to keep silence.
> So Mote it be.[17]

Third chakra work is magical work. Third chakra work can be pretty scary.
Oya can be a pretty scary goddess.

She's a Yoruban Goddess of storms, strong winds, fire, and lightning, Ruler of the marketplace. Luisah Teish calls Her Queen of the Winds of Change, Mother of Transformation, Lady of the Sunset, Boss Lady of the Cemetery. Her consort is Shango, Lord of Thunder, but though She "marries a fierce man, She is fiercer than Her husband."[18]

Judith Gleason, who has studied this goddess in Her manifestations in Africa and the New World, writes that Oya is a "patron of feminine leadership and of persuasive charm reinforced by *aje*—an efficacious gift usually translated as 'witchcraft.'"

Gleason quotes several traditional African Praises of Oya. I especially like the following stanza:

> *She burns like fire in the hearth, everywhere at once.*
> *Tornado, quivering solid canopied trees*
> *Great Oya, yes.*
> *Whirlwind masquerader, awakening,*
> *courageously takes up her saber.*[19]

Let us find out what Oya can teach us about strength of will and sense of purpose.

The Meditation

Find something yellow to sit on, something yellow and warm and billowy. Close your eyes and take several deep, easy breaths and feel the power of yellow rising through your first chakra, spiraling through the second chakra, and spinning in your third chakra. Feel the strength of yellow in your solar plexus and know that it will fan the winds of change through your life.

Pause

Do you still have your wings, the ones you received in the Trust meditation in chapter 3? Find your wings again and put them on and fly to the wilderness. Your wilderness can be the forest, the jungle, the desert, the mountaintop, the inner city. Fly to your wilderness, and as you're flying remember the lesson of your wings: remember to trust the Goddess.

Now you find yourself alone in your wilderness. Spend a moment exploring this lonely, alien place. What is it like in your wilderness?

Pause

You're not alone for long, however. Here comes someone, a tall African woman dressed in billowing white clothing. She wears a dozen white skirts over a dozen ruffled white petticoats. She wears white blouses and scarves. She wears dozens of beaded necklaces and bracelets, and a fine linen headwrap. In one hand She carries a feathered fan, in the other a calabash, or large gourd.

Here comes Oya, Goddess of Edges. Goddess of the edge between what we know and what we don't know. Goddess of the edge between our will and the will of another. Goddess of the edge between what we dare to do and what someone commands us to do. Goddess of the edge between silence and noise. Oya arrives. Make yourself ready to be tested.

Pause

"I know who you are," the Goddess says to you. "I know you now, I know you as you have been, I know you as you will be."

She fans herself and you can feel the breeze of Her feathered fan. The winds of change are stirring around you. "And what do you know?" the Goddess asks.

What do you know? You presumably know your name and address. You know the multiplication tables. You know the alphabet. But what do you know of your place on earth? What do you know of your place in your community?

Pause

Oya shakes Her calabash and a tiny black creature jumps out. This tiny creature symbolizes what you know about *your true self.* Who are you? What is your place in your community upon the earth? Let the tiny black creature help you answer these questions. Let her whisper in your ear, let her draw some magical image in the dust at your feet. Let this tiny creature help you know what you *know.*

Pause

Oya stalks around you, making one circle. One circle for what you know.

She fans Herself again, and you feel the winds of Her feathered fan. They ruffle your hair, these winds do, they ruffle your clothing and make you uncomfortable.

"I have always had great strength of will," the Goddess says, speaking aloud but not looking at you. "I have always been willful." She fans Herself, and you feel the winds from Her fan beating against your skin, pushing at you. "But what is your will?" She suddenly asks.

What is your will? What is your character? What focus of energy directs the way you live your life?

Pause

Oya shakes Her calabash again, and two tiny black creatures leap out. These two tiny black creatures symbolize your will. They represent your life energy, the true goals of your life. Let them help you answer Oya's question. What is your will? Let them whisper in your ears, let them draw magical images in the dust at your feet, let them sing to you. Let them help you see the focus of your life energy.

Pause

Oya stalks around you again, making a second circle. The circle of your will.

She stops and points Her feathered fan at you. The winds are stronger now, they blow harder at you, and you feel your clothing flatten against your skin. The winds of change are disturbing the order of your life. You have to close your eyes against this strong wind. You may gasp for breath.

"I have always dared," She says, as if speaking to Herself, fanning Herself, as if She doesn't even remember that you are here. "I have always dared to seize the horns of the buffalo, to confront the dead, to dance with violence and burn like the fire in the hearth. I have always dared," She says. She spins and points Her feathered fan. "What do you dare?" She asks. "What do you dare to do?"

When your will is strong, what do you dare to do? When you feel your sense of purpose, what do you dare to do? What is the courage of your heart?

Pause

Oya shakes Her calabash once more, and three tiny black creatures fly out. These tiny black creatures symbolize what you dare to do. Let them help you answer Oya's question. Let them whisper in your ears, let them draw magical images at your feet, let them dance and sing what you may dare to do.

Pause

Oya stalks around you. Three circles. One circle for what you know. One circle for what you will to do. One circle for what you dare to do.

She fans Herself, and now the winds from Her feathered fan blow like a tornado. What keeps you from being blown away? Only the strength of your own wings, only the strength of your trust. Only the stability of what you know and will and dare are keeping you on the ground. Grounded. She fans Herself, and the tornado roars through you, and it rips your old useless ideas clear out of you. It leaves spaces for new ideas to take root. She fans Herself with Her feathered fan again and when She opens Her mouth you can hardly hear Her words.

"I speak forth what I must say"—can you hear Her voice?—"and I know when to keep silent." Is the Goddess truly speaking? What do you truly hear?

Pause

She shakes Her calabash one last time, and four tiny black creatures erupt from it. These four tiny black creatures symbolize your ability to know when to speak and when to keep silent. They do not whisper in your ears. They do not draw in the dust at your feet. They neither sing nor dance. They gesture, and in their gesturing you understand the wisdom of silence.

Pause

Oya raises Her feathered fan. The winds stop. The tornado ceases and the ten tiny black creatures become still. "It is said," the Goddess whispers, "it is said that those who speak do not know, and those who know do not speak . . . ."

When you return to ordinary consciousness, get out your journal and write what you know. Write what you will to do. Write what you dare to do. Keep silent about what you have written and do not show your journal to other people.

Heart Chakra: Kuan Yin

We get a lot about love. It's never having to say you're sorry. It's letting go of fear. It's what the world needs now. It's a puppy, a backrub, a cup of fancy coffee, a new car. From Sappho to Shakespeare to Stephen Sondheim, poets (and advertisers) have written voluminously of love. The index of my *Bartlett's Familiar Quotations*, in fact, lists 822 quotations under "love."

Everyone knows that the heart chakra is the love chakra, and so for our heart chakra meditation we focus on love. But not romantic love, or the religicized love the preachers exhort us to hold in our hearts, or the fuzzy love invoked to sell us stuff, or manipulative love. The third chakra issues are specific, useful aspects of love: *compassion, self-acceptance,* and *balance in relationships.*

In the next chapter we will do the Goddess Pillar Meditation, in which we become the Central Pillar of the Qabalistic Tree of Life. Although I call the Central Pillar the Goddess Pillar, traditionally it is called the Pillar of Equilibrium. The Sphere at the heart of this Pillar is Tiphareth[20] (Beauty), and its position on the Tree corresponds to the heart in the human body.

Dion Fortune writes that the Pillar of Equilibrium is "always concerned with consciousness" and "must never be regarded as an isolated factor, but as a link, a focussing-point, a centre of transition or transmutation." In her summary of correspondences, she lists among the attributes of Tiphareth "mediating intelligence," "vision of the harmony of things," and "devotion to the Great Work" of alchemical transmutation.[21]

We like to think that our heart is our spiritual center. The heart chakra thus becomes the midpoint between survival and knowing, between pleasure and imagination, between will and communication. Whether we're dealing with an intellectual construct like the Tree of Life or with earthy, messy "real life," it's in our heart that we find—or create—harmony and balance. And while it's possible in theory to intellectually transmute our soul from lead to gold, it's only in the heart—the alchemical athanor, or oven—that transmutation can truly take place. It's only when we take a new idea "to heart"—not "to head"—that we accept it.

The best sermon I know on issues of the heart chakra isn't a sermon at all. It's a children's story. The hero of Antoine de Saint Exupéry's *The Little Prince* lives on asteroid B-612. One day he meets a rose, a vain creature born exactly at sunrise. He attends to her, waters her, protects her from breezes and tigers, and takes her coquetry all too seriously. At last, confused by his feelings for a creature who appears to have no feelings, he flies away with a migration of birds and eventually arrives on earth. One day he comes upon a whole field of roses. When he realizes that his precious flower was nothing more than a common rose, he begins to cry.

At this point, a fox appears and asks to be tamed. What does it mean, "tame?" the boy asks. "To establish ties," the fox explains. When people spend time together, they come to need each other. They are tamed. "To me, you will be unique in all the world," the fox says. "To you, I shall be unique in all the world."

"There is a flower," the little prince replies. "I think that she has tamed me."

After some wanderings, the little prince meets the author, an aviator who has crashed in the Sahara. Because they spend time together, both become tamed, and the boy comes to understand that he must return to his rose. He goes back to the fox to say good-bye. The fox promises to tell him a secret, but first he must go back to the field of roses. "No one has tamed you," the boy tells the flowers, "and you have tamed no one."

When he returns to the fox, the fox tells him the secret: "It is only with the heart that one can see rightly; what is essential is invisible to the eye . . . . It is the time you have wasted for your rose that makes your rose so important . . . . You become responsible, forever, for what you have tamed."[22]

The little prince has compassion for his rose, but at first their relationship is unbalanced. He's doing all the giving, she's doing all the receiving. His imbalance drives him to escape from her. The time he spends with the fox and the aviator help the child come to understanding and self-acceptance. We can hope that his renewed relationship with his rose will be a balanced, more mature relationship.

Isn't it the same for us all? We've been naive children who care too much. We've tried to love roses who are filled with self-love and don't love us back. Some of us have had the good fortune to meet a fox who teaches us to see with our heart, to see what is essential. What is essential, of course, is acceptance. It has become a cliché that if we don't love (accept) ourselves we cannot love (accept) others or be loved by (accepted by) others. It seems to me that acceptance is the key to balance in relationships, and that compassion is the key to acceptance.

There is another well-known sermon that seems to concern heart chakra issues. This sermon was preached nearly 2,000 years ago by the most compassionate of gods. In the fifth chapter of Matthew, Jesus of Nazareth teaches the multitude, saying:

> Blessed are the merciful, for they shall have mercy.

And:

> Love your enemies, bless anyone who curses you, do good to anyone who hates you, and pray for those who carry you away by force and persecute you.[23]

The most compassionate of goddesses is said to be Kuan Yin, "She who hears the cries of the world." Merlin Stone says that She may be "a relatively recent reflection" of the ancient Chinese goddess Nu Kwa, who created "a race of golden people" and repaired the universe in a time of chaos when the pillars of north, south, east, and west had been destroyed by fire and flood. Because both *Nu* and *Yin* mean "woman" and *K'uai* means "earth," it is possible that both names "refer to a concept of the Goddess as Earth or Nature."[24]

One tradition about Kuan Yin holds that She was originally a male, Avalokites-vara, who achieved Buddhahood and decided to reincarnate in a female body as Kuan Yin. Avalokitesvara/Kuan Yin not only protects us by extinguishing fires, still-ing floods, and calming winds, but also brings fertility to women who pray to Him/Her. "She who brings children" continues to be beloved, and figures of the Goddess standing or sitting on a lotus blossom and holding a boy child named Shan Ts'ai are popular. I have such a porcelain figure myself; Shan Ts'ai looks like a little old man. Lung Nu, the dragon girl, also sometimes accompanies the Goddess.

Let us visit Kuan Yin's residence on Mount Potalaka, which may be in Ceylon, in India, or on the Chusan Islands south of Shanghai. Occultists tell us that we reverse genders on the inner planes, i.e., one who is female in the physical body becomes male in the emotional body, female again in the mental body, and male again in the spiritual body. (And vice versa for men.) Let us, therefore, take Shan Ts'ai or Lung Nu as our other selves, the children of our hearts.

The Meditation

Find something green to sit on, a scarf or a towel or Mother Earth's own green grass. Close your eyes and take several deep, easy breaths and begin to feel the energy of green stirring beneath you. Feel the greening power that Hildegard of Bingen called *viriditas*[25] strengthening your root chakra. Feel the greening power rising through your genital chakra and your solar plexus chakra. The greening power moistens your chakras "just as moisture is infused throughout the Earth." Feel the greening power making your body and soul "green and fruitful so that [you] bring forth noble fruits of virtue." *Viriditas* gives "vitality to the marrow and veins and members of [your] whole body, as the tree from its root gives sap and greenness to all the branches."[26] For a moment, let this greening power travel throughout your body.

Pause

Now you find yourself standing in a meadow beside a wide river. All around you it is green. The whole world is lush and moist and fresh, and the river seems to encircle the land. You have come to a holy island, and before you stands Mount Potalaka, a mountain out of an exquisite Chi-nese brush painting. Its foot in shadows, Mount Potalaka rises into the clouds that shroud its peak. Halfway up the mountain you see flashes of light and color. Are those banners you see? Is that a papier mâché dragon dancing on the mountain? You're wondering how to find the path up the mountain when you hear a cough nearby. Or maybe it's a giggle.

Look around the meadow until you find what got your attention. It's a flower. This flower can be a rose, a tulip or a lily or a lilac or any other flower that has special meaning for you.

"I was born just at dawn," the flower tells you, stretching and yawning. "I am the most special flower in the world." Look around again. There are no other flowers in the area.

The flower coughs again. "Pray have the courtesy to water me," it says. In such a presence you must do as you are told. Find the watering can. As you're watering the flower, you notice that it has a face, and the face is very familiar. This is someone you care for. Who is this flower? Is it a parent or a child? A life partner? This flower is the most important person in your life.

Pause

"That's enough water!" the flower says. "Now pull up those awful weeds. And shade me so I don't get too much sun. But don't shade me too much, for I'm preparing to bloom. Protect me from mealy bugs and caterpillars. You're standing in my light. Maybe a fence would be good. It would protect me from rabbits that might nibble my leaves. Spend more time with me. I'm getting ready to bloom and I am so very bored with the waiting."

How can you meet all the demands your flower makes? Do what you can for your flower. Do what you can with sincere attention, do it with sincere love and patience. Be mindful while you attend to your flower and know that no matter how trivial your flower's demands may seem, what you are doing for your flower is important.

Pause

Nevertheless, you're becoming irritated. Yes, you really are. You're annoyed at the flower's constant demands. You're becoming frustrated. Your flower is too demanding and takes too much of your time. Yes, you have a right to be angry.

Pause

Kuan Yin loves those who are mindful. As you are attending to your flower, you feel someone standing nearby. It's Shan Ts'ai, with Lung Nu nearby. The two children have come while you were paying attention to your flower. They are the children of your heart and they represent compassion and self-acceptance. "Kuan Yin sent us to you," they say. "We are here to invite you to the Lotus Festival. See? The sacred green dragon is already dancing around Mount Potalaka."

Here's a good excuse to escape from your flower. Be sure you water it once more and be sure there are no bugs on its leaves.

Pause

Now you may begin to climb the sacred mountain with Shan Ts'ai and Lung Nu. They take your hands and lead you to the path that circles the mountain. Nearly flying, you go around the base of the mountain, a little higher you go around again, a little higher you go around again and again. You are now halfway up the mountain, and here Shan Ts'ai and Lung Nu stop at the entrance to a large, bright cave. This is Kuan Yin's residence. Here She waits to rush to the aid of all who call to her.

Shan Ts'ai and Lung Nu lead you into Kuan Yin's cave, and it's a wondrous cave indeed. It seems to be as big as Mount Potalaka itself, and it's full of light. The ceiling sparkles with jewels and the painted walls show scenes of the Goddess helping Her devoted followers. Here She is rescuing someone from a fire, there She is standing at the edge of a receding flood. Another scene shows the Goddess rescuing a young child from a wild animal, another shows Her strolling in a garden full of flowers—do any of these flowers look familiar?—and teaching the power of compassion. Spend as much time as you want to studying the beautiful lessons painted on these walls.

Pause

In the center of the cave is a pool with blooming lotuses and swimming *koi* fish. Rising up in the center of this pool is a wondrously carved fountain. A black marble cube supports a blue-green sphere, from which rises a red-orange cone. At the top is a pale alabaster crescent moon. The water that flows out of the curve of the moon is cool and pure. Kuan Yin descends from Her ivory throne and invites you to drink, and one of your heart children hands you a silver cup. Drink. Taste this sweet water, feel its purity flowing into your throat and through your body. Here is the power of *viriditas*, the greening power that moistens the world with its energetic love. Drink again if you want to. There is more than enough of this water for everyone who wants to drink.

You may speak with Kuan Yin now. Tell the Goddess how it's going in your life and ask for Her advice or help. This is your opportunity: tell Her how annoying your flower is, how demanding and selfish. Tell the Goddess everything about your relationship with your flower and ask Her to help you.

Pause

She thinks a moment. "I will tell you, first, what was once taught by my brother bodhisattva from another land," Kuan Yin says, and She raises Her right hand in the "giving" gesture. "Blessed are the merciful, for they shall have mercy." Repeat after the Goddess: "Blessed are the merciful, for they shall have mercy."

Now Kuan Yin seats herself on Her ivory throne again and invites you to sit on an ebony throne nearby. She will speak with you and teach you what you must know about your flower, about all your flowers. Listen to the Goddess and know that you will remember Her teaching.

Pause

At last Kuan Yin rises again. She extends Her right hand and lays Her palm over your heart. "I will tell you what another wise one has said," She says. "It is only with the heart that one can see rightly. What is essential is invisible to the eye." She takes your hands in Hers. "Take the words of these wise ones into your heart," She tells you, "and return to your flower and teach it what I have taught you."

The Goddess sits upon Her ivory throne again and gestures to Shan Ts'ai and Lung Nu. The children take your hands and lead you out of the cave to the courtyard where the sacred green dragon is still dancing. It stops and looks at you. "Remember the words of the wise ones," the dragon says. "And remember that Kuan Yin hears the calls of all who love her. She will come when you call Her."

When you return to ordinary awareness, consider the lessons you have received from Kuan Yin and Jesus of Nazareth and the fox, and speak from your heart to the person who is your flower.

Throat Chakra: Sarasvati

I vaguely remember a crowd scene from a play in which one of the characters shouts, "If everyone will just *shut up,* we can start communicatin' here." The line got a big laugh. It seems as if everyone has something to say.

Just visit your nearest bookstore and count the books. How to say what you mean (and, yes, how to mean what you say). How to speak in public. How to write better memos and letters. How to communicate with your employees, your family, your elected politicians. How to journal and how to write from your right brain. How to use DOS, how to get on the Net and into the Web. There are piles of books on communication.

In the third chakra meditation we learned when to speak and when it's wiser to be silent. Because the fifth chakra is located at the throat, however, now we learn to speak forth what we know, either orally or on paper. The throat chakra issues are *clear communication, self-expression,* and *creativity.*

Communication is not talking to. The word comes from the Latin *communis,* "common." Related English words are "common," "community," "communion," and "commune." The essential idea is to make public, to make common among the people, to share equally. Communication is talking *with.*

Are there any new ideas under our Mother Sun? What does anyone know that is worth communicating?

Let's consider some of our true innovators, the creators of our ovular works in feminist spirituality. Our best writers are people like you and me. They've had to struggle to pay the rent while finding their right livelihood, and they've had to deal with illness and grief. They've built communities and learned to trust and be grateful. They've had great ideas about which they're driven to write and speak, and they've done much to make the Goddess public and to share knowledge of Her among the "common" people. Sometimes they've had to wait for people to catch up with them. Here is a short list of my heras, plus one hero:[27]

- M. Esther Harding, who in 1933 gave the definition of virginity that we still repeat: "A girl belongs to herself while she is . . . unmarried [and] is 'one-in-herself.'"

- Robert Graves, whose *Greek Myths* (1957) and *White Goddess* (1948) gave us the history and linguistics behind mythology and showed the world Who inspires true poetry.
- Elizabeth Janeway, who wrote in the early 1970s that Freudian penis envy is metaphorical, not literal, and that it's the weak of both sexes who are the "second sex."
- Merlin Stone, whose *When God Was a Woman* (1976) shot a feminist arrow right into the heart of the standard-brand religions.
- Susan Griffin, whose *Woman and Nature* (1978) opened our eyes and broke our hearts.
- Mary Daly, whose works are giving us a whole new vocabulary.
- Vicki Noble, creator, with Karen Vogel, of the *Motherpeace Tarot* (1983) and priestess of snake power.
- Carol Christ, whose important essay, "Why Women Need the Goddess" (1987), concludes that "it seems natural that the Goddess would reemerge as symbol of newfound beauty, strength, and power of women."
- Marija Gimbutas, the honored mythoarchaeologist who dug up and described evidence of the Goddess civilization of Old Europe.

Because I work mostly with words, my heras and heros are writers and teachers. I can think of few better examples of communication, self-expression, and creativity.

Stop reading for a moment and consider: who would you add to my list? Who are your heras and heros in the Craft, the Neo-Pagan world, the Goddess religion? Why are they your heras and heros?

Perhaps you work in other media. What musicians or artists or athletes are your heras and heros? What dancers or good cooks or scientists?

Don't be discouraged if you're not as erudite as Graves or as wise as Gimbutas. Who could be? But surely you have some wise thing—perhaps many wise things—worth speaking forth. Maybe you just don't think you have time to communicate your wisdom. Maybe you haven't felt that you have permission to express yourself. Maybe you believe that other people are the creative ones.

In *The Artist's Way*, Cameron sets forth ten basic principles that form the "bedrock" of what she calls "creative recovery." Here is principle number one:

Creativity is the natural order of life. Life is energy: pure creative energy.

Because you are the most precious child of the Goddess, you share Her pure creative energy. Her energy already infuses every cell of your body—of all your bodies, visible and invisible.

Here is Cameron's tenth principle:

Our creative dreams and yearnings come from a divine source. As we move toward our dreams, we move toward our divinity.[28]

This is precisely what you've been doing throughout this book. You've been using *Goddess Meditations* to move closer to your own divinity.

Sarasvati, whose consort is Brahma, is the Goddess of speech, wisdom, and music. Mother of the Vedas and inventor of the Sanskrit alphabet, She is often depicted with four arms, holding a book, to show Her love of learning, and a drum or playing the vina, a stringed instrument. Sometimes a goose stands beside Her, which (though no one else seems to make this connection) reminds me of Mother Goose, who laid the golden egg of the sun and whose nursery rhymes have amused and instructed generations of children. Early on, Sarasvati may have been a river goddess and sister of Ganga, after Whom the Ganges is named. Monaghan calls Her the "very prototype of the female artist" and "the goddess of eloquence, which pours forth like a flooding river."[29]

Z. Budapest writes that the new moon of Aquarius marks the Bengali festival of Sarasvati, which we can celebrate by changing the ink in our inkwell, cleaning all of our writing instruments (including the computer), dusting all of our books, and organizing all of our personal papers. Following Budapest's suggestion, several years ago I bought a modest glass inkwell to keep next to my little statue of Sarasvati; I keep "dove's blood" ink in it to write magical spells with. Budapest says that no writing should be done on Sarasvati's day—with all that cleaning, who has time?—but, instead, we should rest and pray for the energy to study, write, to "accomplish something great." Invoke the goddess with these words:

> Sarasvati of the pen and of the ink, you have caused words to come to being. Eloquent One, open up my soul to your inspiration. Flow through me as your channel, make my words flow better and more clearly, and illuminate my mind.[30]

Let us seek out Sarasvati and ask Her to teach us what true communication is.

The Meditation

Find something blue to sit on, something as blue as pure flowing water, as blue as a clear summer sky. Sit comfortably, close your eyes, and take several deep, easy breaths. Feel the cool blue energy rise into your body. Let it speak to your first chakra, second, third, and fourth. Let blue energy declare, "Creativity is the bedrock of my life," to every cell in your body. Let every cell believe it.

Pause

Soon you find yourself in a place of great mystery, blue and cloudy, without any recognizable features, without visible land or sky. You have a vague sense of water nearby, the ocean, perhaps, or a flowing river, but you can see nothing except fog and clouds. Try looking up. If you squint, perhaps you can make out the new moon's faint crescent.

Listen. Do you hear sounds? Or is that a voice you hear? Yes, it's definitely a voice, and it's reciting a nursery rhyme!

Luna, every woman's friend,
To me thy goodness condescend,
Let this night in vision see
Emblems of my destiny.[31]

Repeat the second couplet with this mysterious speaker—

Let this night in vision see
Emblems of my destiny.

—and know that you may indeed see emblems, or symbols. Perhaps you are already beginning to see something in this unknown foggy place. Perhaps the glow of the new moon is revealing some symbol or vision . . . .

Pause

As the fog begins to clear, you discover that you seem to be standing on a broad, flat plain with few landmarks. It doesn't feel unfriendly, just empty, like canvas waiting to be painted or a sheet of paper waiting to be written on. Look down. You are, in fact, standing on bedrock. You're standing on the solid rock that underlies all of the soil and loose materials on the earth's surface. And the bedrock is beautiful. It's blue. Shining and solid, the bedrock gleams in all the shades of the sky in springtime. Another definition of bedrock is "fundamental principles." You are standing on the fundament of the earth, the bed from which our principles arise.

"The fundamental principle is creativity," says a voice somewhere nearby. "Always remember that." Who's talking? This is not the same voice that was reciting the nursery rhyme. Look through the fog and clouds for the source of that second voice. Who is speaking to you?

The fog clears a bit more. The clouds begin to lift. Now you realize that you're standing at a crossroad. Which direction have you come from? Where are you headed? Have you turned a corner recently? From where and to where?

Pause

As the light becomes measurably clearer, you notice someone walking toward you. It's a four-armed Lady wearing a red tunic and green trousers. This is Sarasvati, with Her goose beside her. They're engaged in conversation, and both Sarasvati and the goose are carrying books that are glowing so beautifully they seem almost to be alive. You are sure that they must be marvelous books, written by world-famous authors and filled with wisdom and humor. You ache to read these rare books.

The goddess smiles. "Welcome," She says, and the goose echoes Her greeting. "Welcome, dear friend."

The fog continues to lift, the clouds drift away, and now you see a crooked little house beside this crossroad where you have met the goddess. Sarasvati beckons to you to enter the crooked little house with Her.

It's a house out of a fairy tale. There are herbs hanging in bunches from the rafters. In the bright fireplace a cauldron is simmering over the fire. In the far corner is a curtained bed. Shelves and cabinets line the walls, and a wooden worktable and chairs stand in the center of the room. And the floor of this room? It's bedrock, the beautiful, shining bedrock of the creative universe, gleaming in all the blue shades of the sky in springtime. You can tell that whoever lives in this crooked little house is obviously a friend of the Goddess. She has apparently just stepped out.

On the table are a tall stack of paper, several elegant quill pens, and an inkwell filled with shining golden ink. Take a seat at the old wooden table with Sarasvati and the goose.

"Let us speak together of fundamental principles," Sarasvati says. "Creativity is your bedrock," She says to you. "It is your life energy in action. Creativity brings force into form, it brings the unmanifest into manifestation. As force yearns to become form, so does creativity yearn to be expressed, and your self-expression is your life force taking form. You can, of course, choose to express yourself in beneficial ways or nonbeneficial ways, for We do not control you. What you choose determines how you live, and you know that the energy you send out is the energy that returns to you.

"If knowledge is to be shared and made common," the Goddess continues, "it must be accessible. However you communicate, you must communicate in a way that people can grasp. These are the fundamental principles," She says, "and I repeat them only to remind you." "Only to remind you," says the goose.

Pause

"Now," Sarasvati says, "these are *your books.* This one," She indicates the book She was carrying, "is the book of your heart." "And this one," says the goose, "is the book of your head."

"In these books," Sarasvati continues, "you have already written much. In your life, you have already been speaking your wisdom."

Did you know that? Do you know your own wisdom? Think for a moment. What do you know? What have you learned?

Pause

You can ask to see your books if you want to. Ask to read your books. Sarasvati and the goose hand them gladly to you. Choose a book, open it, and begin reading. Take as much time as you need and know that you will remember what you need to remember. Read in both books. Read the wisdom of your heart. Read the wisdom of your head. Know also that if you choose not to read very much in either book, you can come back to this crooked little house. Your books will be waiting for you on the shelf beside the fireplace, and she who lives in this house has already agreed to act as guardian to your books.

Pause

Now you have the opportunity to write or express yourself in any way you want to. Look at the pens on the table. Select the most beautiful pen and dip it in the inkwell. The golden ink is pure energy, the life energy given by the Goddess to you. Take a sheet of paper from the stack and begin writing.

Write as long as you need to get your basic principles and ideas on paper. Then use any other medium to express your creativity: painting, fiber art, sculpture, dancing, singing, drumming, instrumental music, sewing, cooking, woodworking, athletics, hands-on healing, gardening. Whatever supplies you need, you can find them in the cabinets and on the shelves of this magical little house.

Pause

Do what you do best and know that your work is as good as it currently can be. Know that you are expressing your dreams and yearnings, that you are expressing the wisdom of your life. Work from your heart and your head. Express the principles you have learned in your life. Express what you would teach. Take as much time as you need.

When you return to ordinary awareness, write in your journal. Make notes of what you did in this meditation and do what you can to manifest your wonderful work in "real" life.

Brow Chakra: The Cumaean Sybil

Well, here we are—up in our heads, up where just about every metaphysical person I've ever met is most comfortable. We have, however, already grounded ourselves in earthly survival, enjoyed physical pleasures, discovered what we know and will and dare to do, found love and compassion, and spoken forth our true wisdom. Because we are moving our life energy up through our chakra system, we can perhaps avoid becoming too spacy, or spacily speculative, as we work with our two head chakras.

The brow chakra issues are *intuition, imagination,* and *psychic perception.*

I've been pondering intuition and imagination for some time. They're both right-brain mental processes, both nonrational ways of learning. So what's the difference?

As usual, I find etymology a useful beginning. *Intuition* comes from the Latin *intueri,* "to look at, contemplate." Intuitive knowledge is "knowing without the use of rational processes, immediate cognition, a capacity for guessing accurately, sharp insight." *Imagination*'s Latin root is *imaginari,* "to picture oneself," from *imago,* "image." The first definition of imagination is "the formation of a mental image or concept of that which is not real or present." Both intuition and imagination are thus about *inner seeing.*

That's what's been happening in the guided meditations you've been doing. In your *imagination* you've been going to fantastic places (i.e., places of fantasy) and meeting goddesses and fantastic beings. You've had imaginary experiences and been asked questions, which you've answered from your *intuition*.

It seems to me that intuition is metaphorical seeing, as in "I see," meaning "I understand." Intuition generally comes in an unexpected flash—the famous "Aha!" It also seems to me that intuition comes as much from the gut and the heart as from the inner eyes. As we learned in the BodyKnowing meditation in chapter 4, page 96 our body's reactions give us insights our brain does not. When I get an intuitive insight, for example, I often feel something like a hot flash. I've also learned that my most truthful intuitive insights wake me up at four in the morning. What are the mechanics of your intuitive insights? Stop reading for a moment and consider how you know what you don't learn from left-brain processes.

Imagination, on the other hand, is more deliberate. We use our imagination to build, shape, and order a separate reality, one that coexists with our "real" (mundane) reality. Sometimes that other reality is patently false. The first example that comes to mind is unrequited love, wherein every little thing is a hidden message—of which the object of your affections may be totally unaware. When this happens, your saner friends tell you, "It's all in your head." And it is. You've built a whole different world in there.

Novelists build the best alternate realities, however, and Serious People who read only nonfiction books that are Good For Them are missing out on a lot. Dion Fortune explains why we need novels:

> People read fiction in order to supplement the diet life provides for them. If life is full and varied, they like novels that analyse and interpret it for them; if life is narrow and unsatisfying, they supply themselves with mass production wish-fulfilments from the lending libraries.[32]

As the ancient teachers taught with parables, today we can learn much from our novelists.

Here are eight of my favorite Goddess novels, which are, alas, usually found on the fantasy and science fiction shelves in bookstores and libraries.[33]

- Gael Baudino, *Gossamer Axe*
- Marion Zimmer Bradley, *The Mists of Avalon*
- Kim Chernin, *The Flame Bearers*
- Elizabeth Cunningham, *The Return of the Goddess*
- Cerridwen Fallingstar, *The Heart of the Fire*
- Dion Fortune, *The Sea Priestess*
- Ellen Frye, *Amazon Story Bones*
- Diana L. Paxon, *The Serpent's Tooth*

Rooted in sound scholarship, these novels are fertilized with grand imagination and good stories. They're filled with the vital details that show us how people actually live when the Goddess is in their lives. Some of these novels take place in the present, some in historical settings, some in purely make-believe settings. Some are based on literature and myth, others are autobiographical. As in any good novel, when you identify with the protagonist and get lost in the narrative, you learn without realizing that you're learning.

After you finish your goddess meditations, go out and find a Goddess novel or three and see what magic you find in them.

In *Moon Magic*, one of her two Isis novels, Fortune shows the effectiveness of imagination in magic when Vivien, the sea priestess, and a friend create a temple of Isis: "And this is how we do it—we sit down and imagine it—nothing more—*but*—it is the imagination of a trained mind!"[34] The novelist is likewise a magician, one who also uses her trained mind to create alternate realities.

"Trained mind" leads us to the third brow chakra issue, psychic perception, or using the third eye to see what is usually invisible to the physical eyes. Psychism is a kind of adjunct to spiritual development, not, in my opinion, really necessary but interesting. It's useful to study some of the psychic sciences and know something about astrology, numerology, and the many varieties of divination and to be able to see "invisible" things, but remember that using psychism to manipulate another person is hazardous to your karmic health. Jade lists thirty-six psychic skills, from "psychic artist" to "xenoglossia" (knowledge of a language you've never heard), and comments that "in a society which has taught us to deny our reality, it is not surprising that women of spirit have found ways to validate themselves, their actions, and their intuitions. . . ."[35]

The Sibyls are believed to have lived at ten ancient sacred sites in Cimmeria, Cumae, Delphi, Erythraea, Libya, Marpessus, Persia, Phrygia, Samos, and Tibur. The most famous of these ancient priestess/prophets was the Cumaean Sybil, whose cave was discovered near Naples in 1932. In the fifth century B.C.E., the Cumaean Sybil wrote her prophecies on leaves, which she scattered at the mouth of her cave. Anyone who happened by could pick them up and read them. If no one came, however, the leaves just blew away.

It is said that the Cumaean Sibyl once bound her Sibylline Leaves into nine books and offered to sell them—at an outrageously high price—to the Roman king, Tarquin II. When he said no, she burned three of the books and offered him the remaining six for the same high price. He said no again, she burned three more. Tarquin purchased the remaining three books. These were filled with prophecies about the Roman Empire (to be founded four centuries later) and instructions for gaining the favors of foreign gods.[36] It is also said that the Sibylline Leaves are still shelved in the Vatican.

In the Middle Ages, it is furthermore said, the Sibyl left her Cumaean cave and moved to a new cave high up in the Apennines. This cave was known throughout Europe to be a paradise; one of its names was Venusberg, where Tannhauser and other heroes so famously lingered. Here the Sibyl became famous as a storyteller who, Marina Warner writes, "offers the suggestion that sympathies can cross from different places and languages, different peoples of varied status." She also "exists as a Christian fantasy about a pagan presence from the past," and thus "fulfils a certain function in thinking about forbidden, forgotten, buried, even secret matters."[37] Does the reputation of the medieval Sibyl remind us of the functions of our Goddess novelists?

The hero of the *Aeneid* (an epic poem composed in 30-19 B.C.E. by the Roman poet Vergil) is Aeneas, a Trojan warrior and son of Venus who escapes from Troy and becomes the founder of the Roman people. In Book VI, Aeneas consults the Cumaean Sibyl to guide him to the Underworld. The Sibyl requires that he pluck a golden bough from a grove near her cave. After he has done so, they descend to the Underworld through her cave and tour Tartarus and the Elysian Fields. After Aeneas has visited his father, they depart through ivory gates.

Let us see what Sibylline Leaves we might find if we visit the Sibyl's cave and visit the Underworld with her.

The Meditation

Find something indigo to sit on, something as deep and dark as the nighttime sky. Close your eyes and take several deep, easy breaths and feel the energy of indigo rising through your body. Let it touch each of your chakras with intuition and imagination and let the energy of indigo help you see what you have never seen before.

Pause

In your imagination, find yourself in the night, alone on a dark plain. You are walking along a winding road, and in the distance, you can see the lights of a beautiful city built on seven hills. Do you want to visit this city? What might you find there?

But the city is not your destination. You must walk alone to the sacred grove, which is far across this dark plain. Walk through the dark night until you find the grove where numerous golden trees are growing—oak and cypress, willow and almond, birch and ash.

Pause

If you wish to travel with the Sibyl, you will need a branch from this grove. What tree are you drawn to? We cannot, of course, take anything without paying for it. What do you have to exchange for a golden branch? Walk among the golden trees until you find the one that calls to your soul. As you stand before it, search your pockets. When you find the proper payment, lay it on the ground before the tree. Now you may ask the tree to give you one of its golden branches. Within minutes, a small branch falls gently from the tree. This branch is about as long as your forearm and has a cleft at one end. Its golden leaves rustle in a breeze that you do not feel.

Pause

As you hold the golden branch you realize suddenly that you can hear a whispering, or perhaps you feel a nudging. You can see a path you could not see before. Trust this guidance and walk out of the grove. Soon you come to a deep gorge. Above this gorge is a steep hill crowned by a temple of shining marble. Do you want to visit this temple? What might you find there?

But the temple is not your destination. Touch the golden branch to your eyes. Suddenly you notice a cave near the bottom of the gorge. This is the cave of the Cumaean Sibyl, and it lies far below the roots of the hill, far, far below the temple.

Pause

An old woman is seated near the mouth of her cave, and she is wearing a robe of many colors, a robe of all the colors of the earth. This is the Sibyl herself, and she is seated upon a three-legged stool before something that may be an altar, though she is currently using it as a desk. As you watch, she writes on large golden leaves and waves them to dry the ink. And after she has written, she carelessly lets the leaves fall where they may.

Suddenly she looks up. "What are you waiting for?" she asks in her sharp voice. "Come here!"

It is unwise to disobey a Sibyl. Approach her cave. When you are close enough to look inside, you can see that it must be as high as a six-story building. Behind the Sibyl is the opening of the long, winding passage that leads down into the earth.

"Anyone who comes here may read my leaves," the Sibyl says, pointing at the litter of leaves just outside her cave. Do you want to read a leaf? If you do, pick one up. Like most prophecies, many of the Sibyl's prophecies are written as enigmatic poems that mean different things to different people. Read your Sibylline Leaf. Know that when you return to ordinary awareness, although you may not remember the poem you will retain the sense of the prophecy.

Pause

You see that some of the leaves on the ground have simpler dicta written on them: "Existence is the mother of all things." "As above, so below." "Do what thou wilt, an it harm none." "Blessed are the peacemakers." "The phenomena of life may be likened unto a dream, a shadow, the glistening dew, a lightning flash." "Know thyself." "The unreal has no being; the real never ceases to be." "We must be mild, and humble, as if we were perched on trees." "The miraculous comes so close/ . . . something not known to anyone at all,/ but wild in our breast for centuries." "All shall be well."[38] You may pick up one of these leaves and carry it with you to guide your life.

Pause

As the Sibyl beckons you into her cave, she packs her pen and ink into a basket. "Let us go," she says, "for it is time to see what we must see." Be sure to carry your golden branch with you. Go with the Sibyl, down, down, down along the passage behind her cave. Follow her down hundreds of worn stone steps until at last you come to the dock on the River Styx. Charon, the infernal boatman, is waiting with his boat, and when he demands your fares, the Sybil points to the golden branch you carry. Charon finds this an acceptable ticket and rows you both across the black river. After you land, follow the paved road before you until you reach a tall iron gate. Touch the gate with your golden branch and it swings open. When you are inside, however, the Sibyl suddenly and without explanation takes your golden branch away from you.

When Aeneas went to the Underworld with the Sibyl, he went to visit his dead father to ask for advice on how to carry out his mission in life. You may also seek advice on how you will live. In an elegant corner of the Elysian Fields, under the portico of a magnificent library, are gathered the protagonists of novels you have read and will read. You may sit down with these people and ask them to tell their stories. They tell you about their comedies and tragedies. They tell you about their struggles, how to use your head and overcome obstacles you think no one could possibly overcome. They tell you how to call on the powers of the Goddess and use the psychic powers and magical tools She has given you. They tell you how to live heroically or lightly upon the earth. Sit with these heras and heros for as long as you want to and listen to their stories.

Pause

At last the Sibyl protests that you cannot spend your whole life in conversation with imaginary characters. She drags you away and sets you back on the road through the Underworld. Follow the Sibyl once more until you reach the ivory gate that opens upon the world above. Here the Sibyl halts. "Beyond this gate," she tells you, "the road forks. You may go to the city or to the temple. Choose where you will go."

Pause

She gives you a moment to think, then inserts the cleft tip of the golden branch into the lock that secures the gate. As the gate slowly opens, you can see the two roads under bright sunlight. After you have passed through the gate, you look at your golden branch and notice that the Sibyl has written on its leaves. The branch now bears principles that will guide you through the city or the temple.

Choose now where you will go. If you choose the city, you will live in the world. If you choose the temple, you will spend your life serving the Goddess. Know, however, that city and temple are not mutually exclusive and that you may move at will from one to the other as long as you live, both in "real" life and in dreams.

When you return to ordinary awareness, consider what gifts you have received from the Goddess, and why. Consider how you can use these gifts.

Then take some time out from all your hard work and read a good Goddess novel. Use your imagination in other ways, too.

Crown Chakra: Sophia

Whereas the fundamental (root chakra) issue is living on earth, the essential (crown chakra) issue is living in the universe. The earth is our fundament, or base: we're planted here and what we do, we do on earth. The universe is our wider field of endeavor, the true home of our body, soul, and spirit. In the universe are all the paths of all our lives.

Taoist scholars thousands of years ago taught, and the scientist-philosophers of twentieth-century quantum physics affirm, that the essence of the universe—its intrinsic and indispensable quality—is consciousness.[39] The apparently solid things we know through our physical senses are mostly empty space, but what looks empty is really filled with consciousness.

And what does meditation teach us? To be mindful. To live consciously. To participate in consciousness.

The crown chakra issues are thus consciousness issues. They're issues that reach beyond living on earth and address living in the universe: *knowing, understanding,* and *connecting.*

Notice that the crown chakra issues are stated as gerunds. In English grammar, a gerund is a word that was born a verb but grows up to be used in a sentence as a noun. Somewhere along the line it's had a life-change operation from state-of-being to name-of-something. In the lower chakras, the issues are stated as nouns (or noun phrases): they name qualities, intentions, feelings, etc. Even though they're abstract nouns, naming things we cannot see or touch, like survival and pleasure and compassion, nouns seem to stand squarely on the earth, to stand firmly on their own two feet. But a gerund is loftier; it has wings and rises from being-in-the-world to naming.

Whoa! Existential creation is a lot of weight for a defenseless gerund to bear. But let me lay just one more brick on its load. Maybe a gerund is like a thoughtform.

Lamsa writes that "God is the spiritual essence and the intelligence which governs the universe," and Fortune writes that "the universe is really a thought-form projected from the mind of God."[40] Although Lamsa and Fortune were working within the standard-brand religious paradigm and got the Creator's gender wrong, their teachings are nevertheless true: consciousness precedes and governs manifestation. It's true whether you're making a universe or a sandwich.

Manifestation as a projection of thought is a third chakra process. You remember—to know, to will, to dare. Now, at the seventh chakra, we're working on the same process again, but on a higher (or wider) plane. We're adding *understanding* to knowing, willing, and daring, and I think that's a useful distinction. Perhaps if Dr. Frankenstein had truly understood what he was doing—what creation really signifies—he and his Creature wouldn't have ended up on that glacier destroying each other.

I like Judith's description of the crown chakra. It "blossoms forth," she writes, "with its thousand petals radiating out from the top of the head like a private antenna, reaching to higher dimensions."[41] When that antenna is operational, it pulls in signals from a metaphorical thousand directions. It *connects* us with everyone and everything in the universe.

Connection is a pivotal motif in quantum physics. In 1964, J. S. Bell noticed the "strange connectedness" of quantum phenomena and published the mathematical proof now known as Bell's theorem, which works roughly this way: Imagine a pair of particles separated from each other by vast distance and experimental apparatus. They can't possibly talk to each other. Shine a light on one and it moves. *The other particle moves at the same time in the same direction.* One of the implications of Bell's theorem, Zukav writes, "is that, at a deep and fundamental level, the 'separate parts' of the universe are connected in an intimate and immediate way."[42] The physicists are telling us that consciousness is the only possible connection between particles.

What does this connection mean to you and me? It means that there is no essential difference between us. It means we're linked to people we don't know we know until we run into them in this lifetime. It means community, the topic of one of our Great Goddess meditations in chapter 3. It means our communities are responsible for what our governments and armies do . . . or don't do. It means ecological interdependence, understanding that the trash we casually toss away can end up in the ocean or a landfill for a thousand years, and the radioactive trash we think we're burying safely in the desert will still be deadly when someone digs it up ten thousand years from now. Connection is spatial and temporal, personal and global. Maybe supra-global.

Sophia is not a goddess *of* wisdom. She *is* wisdom, Holy Wisdom, and we find Her (using many aliases) in the Hebrew Bible and other ancient texts from the Near East, Egypt, and Greece. In the apocryphal Book of Wisdom of Solomon (written in Alexandria in the first century C.E.), She is Hochma, "a divine female figure [who is] independent of the traditional concept of God" and is the "architect of creation." Hochma (also spelled Chokmah) is the second Sphere on the Tree of Life, the head of the—masculine—Pillar of Mercy. Fortune quotes texts that apostrophize Chokmah as "Illuminating Intelligence," the "Crown of Creation, the Splendour of Unity," and "the Vision of God face to face."[43]

Sophia is best known, however, as the Gnostic goddess:

> . . . the First Thought, His image,
> She was the Mother of the All, because she was before them all,
> Mother-Father, First Man, Holy Spirit, triple male,
> triple power, triple male-female name, and eternal aeon of the invisible
> ones, and the first to come forth.[44]

Briefly, the Gnostic Sophia is the youngest aeon, or offspring, of God. Her "passion or desire for knowledge becomes the source of the god and substance for this world." She "plays an ordering and providential role" and is a revealer of *gnosis*, or knowing, to humans. She is our redeemer, who "must protect her seed/light from destruction by the hostile powers who do not want the truth about their inferiority [and] lack of real divinity to become known among humans."[45]

Sophia is sometimes Holy Wisdom, sometimes a prostitute—the famous "Thunder: Perfect Mind" poem from the Nag Hammadi codices endlessly lists Her paradoxical characteristics.[46] In another Gnostic codex, the *Pistis Sophia* ("Faith Wisdom"), She is identified with Mary Magdalen as the favorite and wisest disciple of Jesus and perhaps his lover or wife, much to the disgust of Peter and the other male apostles. Begg identifies both Sophia and Mary Magdalen with the enigmatic, miracle-working Black Virgins found in hundreds of sites throughout Europe.[47]

A thousand years after the Gnostic texts were written, Hildegard of Bingen was devoted to Holy Wisdom. In the poems and music the abbess wrote for her nuns to sing as part of the Holy Office, we find this antiphon:

> Sophia!
> you of the whirling wings,
> circling encompassing
> energy of God:
>
> you quicken the world in your clasp.
>
> One wing soars in heaven
> one wing sweeps the earth
> and the third flies all around us.
>
> Praise to Sophia!
> Let all the earth praise her![48]

When I read the Tarot, I interpret Card XXI, The World, as "meeting the Goddess face to face." We will soon encounter dancing Wisdom in our crown chakra meditation.

The Meditation

Find something lavender, violet, magenta, or deep, royal purple to sit on. Close your eyes, take several deep, easy breaths, and feel the energy of the purple begin to rise through your chakras. Feel the power of *knowing, understanding,* and *connecting* touch each of your chakras and intensify its special energy. Feel it adding power to survival at your first chakra. To your emotions and sexual feelings at your second chakra.

Feel the power moving up through your body. Feel it touching and strengthening your will at your third chakra. Strengthening love and compassion at your fourth chakra. Feel it strengthening communication and creativity at your fifth chakra. Strengthening your imagination and intuition at your sixth chakra.

Let knowing, understanding, and connecting flood your entire body, soak into every cell of your being.

Pause

Soon in your imagination you find yourself on the road in an unknown land, in a place of wonder and magic. And look at yourself. You're wearing a purple cockscomb headcovering with bells on it. A threadbare yellow shirt with harlequin patches of blue and green. Orange trousers with more patches, trousers that are so short and threadbare that you can see your red socks and shoes. On your back is a knapsack of black and white, and here you carry your most secret treasures. You're the Fool of the Tarot deck, the Wise, Naive One, the seeker who appears foolish and silly only to ordinary people who lack proper vision.

Spend a moment feeling Fool-ish. Spend a moment knowing your innocence and your wisdom.

Pause

And look where you're standing. You're on a narrow path on the edge of a precipice. Unless you're feeling very brave today, don't look down, for the abyss is exceedingly deep and dangerous. Tiptoe forward a few steps and peer around the next curve. Good grief—your path disappears under a wall of solid rock.

It's impossible to go forward and you'd never go back. There's no place else to go, nothing else to do. You have to step off. *You have to make a leap of faith.*

Take that step. Make that leap . . . and you float up into the sky supported by a migration of scarlet butterflies.

Rise with the butterflies, ancient symbols of the soul, and let them support you in your flight. Pass over the abyss and rise until you come to a glass mountain floating in a cerulean sky under a bright golden sun.

Pause

You have come home. You have come home to Holy Wisdom's residence, and you are able to move easily and without fear on Her glass mountain. Spend a moment exploring Wisdom's glass mountain and meeting the beings who dwell there.

Pause

Soon you hear a step on the path and look up. Holy Wisdom Herself is coming to lead you to Her household. Sophia appears, wearing a blue gown tied with scarlet sashes that make an X across Her heart. She wears a wreath of green leaves and carries a golden wand. Smiling, She beckons to you and asks you to walk with Her. Walk beside Sophia along the royal road that winds through Her glass mountain and until you come to the homestead of Holy Wisdom. Sophia lives in a shining mansion of many rooms. She leads you directly to the atrium in the center, where you find a reflecting pool with a fountain of gentle music and a multitude of green and flowering plants. Spend a moment exploring Wisdom's garden. What do you find here?

Pause

Holy Wisdom speaks. "Welcome home," She tells you. "Welcome to your proper home, and know that you are forever welcome in this place." When Sophia smiles the air itself glitters. Now you notice children playing in one part of the garden. Two or three are blowing bubbles, and the bubbles begin drifting on the breeze toward you. Other children are playing tambourines and small drums, and still others are gathering herbs and flowers. You can smell rosemary and lavender and jasmine and rose.

"This is a place of knowing and understanding," Sophia tells you. "It is a place of connecting. Here you will meet four who will be your friends and helpers. Here you will connect with your guides. Though you may not have known it, they have been with you for a long time already. Your guides accompany you wherever you go, even back in the mundane world where you ordinarily live. Make ready to meet your guides."

Take a moment to breathe or pray or say a mantra.

Pause

Your first guide now appears. This is a guide from the realm of plants,[49] one who will be with you in spirit and perhaps in person, for if you have a garden or a windowsill you can plant her there. Who is your plant guide? A tree? Which one? An herb or a flower? Which one? Spend a moment renewing your acquaintance with your plant guide.

She gives you a leaf or a petal or a sprig to tuck into your knapsack. Spend some time with your plant guide.

Pause

When you're ready, your second guide appears. This is a guide from the realm of animals and can be four-legged, feathered, finned, or reptilian. This guide can live with you in spirit form and become your totem or familiar or she can adopt you in person.[50] Who is your animal guide? A wolf or eagle or cat? A lizard or turtle or dolphin? Spend a moment renewing your acquaintance with your animal guide. She gives you a bit of fur or feather, a tooth or a claw to tuck into your knapsack. Spend some time with your animal guide.

Pause

When you're ready, your third guide appears. This is a "shining one," a deva, whom some would call an angel.[51] Devas, or angels, are not the winged frou-frou ladies of popular sentiment but muscular counselors and messengers of pure radiant energy.[52] A being of elemental fire, your deva or angel is your friend and protector. Spend a moment renewing your acquaintance with this protector. He or she may tell you his or her name. He or she gives you a token or a magical word written in an angelic alphabet to tuck into your knapsack. Spend some time with your deva or angel.

Pause

When you're ready, your fourth guide appears. This is a spirit guide, someone who is either between incarnations or has perhaps never incarnated on earth. It's likely that you have known this person, either in another lifetime or possibly in this lifetime. Your spirit guide is a healer or teacher, or both, and has forever been your dearest friend. Perhaps your guide will give you his or her name and establish a means of communication so that you become aware of him or her and can pay attention when you're spoken to. Like the others, your spirit guide gives you a token to tuck into your knapsack. Spend some time renewing your acquaintance with this guide.

Pause

Now you will dance with Holy Wisdom and your guides. As you take their hands, you notice that others join the circle, other members of your community—human, spirit, and animal—and they are here to dance your crown chakra with you. The beating of the drums and jingling of the tambourines grow louder and you begin to move. Sunwise you move, step by step, weaving a vine of spirit and grace with your dance, weaving and spiraling. And the circle rises into the air! You are dancing on air, dancing in perfect balance, spiraling sunwise with Sophia and your guides around Her glass mountain. Dance with Holy Wisdom. Dance with your guides, dance in perfect balance.

Dance sunwise, dance outward into the universe, outward into manifestation and as you dance, feel yourself connecting with the universe.

Pause

Time comes, however, when the dance must turn, and now you must dance moonwise. Dance moonwise with Holy Wisdom and your guides, dance into the center of Sophia's glass mountain. Dance into a place of resting, into a clear, dark place of pure energy. Dance where there is nothing but formless knowing and understanding. Dance moonwise in perfect balance, dance moonwise into the center.

Pause

And time comes again, and the spiral turns sunwise again, and you must dance back out into the world. And here you find yourself dancing alone beside Holy Wisdom, for your four guides have taken their places at the four corners of the world. From their proper places, your guides watch over you, they lead and teach and heal you as you dance with Holy Wisdom. Know that even when you think you are dancing alone, you are always dancing with Holy Wisdom and that your four guides are always in their proper places.

Dance as long as the dance can last, and when the dance comes to its end, know that still you dance. You dance in the empty spaces between the atoms of your body and in the spaces between the stars of Her body.

Other Chakras: Found Goddesses

If you are willing to find your own goddesses and create your own meditations, you can explore chakras beyond the seven major ones.

We have chakras in the palms of our hands, at our knees, and in the tops or soles of our feet. Goddesses for the hand chakras might be the goddesses of handicrafts, like the weavers and potters. Goddesses for the knee and foot chakras might be dancing goddesses.

In her book on nontraditional Reiki, Diane Stein discusses an alternative chakra system that begins above the head, follows the Hara Line (which sort of parallels the spine), and extends below the feet.[53]

The following "developing" chakras lie along the Hara Line:

1. Transpersonal Point (clear), above the crown chakra
2. Causal Body center (crimson), at the base of the skull
3. Thymus (aqua), between the throat and the heart
4. Diaphragm (lime green), between the heart and the solar plexus
5. Hara (orange-brown), between the solar plexus and root chakras
6. Perineum (ruby red), between the vaginal opening and the anus
7. Earth/grounding (black), directly below the feet.

I have also learned that in the fourth through ninth dimensions there may be fifty-odd chakras, and there may also be twenty-two other chakras, many of them above the Transpersonal Point, and a "deep root" chakra, which is five or six feet beneath the feet.[54]

Perhaps, with psychic help, you can find these alternative chakras. Using research from Monaghan, Farrar, Graves, and other good books and *relying on your intuition and imagination,* you can next choose goddesses for them. Because these are alternative chakras, you may want to have some fun with them and choose Found Goddesses whom you find and name yourself. The best book for learning how to find a goddess is *Found Goddesses,* by Grey and Penelope.

Endnotes

1. Originally, I wrote "invisible body." Then I remembered that some people see it quite clearly.
2. Anodea Judith, *Wheels of Life* (St. Paul: Llewellyn Publications, 1988), p. 1.
3. Judith, *Wheels of Life*, p. 9.
4. Anodea Judith and Selene Vega, *The Sevenfold Journey* (Freedom, CA: Crossing Press, 1993), pp. 12–13.
5. Judith and Vega, *Sevenfold Journey*, pp. 12–13.
6. Information in this column is taken from the Table of Correspondences in Judith and Vega's *Sevenfold Journey*, pp. 8–10. Used with permission.
7. See Maslow's "hierarchy of needs" in Frank G. Goble, *The Third Force*, p. 50.
8. Does it seem to you, as it does to me, that the famous "they" consists mostly of hyper-rational scientists, politicians, and parents?
9. Diane Ackerman, *The Natural History of the Senses* (New York: Random House, 1990), p. xix.
10. Judith and Vega, *Sevenfold Journey*, p. 86, their emphasis.
11. Monaghan, *O Mother Sun!* (Freedom, CA: Crossing Press, 1994), ch. 3, *passim.*
12. Jean Houston, *The Passion of Isis and Osiris*, p. 344.
13. Farrar, *Witches' Goddess*, p. 227; Exodus 32:6, Authorized Version.
14. From Ackerman, *Natural History of the Senses*, p. xix.
15. From *The Charge of the Goddess* in Starhawk, *The Spiral Dance*, p. 91.
16. Starhawk, *Spiral Dance*, p. 125; Judith and Vega, *Sevenfold Journey*, p. 129.
17. Jade, *To Know*, p. 18. Used with permission. For information on the Re-Formed Congregation of the Goddess (RCG), see the Resources.
18. Luisah Teish, *Carnival of the Spirit* (San Francisco: HarperSanFrancisco, 1994), pp. 160–61.
19. Judith Gleason, *Oya* (Boston: Shambhala, 1987), pp. 1–3.
20. Pronounced TIFF-a-reth.
21. Fortune, *Mystical Qabalah*, pp. 190, 188.
22. Antoine de Saint Exupéry, *The Little Prince*. Trans. Katherine Woods (New York: Harcourt Brace Jovanovich, 1971), pp. 33–34, 80, 87–88.
23. Matthew 5:2, 7, 44, *The Holy Bible From Ancient Eastern Manuscripts*, trans. by George M. Lamsa (Philadelphia: A.J. Holman, 1968).
24. Merlin Stone, *Ancient Mirrors of Womanhood* (Boston: Beacon Press, 1979), pp. 27–30.
25. A Latin word, pronounced vir-ID-i-tas.
26. Hildegard of Bingen, *Book of Divine Works*, quoted by Eileen Conn in "The Interconnected Universe: Hildegard of Bingen," in *Visions of Creation*, ed. by Eileen Conn and James Stewart (Alresford, Hunts.: Godsfield Press, 1995), p. 39.
27. Their books are listed in the Bibliography.
28. Cameron, *Artist's Way*, p. 3.
29. *Larousse Encyclopedia of Mythology*, pp. 358–59; Monaghan, *The Book of Goddess and Heroines*, p. 305.
30. Z. Budapest, *Grandmother Moon* (San Francisco: HarperSanFrancisco, 1991), pp. 48–49.
31. William S. and Ceil Baring-Gould, *The Annotated Mother Goose* (New York: Clarkson N. Potter, 1962) p. 203.

32. Dion Fortune, *The Sea Priestess* (York Beach, ME: Samuel Weiser, 1978), p. 7.

33. Publishing information is given in the Bibliography. I'm listing only one novel by each author; after you've fallen in love, it's up to you to find their other novels.

34. Dion Fortune, *Moon Magic* (York Beach, ME: Samuel Weiser, 1978), p. 81.

35. Jade, *To Know*, pp. 105–07.

36 Monaghan, *Goddesses and Heroines*, pp. 317–18; *Larousse Encyclopedia of Mythology*, p. 233.

37. Marina Warner, *From the Beast to the Blonde* (New York: Noonday Press, 1996), ch. 1, *passim*.

38. Sources: The Tao, the Emerald Tablet of Hermes Trismegistus, the Wiccan Rede, the Sermon on the Mount, the Diamond Sutra, the temple at Delphi, the Bhagavad Gita, Confucius, Anna Akhmatova, Dame Julian of Norwich.

39. Books by Bentov, Capra, White, Wilbur, Wolf, and Zukav are listed in the Bibliography.

40. Lamsa, *Old Testament Light* (Philadelphia: A. J. Holman, 1978), p. ix; Fortune, *Mystical Qabalah*, p. 17.

41. Judith, *Wheels of Life*, p. 368.

42. This description is greatly oversimplified. For greater clarity, see Gary Zukav, *The Dancing Wu Li Masters* (New York: Morrow, 1979), pp. 305–09, 298.

43. Asphodel P. Long, *In a Chariot Drawn by Lions* (Freedom, CA: Crossing Press, 1993), p. 26; Fortune, *Mystical Qabalah*, p. 122.

44. Pheme Perkins, "Sophia and the Mother-Father: The Gnostic Goddess," in *The Book of the Goddess*, ed. Olson, p. 99. This description of Sophia is from the Nag Hammadi codices, written during the second through fourth century C.E.

45. Perkins, "Sophia and the Mother-Father," pp. 102–05.

46. "For I am the first, and the last./ I am the honored one, and the scorned./ I am the whore and the holy one . . . ."

47. Susan Haskins, *Mary Magdalen* (New York: Riverhead, 1993), pp. 46–49; Ean Begg, *The Cult of the Black Virgin* (London: Arkana, 1985).

48. Quoted in Jane Hirshfield, ed., *Women in Praise of the Sacred* (New York: HarperCollins, 1994), p. 67. Used with permission.

49. When you return to ordinary awareness, you can get more information about your plant guide from any of the herb and gardening books you can find in bookstores or libraries. Jeanne Rose's *Herbs and Things* (New York: Putnam, 1972) and Cunningham's *Encyclopedia of Magical Herbs* are particularly useful.

50. When you return to ordinary awareness, you can likewise learn more about your animal guide. Jamie Sams' *Medicine Cards* and Timothy Roderick's *The Once Unknown Familiar* (St. Paul: Llewellyn, 1994) are useful sources.

51. It is important to understand that angels and archangels exist primarily in the Judeo-Christian-Islamic traditions and are thoughts projected by the Father God. There are nine classes of angels and all of the named angels are masculine.

52. See Lamsa, *Old Testament Light*, pp. 53, 81, 149.

53. Diane Stein, *Essential Reiki* (Freedom, CA: Crossing Press, 1995), pp. 33–34. Stein gives the sources of these alternative chakras. The Hara Line is attributed to Barbara Brennan.

54. Many of the sources for this information are undocumentable photocopies of pages from unidentified books, though some of this information is apparently based on the work of Alice Bailey. Thanks to my friend Kitari Om, the StarWalker, for sharing with me.

7

The Goddess Pillar Meditation

Brigid

As devised by Israel Regardie, the famous scholar of ceremonial magic, the Middle Pillar Meditation is based on the Pillar of Equilibrium, which is the central Pillar of the Qabalistic Tree of Life. The Qabalah (also spelled Kabbalah) is a medieval Judaic mystical system believed to reach back to the beginning of time. It has been adopted (and adapted) by members of the Hermetic Order of the Golden Dawn[1] and others, past and present, who follow the path of ceremonial magic for various magical purposes.

The best books I know on ceremonial magic are by Dion Fortune. In *The Mystical Qabalah*, originally written in 1935, Fortune called the Qabalah "the yoga of the West." Mysticism, she writes, "is inherent in the human race" and during the Middle Ages, "devout spirits" in Europe developed a "technique of the soul's approach to God . . . a characteristic Yoga of their own, closely akin to the Bhakti Yoga of the East."[2] A psychologist as well as a ceremonial magician, Fortune also wrote two novels about the Goddess and recommended the Qabalah to Westerners as an appropriate way to seek God (or the Goddess).

The goal of Regardie's meditation (which was written in 1932) is to create a direct, mystical connection from the top of the Tree to its bottom, that is, from the Crown (Kether) to the World (Malkuth). As they say in the standard-brand religions, it's a direct link from God to man. It's a lightning bolt, a conversion experience. A well-known example of such a lightning bolt link—without the Qabalistic apparatus—is given in the Bible (Acts 9:1–9), wherein one Saul of Tarsus is blinded by a great light on the road to Damascus and remains blinded for the traditional, magical three days and nights. At his recovery, he becomes St. Paul; the experience of the direct link with his god has changed his life.

As Regardie gives the meditation, he assigns a "shaft of silvery light, studded as it were with five gorgeous diamonds of incomparable brilliance, stretching from the crown of the head to the soles of the feet."[3] The light above the head is the "light of spirit" and the four lower lights are the lights of the four magical/alchemical elements: earth, air, fire, and water. The light of spirit represents the center (the quintessence). You have already met the four elements in the generic ritual in chapter 2.

Regardie's diamonds are roughly equivalent to the chakras, and the meditator is instructed to intone god names, which are taken from the Hebrew.

Unregenerate feminist and cantankerous Witch that I am, however, I prefer to meditate to goddess names and to partake of an experience less extreme than a lightning bolt.

The Goddess Pillar Meditation can put you in a whole new space. One of my circle sisters has been meditating for forty years; the morning after I introduced this meditation to my circle, she phoned me to say she'd gotten lost driving home, and she *never* gets lost. I have thus learned to ground people thoroughly after we've done this meditation. Not everyone becomes disoriented, of course, but most people experience visions or healing or the beginnings of visions or healing.

At the beginning of the meditation, you will find yourself standing before the right and left Pillars (as you face them) of the Tree of Life. The right Pillar is the masculine Pillar, which contains the mystical Spheres of Wisdom (in Hebrew, Chokmah), Mercy (Chesed), and Victory (Netzach). The left Pillar is the feminine Pillar, which contains the mystical Spheres of Understanding (Binah), Strength (Geburah), and Glory (Hod). At the head (top) of the Tree is the Crown (Kether) and at its foot (root) are the Moon (Yesod) and the Kingdom or the World

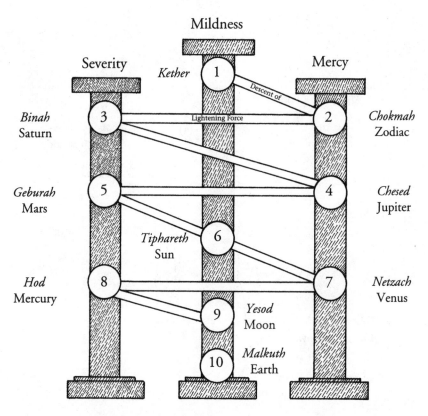

Figure 4. **The Three Pillars of the Tree of Life.**
(Adapted from Dion Fortune, *The Mystical Qabala*.)

(Malkuth). Energy moves in a zigzag (lightning bolt) pattern from the unmanifest heavens above Kether through all ten Spheres and down to the earth. These two Pillars have come to be associated with the pillars at the entrance to Solomon's Temple, which you can see illustrated on Card II, The High Priestess, of the Rider-Waite Tarot Deck. Figure 4 (above) shows the three Pillars that make up one diagram (of many) of the Tree of Life.[4]

Figure 5 (page 202) shows the basic model for the Goddess Pillar Meditation, with the colors, Goddess names, and affirmations that are used in the meditation.

If you do this meditation under a full moon, it will be even more powerful.

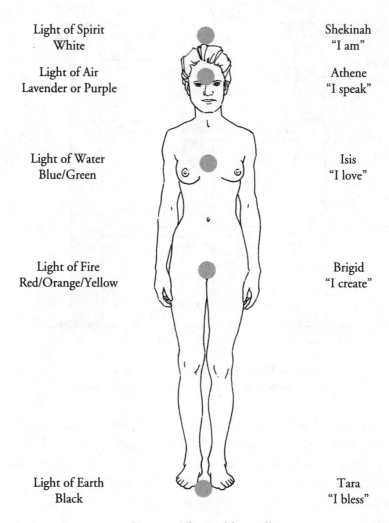

Light of Spirit
White

Light of Air
Lavender or Purple

Light of Water
Blue/Green

Light of Fire
Red/Orange/Yellow

Light of Earth
Black

Shekinah
"I am"

Athene
"I speak"

Isis
"I love"

Brigid
"I create"

Tara
"I bless"

Figure 5. **The Goddess Pillar.**

The Meditation

Lie on your back with your hands at your sides or sit with your spine erect and your hands on your thighs. Take two or three deep, easy breaths and close your eyes. Take a few more deep, easy breaths and feel your body begin to relax.

With your inner eyes, the true eyes of your soul, visualize two pillars that extend from the center of the earth up into the heavens. The pillar to your right is white or silver. On the Qabalistic Tree of Life, this is the Pillar of Mercy, the masculine Pillar. The pillar to your left is black or indigo. On the Tree of Life, this is the Pillar of Severity, the feminine Pillar. Just as, in Taoist philosophy, every yin requires and is incomplete without a yang, so do light and dark, masculine and feminine, require each other. So is each incomplete without the other. Feel the complementary powers of these two Pillars as they shimmer before you. Feel the strength, the intelligence, the integrity of each Pillar, knowing that no quality is the exclusive property of either gender. Feel the *balance* of the two Pillars.

Pause

Now step forward and stand between the Pillars. Feel their power moving into your mind and into your physical body. Feel their masculine and feminine energies touching your own masculine and feminine elements. Know that as the Middle Pillar of the Tree signifies balance, so will you find balance, for as you continue this meditation, *you will become the Middle Pillar.* This is the Goddess Pillar. You will know that your base is rooted in the center of the earth and that your crown blossoms in the heavens. For a moment, contemplate yourself as a pillar connecting heaven and earth.

Pause

Still standing between the dark and light Pillars, look up and see the Light of Spirit begin to take form above your head. It becomes a circle of light whose bottom gently brushes the top of your head. You can feel the tingling of your crown chakra. The Light of Spirit is a pure, warm, white light, a beautiful crystalline light shining and sparkling above you. The

Goddess of the Light of Spirit is Shekinah ("Brightness"). Shekinah is the formless, invisible Hebrew goddess envisaged as a cloud of fire or a flaming torch.[5] She is a compassionate emanation of Yahweh and shows us His hidden and suppressed feminine side. It is said that, like Astraea, Shekinah fled the earth when mankind became too wicked.

Sound Shekinah's name aloud (or silently), stretching out the vowel sounds as long as your breath can last:

SHEH . . . . KEE . . . . NAH . . . .

Slowly sound Her holy name three times. As you do so, you are pulling Her compassionate energy into your crown and into your thoughts. In this rational world, where people think more than they feel, we need more compassionate thinking. Let Shekinah's loving energy flow down into your body. Take as much time as you need for this.

Pause

When you're ready, see one ray of white light reach down into your head and throat (forehead and throat chakras). The white light changes color as it moves, forming a ball of blue-violet light that fills your head and throat. This is the Light of Elemental Air, which is associated with intellect, discernment, and intuition. The Goddess of the Light of Air is Athene, "goddess of the brilliant eyes."[6] Athene is the Greek Goddess of prudent intelligence, civilization, crafts, and defensive warfare.

Sound Athene's name aloud (or silently), pulling Her intellectual and intuitive energy into your head and throat:

AH . . . . THEE . . . . NAH . . . .

Sound Her holy name three times, letting Her energy spread throughout your body. Take as much time as you want to.

Pause

When you're ready, see one blue-violet ray reach down to your heart and change color to soft green. See and feel this soft green light become a ball of light that fills your heart chakra. Let this green light expand and fill your entire chest, from your shoulders to your waist. This is the Light of Elemental Water, which is associated with love, sensitivity, spirit, the emotions, and instinct. The Goddess of the Light of Water is Isis, "star of the sea." Isis is the Egyptian Mother-Creatrix and throne upon which the pharaohs sat. Her love for Her husband-brother Osiris was so great that after He was killed and dismembered, She sought Him through lands and waters, re-membered Him, and bore His son.

Sound the name of Isis aloud (or silently), pulling Her liquid, loving energy into your heart:

I . . . . .SIS . . . .

Sound Her holy name three times, letting the power of love spread throughout your body. Take as much time as you want to.

Pause

When you're ready, see one ray of green light reach down to your solar plexus (just above your navel) and change color to red-orange-yellow. It fills your solar plexus chakra, your belly and womb and ovaries, your entire lower abdomen with a ball of red-orange-yellow light. This is the Light of Elemental Fire, which is associated with inspiration, creativity, and passion. It's the famous "fire in the belly" that drives what we do when we love what we're doing. The Goddess of the Light of Fire is Brigid, the Celtic triple goddess of poetry, smithcraft, and healing. Brigid is also a sun goddess. Her sacred fire burned at Cill Dara (Kill-dare) for 1500 years until it was extinguished by soldiers serving King Henry VIII of England. It was relit on Brigid's Day (February 2), 1995, after having been dark for nearly 500 years.

Sound Brigid's name aloud (or silently), pulling Her fiery energy into your solar plexus:

BRI . . . . GID . . . .†

Sound Her holy name three times, letting Her energy spread throughout your body. Take as much time as you want to.

Pause

When you're ready, see one ray of red-orange-yellow light move down your legs and through your feet. See it form a glowing ball of black, deep green, and russet (earth colors). The top of this ball of earthy light touches the soles of your feet and supports you firmly and comfortably upon the earth. This is the Light of Elemental Earth, which is associated with groundedness, rootedness, growth, blooming, and abundance. The Goddess of the Light of Earth is Tara, the Glorious Mother who eliminates all fears and grants all successes. Eons upon eons ago, this wise and

† Pronounced bri-jid.

compassionate Tibetan mother goddess vowed to remain in a female body until all sentient beings have found blessing and liberation. She is the Blessed One "who knows all things as they are."[7]

As you feel Tara's energy supporting you upon the earth, sound Her name aloud (or silently):

TAH . . . . RAH . . . .

Sound Her holy name three times, letting Her energy move up into your entire body. Take as long as you want to.

Pause

You are now connected with both the heaven above and the earth below. You are a link between the universal heavens and the center of the earth. *You are the Goddess Pillar.*

Spend some time exploring what this feels like.

Pause

Now you will ascend the Goddess Pillar. As you drew in the energies of five goddesses, now you will project those energies into a world that cries out for them.

Still standing on the Light of Elemental Earth, sound the first affirmation, *I bless,* three times and think about what you're blessing. Project both energy and blessing outward. Bless the earth and Her children—two-legged, four-legged, many-legged, feathered, finned, leafy, and crystalline. Send blessing to all the creatures of the world.

When you're ready, see one ray of the Light of Elemental Earth reach up and connect with the Light of Elemental Fire. The affirmation is *I create.* Sound *I create* three times and project the creative energy out into a world that cries for beauty and music and art and life. Project the power and beauty of creativity to all the world.

Pause

When you're ready, see one ray of the Light of Elemental Fire reach up and connect with the Light of Elemental Water at your heart chakra. The affirmation is *I love.* Sound *I love* three times, again projecting the energy outward into a world that knows too little about love. Project love, understanding, and acceptance into the minds and hearts of all the people of the world.

Pause

When you're ready, see one ray of the Light of Elemental Water reach up into your head and connect with the Light of Elemental Air. The affirmation is *I speak*. Sound *I speak* three times, speaking forth what you want to say to the world. Speak of truth to all the people of the world. Speak forth the love and truth of the Goddess into all the world.

Pause

Finally, see one ray of the Light of Elemental Air reach up and connect with the white Light of Spirit. The affirmation is *I am*. Sound the words *I am* three times and project the strength, intelligence, and compassion of the Goddess into the world. Send word that the Goddess is alive, that She is returning to Her children.

Pause

Be still for a while. You can return your focus to the energy of a specific goddess and pull more of Her energy into your body, mind, and spirit for inspiration in work you have to do. You can continue to project the energies of the goddesses out into the world. Or you can simply relax and cruise through the universe and up and down the pillars of the Tree of Life. If you encounter any Beings on paths of the Tree, greet them courteously but do not disturb them.

During this time, a goddess may come to you with lessons or a message. Listen carefully and know that you will remember what you need to remember when you return to ordinary awareness.

When you are finished, *be sure to ground yourself.* Know that you will intuitively know which goddess energy to retain and how much. Be warned, however: even after you've grounded yourself, you may not want to sleep tonight. Not to worry. With the energy from this meditation, you'll probably clean house, reorganize all your files, alphabetize your spices, catch up on your ironing, and write letters to all your friends. I'm not making this up. I know people who have done all these things, and more, after doing the Goddess Pillar Meditation.

	Goddesses		**Gods**
Spirit	Devi (India)	Mary (Europe)	Shiva (India)
Air	Ninlil (Nippur)	Feng-Po-Po (China)	Aeolus (Greece)
Water	Ix Chel (Mexico)	Oshun (Brazil)	Rainbow-Snake (Africa)(Australia)
Fire	Pele (Hawaii)	Hestia (Greece)	Shango (Africa)
Earth	Gaia (Greece)	Frigg (Norse)	Inari (Japan)

Table 3. **Additional Goddess and God Names for the Goddess Pillar Meditation.**

Table 3, above, lists additional goddess and god names you can meditate with. Be sure to select goddesses and gods who are meaningful to you and do enough research so that you know who you're invoking. I've found that diversity of cultures and ages brings me the most powerful energies, but many people find that specialization with a single pantheon (all Celtic, all Native American, all Greek, all Egyptian, all Asian) works very effectively. I think it depends on the path you're following.

Endnotes

1. My favorite book on the Golden Dawn is Mary K. Greer's *Women of the Golden Dawn* (Rochester, VT: Park Street Press, 1995). Israel Regardie and other scholars have also written many books about the Order.
2. Dion Fortune, *The Mystical Qabalah* (London: Ernest Benn, Ltd, 1976), p. 5.
3. Israel Regardie, *The Art of True Healing*, ed. Marc Allen (San Rafael, CA: New World Library, 1991), p. 30.
4. This is much oversimplified. See Fortune's *Mystical Qabalah* for a complete explanation of the Tree and the Spheres.
5. Janet and Stewart Farrar, *The Witches' Goddess* (Custer, WA: Phoenix, 1987), p. 272.
6. *Larousse Encyclopedia of Mythology*, ed. Robert Graves (London: Paul Hamlyn, 1959), p. 117.
7. Stephan Beyer, *The Cult of Tara* (Berkeley: University of California Press, 1978), pp. 333–336.

8

Goddesses for Pure Meditation

Primavera

The Goddess meditations in this chapter are not guided visualizations but, instead, little suggestions and hints for pure, free-form meditation.

Try this. Light a candle. Burn a pinch of summoning incense. Invoke your chosen Goddess into your circle and into your heart. Call Her into your mind, too; imagine Her presence filling your space. Call upon some quality or characteristic that is Hers. Contemplate some part of Her story. Embrace some correspondence or association that touches you. Now still your thoughts. Breathe. Become passive and alert at the same time. Wait. Watch and wait . . . and see what you will see.

Understand with your mind what these Goddesses can mean in the world today. Receive with your heart the blessings these Goddesses bring to those in need of blessing. Acknowledge their powers to change our lives, and use those powers to change your own life.

Darkness: Nyx

And who is older than the Night? Only Chaos. Before light, before order, before creation—before all things, there is darkness. In Her we rest. In Her we dream. In Her we are refreshed. And from the darkness we rise again to a new life. Mystery comes in the dark, and so do magic and prophecy. Welcome the shadows of your life, wrap yourself in dark wings and soar again.

Light: Lucina

We see Her in the candle's flame, in the lantern, in our child's brave nightlight, in the humor of dancing neon, in the corona of our mother sun. By Her blessed light we see ourselves. We see what is around us, too. When we are enlightened, we "see the light." Walk through shadowed valleys with Lucina, find a mirror and look at yourself. Hooray for the day! With Her, we see!

Fire: Aetna

Dancing in Her great explosive mountain, Aetna flares and burns, She flows unstoppably. Like Her fiery sisters across the world, Pele and Fuji, She is light in darkness, the fearsome scalding power that rises through earth and water. She is destruction and creation in action. But She is also our passion, our inspired dance. She burns in our bellies and compels us to creativity.

Water: Mere-Ama

Ancient Sea-Mother of the Saami people, She lives in streams, rivers, and oceans and carves the solid earth to be Her mighty bed. In steam, She is ephemeral, nearly invisible. In ice, where She hides through the winter, She is cold and hard. No obstacle can resist the power of Her flood, and who can survive Her drought? Caretaker of our emotions, water is our true sacrament, washing the newborn and the newly dead alike. She holds us always in Her welling power.

Air: Poldunica

Mistress of the winds, She sends the fresh breeze at dawn, the gusting wind at midday, the falling wind of dusk, and She contains the breathless quiet of midnight. Air that enlivens us, She is the truest Holy Spirit, for we breathe in Her breath and are inspired, and when She deserts us, we have expired. But listen—she is our herald, carrying news and the scent of far-off lands and wonders. So when She comes with Her riddles, use your sharp mind to find the answer.

Earth: Al-Lat

In Arabia, before the Prophet Mohammed and before the capricious god Allah, there was Al-Lat: "Goddess." Goddess of deserts and green pastures, Al-Lat revealed Herself to Her people as a mighty block of white granite, betokener of earth, of the sweet land on which we live. We are grounded in the Earth, our roots reach down to Her center, and Her nourishment lets us grow, bloom, and bear our fruits. Spirit manifests on Earth and as Earth, and here we find our great green abundance.

Spring: Primavera

Her name means "first truth." She is the virgin truth of the year's rebirth. She is the original truth of new light, of returning warmth, of innocent green leaves. Let us sow our new seeds and welcome the new rains, for we've survived another winter. We'll gambol in the spring with maidens, calves, foals, and fawns, we'll greet returning birds. Now is the year's true beginning, the opening of new hope. Let's dance under the newborn sun and sing new words. Let's give thanks.

Summer: Aine

Midsummer. Buzzing growth. Swelling heat. The red Irish mare whom none could outrun, Aine is the Sun Herself. She is the force of dizzying growth, the hinge of the year when growing turns into harvest. Bake and eat Her precious bread, but give Her the first loaf. Feel the heat on your skin, feel Her fire in all your private places, sweat and pant and pour out and dry up and know the power of the summer sun. It is our boon, these lazy days when our Mother Sun is shining and our wealth of wheat is flooding all around us. Give thanks.

Fall: Anna Purna

Food-giver, supervisor of harvest and production, She is the august Mother of our bounty. Reap in autumn what you sowed in the spring, She tells us, and lay away the abundance of summer, for, yes, winter is coming. Harvest now what you planted a season ago, and remember Her son, the great reaper. Feel his sharp scythe, know the willing sacrifice life gives us every year. Such sweet melancholy, this mystery of dying back and rising up. Celebrate the year's harvest-time and remember those who have less than you. Give equal shares to those in need and give thanks.

Winter: Frau Holle

When She combs Her long hair, bright sunshine touches the frozen earth. When She shakes out Her featherbeds, soft snow falls. Her birthday is midwinter's day, Yule, and so much is this old woman beloved that we celebrate for twelve days. Her gifts are the indoor crafts, our golden treasures, the blessed evergreen, the refreshing sleep that follows a holiday's enthusiasm. Watch the soft and silent snow fall, rest, and cherish your magical dreams tonight. Give thanks.

The Sun: Saule

Shining sun, sky weaver, we greet Her every morning, and for holy days we light our bonfires to mirror Her greater light. Like solar deities from sea to sea across the earth, this Baltic Mother Sun drives Her golden chariot across the sky and shines on us from birth till death. In northern lands, She is a nurturing mother, but in southern lands She may shine too hot; thus She becomes a destroying mother. Bathe in Her sweet light, in the heat of Her love, but beware the danger of too much light and too much heat.

The Moon: Luna

Ever-changing, ever constant in Her monthly changes, She drives Her silver chariot through the starry fields. Some say She never married, is ever virgin, but others say She married in the springtime and gave birth to all the stars. She took Her leave of men, a battering husband, and now wanders through the night, hiding herself when he comes too near. Is She lonely? How does She spend Her days? She rules the ocean tides, and our emotional tides, too; when you worship her, remember the perils of lunacy. How do we live, moonstruck, new and full?

The Stars: Ishtar

Lustful Star-Maiden, great-breasted Mother, luminous glad-eyed Goddess of peace and war, She is Queen of Heaven first and last. She is the morning star who sets off each dawn to hunt. She is the evening star upon whose twinkle we cast our wishes. She is the goddess of sexual desire served by holy women. Even as the stars sing their invisible songs to us each night, so does the starry power of Ishtar echo in our blood from the ancient of days. She shines. She lives. Her dancing patterns direct our little lives.

Birth: Eileithyia

The birth goddess spins, and the thread of life streams through Her fingers. From Her eternal womb the world-egg comes forth, from Her wide womb the universe bursts forth, from Her secret womb is the sacred serpent wisdom born. From Her womb of plenty spring out all our kin, all our gods and goddesses. She is the bloody tunnel, the cave painted with red ocher, the simmering pot and the fruitful cauldron. We are born of woman, midwived by our grandmothers and our goddesses. Honor Her laboring. Honor Her cycles. Honor Her.

Death: Ereshkigal

Betrayed by all She loved, now living solitary in the underworld, She grieves. When Her sister comes to visit, She falls to murder. What do we find when we go down to Her deep land? Peaceful fields and a throne room. The feather in the scales and the three awful judges. Vast hidden wealth and the green god of rebirth. Death is not evil but necessary. She is the mystery that comes after "the end." Her lessons are great and Her cycles are just.

Prophecy: Egeria

Nymph of a sacred grove in archaic Italy, She taught us the rites of worship and pronounced our first laws. Wisdom is hers, and foresight, too, though She may speak of what She knows or She may hold Her secrets. Speak to Her of divination, of the magic that makes our future as we will it. Speak to Her of life and death, of worship and law, and find an answer in the whispers of the leaves of Her holy trees. Would you meet the oracle? Pay attention to Her. Honor Her words.

Learning: Sheshat

She is Mistress of the House of Books, this ancient Egyptian scholar-goddess who, like Her sister goddesses around the world, invented writing and mathematics. Listen! Her gifts are intellect, discernment, intuition. Attend to her! What do our minds measure? What is the good of learning? Where does wisdom lie? Listen to the words of Sheshat and learn what is holy and good. Learn to know, to dare, to will. Learn to be silent.

Magic/Shamanism: Sigurdrifta

Wisest of the Valkyries, She is able to transform herself to wolf or raven. With Her Sisters She weaves war and peace, They spin the fates of heroes. Punished by Odin for overreaching, She fell into sleep, into trance, and somewhere She learned—what? Awakened by a man who knew no fear, She saluted east, south, west, north. After long silence, She spoke of magic, She spoke of the runes, She spoke of sorcery. What conjuration did She know, what spirit visits? What worlds did She tell of? Where did She go?

Art: The Muses

Go to the museum and see what they inspire, these nine dancing maidens, daughters of Memory. They brought us poetry, music, drama, dance. They bless all the arts and teach us what design human hands can make. Though They live in great public places, They dance most brightly in our studios, in all the hidden little corners where we bring beauty forth.

Beauty: Oshun

Dressed in yellow silk, dancing, flirting, as cool as the broad river, as hot as all-night drumming—here comes the Beauty of Africa. Call Her "Afrodite,"[1] call Her Golden Lady, greet Her as Daughter of Lush Mountains. She gestures, and we are enchanted. How can we not adore Her, this golden black Lady whose soul shimmers brighter than Her jewelry? We hunger for Her honey-sweet smile. We pray for Her generosity. Gaze into the moon, Her mirror, and see what She reflects.

Health and Healing: Panacea

Healing herbs, healing touch, healing scent, healing sound. Her name means "all-curing," and Her promise is that we shall be whole. We shall be well. We shall thrive and flourish. The Earth Herself will nourish us and heal us. Her energy spirals in us from crown to sole, and we know that all will be well. All is well, all must be well, all can only be well.

Prosperity: Habundia

How sweet is our prosperity! See how it springs up from the earth and pours down from heaven, how it grows in the community around us. We draw it to us, this bounty of Habundia, by our thoughts and actions. And how do we count our prosperity? In the love of family and friends. In our continued good health. Home. Right livelihood. Books, art supplies, a well-stocked kitchen, electronics, all our earthly treasures. In gifts of spirit, gifts of grace, gifts of lovingkindness . . . in all these things, and more, lies our perfect prosperity. Give thanks that She loves us and always will.

Justice: Astraea

They say She fled from earth. Long ago, when the age of gold ended and an age of iron began, mankind became too cruel. So She flew away. Now She waits, among the stars She watches us and waits. She's waiting till we call her. She's waiting for the just ones to arise. She's waiting for harmony and balance to come to earth again. She's waiting for colors and classes and faiths to live in peace together. Let us work to call Her back to us. Let us work together to bring Astraea home again.

The Maiden: Kore

This little one is our daughter, this girl is our granddaughter. She's our potential all over again, virgin fearlessly climbing trees, nymph puzzling over algebra. She's our trust, and She will lead us. She will dazzle us. But until She is grown, we must keep Her safe. We must help Her dream and teach Her to hope. We must feed her, clothe her, protect her, for She's our precious daughter. Let Her play, let Her be wise.

The Warrior Queen: Penthesilea

Greatest Amazon, wisest and most fearless of queens, She came to Troy and fought brutal Achilles and fell. But look—She is with us again today. The first female general, a learned admiral, ferocious sergeants. Today's Warrior Queen is the cop who negotiates and brings calming words instead of violence. She is strong and smart and tough. In times like these, we need this Warrior, and She is here. Her army is growing. She will not fall again.

The Mother: Cybele

Proud Lady walking with lions, Lady of the frame drum, Lady of cities and green lands. Two hundred years before Caesar, when Rome was threatened, it was foretold that when the black meteorite of the Phrygian Mountain Mother could be brought to the city, the invaders would be defeated. Thus She came to the West, Her power planted in our earth, too. All honor and praise to our Ancient Mother. All honor and praise to our earthly mothers, may they always bless us.

The Crone: Cailleach

The Hag is old. The Crone is holy, ugly, and wise. She controls the seasons and the weather and She can outwork any man. She is our beloved Granny, and we fear her. She is our familiar Nana, and we run from Her power. Endlessly old and eternally renewing Her maidenhood, She knows all the stories. She can answer the riddles and She'll sing the silly old songs. She invented the nursery rhymes and She's flown through the air. She's seen it all, and She'll be glad to tell you about it . . . if you know the right questions to ask.

Endnote

1. Luisah Teish, *Jambalaya* (New York: Harper and Row, 1985), pp. 121–22.

Afterword

This meditation is mine, but you can listen in.

I sit quietly, close my eyes, take a few deep, easy breaths, open my eyes, breathe again. All I have left to write is the poem that opens the book. I close my eyes again. My son the poet says I write guerrilla poetry: because no one else will publish my poems (not true), I sneak them into my books. Now I breathe and wonder, *Where's that pesky poem gonna come from?*

I open my eyes again and pick up the book I'm rereading, *Ordinary Magic.* Allen Ginzberg says that

> Real poetry practitioners are practitioners of mind awareness, or practitioners of reality, expressing their fascination with a phenomenal universe and trying to penetrate to the heart of it. Classical poetry is a 'process,' or experiment—a probe into the nature of reality and the nature of the mind.[1]

My eyes close, my lungs breathe, the image comes.

I'm writing, awash in paper, most of it printed on both sides because I recycle. Books are stacked all around me, looming over my keyboard, on the floor, on chairs. My television set is serving (as usual) as a dictionary stand.

And Her eyes are suddenly open inside my closed eyes. Her lungs are now breathing me, deeply, easily, fully. Her hands are upon my hands as gently as mine were upon my son's small hands twenty-five years ago, when I helped him form his first letters. Her muscles hold my spine erect, Her mind pushes my restless thoughts out of the way.

She oversits me at the keyboard. She writes me.

And the images come again—the cauldron of sacred space that is the whole universe, wings and security blankets and trees and a river and the chambered nautilus.

She is meditating me, imagining me, grounding and connecting me.

And I am in Her heart. She has spent time with me, watered and weeded me, tamed me. Creating this book, I leap from the bedrock of Her wisdom and spiral in Her energy . . . and all these words spin out.

When I return to everyday awareness, I know that you're in my imagination now. We've also spent time together, you and I, and you're in my heart. I sit here imagining you imagining Goody Getty and General Terminatrix, seeing Hestia's flame, walking with Athene, dancing with Grandmother Spider. We've found grounding, pleasure, compassion, intuition, creativity, and understanding together. We've become the Goddess Pillar, both of us, connecting the deepest Earth with the highest Heaven. We're connected in mindfulness.

I send these Goddess Meditations to you with all my love. Brightest blessings to you!

Endnote

1. Allen Ginzberg, "Meditation and Poetics," in *Ordinary Magic*, p. 99.

Resources

American Association for the Study of Mental Imagery (AASMI). Disseminates experimental and clinical studies of imagery by sponsoring conferences and supporting publications. For information write to Department of Psychology, DePaul University, 2219 N. Kenmore Ave., Chicago, IL 60614-3504.

Blair, Nancy. Sculpture and jewelry. The Great Goddess Gift Collection Catalog. Star River Productions, P.O. Box 510642, Melbourne Beach, FL 39251. Phone 800/232-1733. $2 for color catalog.

Cards, Tarot or Medicine. See your local metaphysical bookstore or write to U.S. Games Systems, 179 Ludlow St., Stamford, CN 06902, for a catalog. Or see www.usgamesinc.com.

Fellowship of Isis. The FOI currently has over 10,000 members throughout the world. Membership is free. Write to the Membership Secretary, FOI, Huntington Castle, Clonegal, Enniscorthy, Eire.

JBL Statues. Indoor and outdoor figures of goddesses and gods from cultures all around the world, neolithic to modern. For their catalog, write to P.O. Box 163, Rt. 1, Box 246, Crozet, VA 22932. Or see www.jblstatue.com.

Just, Jeanine. Workshops, lectures, and books on "Values, Vision, and Victories," "Evology," and other motivational topics. For information, write to Kreative Solutions, P.O. Box 4649, Laguna Beach CA, 92652.

Kali Evador, Judith. Woman Mysteries, P.O. Box 39A59, Los Angeles, CA 90039. Write for information about classes, lectures, and performance.

Music. Visit your local metaphysical bookstore or the New Age section of any music store. Judith and Vega provide music lists for the chakras in *The Sevenfold Journey.*

Re-Formed Congregation of the Goddess (RCG) and *Of a Like Mind.* An international network of women's spirituality and newspaper. For information, write to Jade at RCG, P.O. Box 6677, Madison, WI 53716, or phone her at 608/244-0072.

Bibliography

Ackerman, Diane. *A Natural History of the Senses*. New York: Random House, 1990.

Allen, Paula Gunn. *Grandmothers of the Light: A Medicine Woman's Sourcebook*. Boston: Beacon Press, 1991.

Ardinger, Barbara, Ph.D. *Seeing Solutions: Brief Visualizations to Help You Control Your Anger, Anxiety and Frustration and Create a Better Reality*. New York: Signet New Age Book, New American Library, 1989.

———. *A Woman's Book of Rituals and Celebrations*, rev. ed. San Rafael, CA: New World Library, 1995.

Awiakta, Marilou. *Selu: Seeking the Corn-Mother's Wisdom*. Golden, CO: Fulcrum Publishing, 1993.

Baring-Gould, William S. and Ceil. *The Annotated Mother Goose: Nursery Rhymes Old and New, Arranged and Explained*. New York: Clarkson N. Potter, 1962.

Bartlett's Familiar Quotations, 4th ed. New York: Little, Brown and Co., 1968.

Baudino, Gael. *Gossamer Axe*. New York: ROC Book, Penguin Books, 1990.

Begg, Ean. *The Cult of the Black Virgin*. London: Arkana, 1985.

Bender, Sue. *Everyday Sacred: A Woman's Journey Home*. New York: HarperCollins, 1995.

Bentov, Itzhak. *Stalking the Wild Pendulum: On the Mechanics of Consciousness*. New York: E. P. Dutton, 1977.

Bernal, Martin. *Black Athena: The Afroasiatic Roots of Classical Civilization*. New Brunswick, NJ: Rutgers University Press, 1987.

Beyer, Stephan. *The Cult of Tara: Magic and Ritual in Tibet*. Berkeley: University of California Press, 1978.

Blair, Nancy. *Amulets of the Goddess: Oracle of Ancient Wisdom*. Berkeley, CA: Wingbow Press, 1993.

———. *Goddesses for Every Season*. Shaftesbury, Dorset: Element Books, 1995.

Bogdanovich, Peter, ed. *A Year and a Day Engagement Calendar: Adapted from the Works of Robert Graves*. New York: Overlook Press, 1993.

Bolen, Jean Shinoda, M.D. *Goddesses in Everywoman: A New Psychology of Women*. New York: Harper and Row, 1984.

Bonheim, Jalaja. *The Serpent and the Wave: A Guide to Movement Meditation*. Berkeley, CA: Celestial Arts, 1992.

Boorstein, Sylvia. *Don't Just Do Something, Sit There: A Mindfulness Retreat*. San Francisco: HarperSanFrancisco, 1996.

Bradley, Marion Zimmer. *The Mists of Avalon*. New York: Del Rey Book, Ballantine Books, 1982.

Breathnach, Sarah Ban. *Simple Abundance: A Daybook of Comfort and Joy*. New York: Warner Books, 1995.

Briggs, Katharine. *An Encyclopedia of Fairies*. New York: Pantheon Books, 1976.

Brother Lawrence of the Resurrection. *The Practice of the Presence of God*. Ed. and trans. by John J. Delaney. New York: Image Book, Doubleday, 1977.

Budapest, Z. *Grandmother Moon: Lunar Magic in Our Lives*. San Francisco: HarperSanFrancisco, 1991.

Burkhardt, Titus. *Alchemy: Science of the Cosmos, Science of the Soul*. Trans. William Stoddart. Shaftesbury, Dorset: Element Books, 1986.

Butterworth, Eric. *Spiritual Economics: The Prosperity Process*. Unity Village, MO: Unity School of Christianity, 1983.

Cameron, Julia. *The Artist's Way: A Spiritual Path to Higher Creativity*. New York: Tarcher/Putnam, 1992.

———. *The Vein of Gold: A Journey to Your Creative Heart*. New York: Tarcher/Putnam, 1996.

Campanelli, Dan and Pauline. *Circles, Groves and Sanctuaries: Sacred Spaces of Today's Pagans*. St. Paul: Llewellyn, 1992.

Campanelli, Pauline. *Wheel of the Year: Living the Magical Life*. St. Paul: Llewellyn, 1989.

Campbell, Don G. *The Roar of Silence: Healing Powers of Breath, Tone and Music*. Wheaton, IL: Thosophical Publishing House, 1989.

Capra, Fritjof. *The Tao of Physics: An Exploration of the Parallels Between Modern Physics and Eastern Mysticism*. New York: Bantam Books, 1975.

Chernin, Kim. *The Flame Bearers*. New York: Random House, 1986.

Christ, Carol P. *Laughter of Aphrodite: Reflections on a Journey to the Goddess*. New York: Harper and Row, 1987.

———. *Odyssey with the Goddess: A Spiritual Quest in Crete*. New York: Continuum Publishing, 1995.

Collinge, William, Ph.D. *The American Holistic Health Association Complete Guide to Alternative Medicine*. New York: Warner Books, 1996.

Collins, Terah Kathryn. *The Western Guide to Feng Shui: Creating Balance, Harmony, and Prosperity in Your Environment*. Santa Monica, CA: Hay House, 1996.

Conn, Eileen, and James Stewart, eds. *Visions of Creation*. Alresford, Hants.: Godsfield Press, 1995.

Conway, D. J. *The Ancient and Shining Ones: World Myth, Magick and Religion*. St. Paul: Llewellyn, 1993.

Cooper, J. C. *The Aquarian Dictionary of Festivals*. London: Aquarian Press, 1990.

Cunningham, Elizabeth. *The Return of the Goddess*. Barrytown, NY: Station Hill Press, 1992.

Cunningham, Scott. *Cunningham's Encyclopedia of Crystal, Gem and Metal Magic*. St. Paul: Llewellyn, 1987.

————. *Cunningham's Encyclopedia of Magical Herbs*. St. Paul: Llewellyn, 1988.

————. *The Magic of Incense, Oils and Brews*. St Paul: Llewellyn, 1988.

Daly, Mary, *Gyn-Ecology: The Metaethics of Radical Feminism*. Boston: Beacon Press, 1978.

Daly, Mary and Jane Caputi. *Webster's First New Intergalactic Wickedary of the English Language*. Boston: Beacon Press, 1987.

Davidson, Gustav. *A Dictionary of Angels, Including the Fallen Angels*. New York: Free Press/Macmillan, 1971.

Davis, Elizabeth and Carol Leonard. *The Woman's Wheel of Life: Thirteen Archetypes of Woman at Her Fullest Power*. New York: Viking Arkana, 1996.

Dictionary of Mary. New York: Catholic Book Publishing Co., 1985.

Drury, Neville, ed. *Inner Health: The Health Benefits of Relaxation, Meditation and Visualization*. Prism Press, 1985.

Durdin-Robertson, Lawrence. *The Year of the Goddess: A Perpetual Calendar of Festivals*. London: Aquarian Press, 1990.

Durham, Michael S. *Miracles of Mary: Apparitions, Legends, and Miraculous Works of the Blessed Virgin Mary*. San Francisco: HarperSanFrancisco, 1995.

Edwards, Tilden. *Living Simply Through the Day: Spiritual Survival in a Complex Age*. Mahwah, NJ: Paulist Press, 1977.

Fallingstar, Cerridwen. *The Heart of the Fire*. P.O. Box 282, San Geronimo, CA, 94963: Cauldron Publications, 1990.

Farrar, Janet and Stewart. *The Witches' God*. Custer, WA: Phoenix Publishing, 1989.

————. *The Witches' Goddess*. Custer, WA: Phoenix Publishing, 1987.

Fortune, Dion. The Esoteric Orders and Their Work. St. Paul: Llewellyn, 1978 (originally written in 1928).

————. *Moon Magic*. York Beach, ME: Samuel Weiser, 1978 (first published in 1956).

————. *The Mystical Qabalah*. London: Ernest Benn, 1976 (originally written in 1932).

————. *The Sea Priestess*. York Beach, ME: Samuel Weiser, 1978 (first published in 1938).

Frye, Ellen. *Amazon Story Bones*. San Francisco: Spinsters Ink, 1994.

Galland, China. *Longing for Darkness: Tara and the Black Madonna, A Ten-Year Journey*. New York: Viking, 1990.

George, Demetra. *Finding Our Way Through the Dark: The Astrology of Dark Goddess Mysteries*. San Diego: ACS Publications, 1994.

————. *Mysteries of the Dark Moon: The Healing Power of the Dark Goddess*. San Francisco: HarperSanFrancisco, 1992.

Gimbutas, Marija. *The Civilization of the Goddess: The World of Old Europe*. San Francisco: HarperSanFrancisco, 1991.

Gleason, Judith. *Oya: In Praise of the Goddess*. Boston: Shambhala, 1987.

Goble, Frank G. *The Third Force: The Psychology of Abraham Maslow.* New York: Grossman Publishers, 1970.

Goliszek, Andrew G. *Breaking the Stress Habit: A Modern Guide to One-Minute Stress Management.* Winston-Salem, NC: Carolina Press, 1987.

Gordon, Stuart. *The Encyclopedia of Myths and Legends.* North Pomfret, VT: Headline/Trafalgar Square, 1993.

Govinda, Lama Anagarika. *Creative Meditation and Multi-Dimensional Consciousness.* Wheaton, IL: Quest Book, Theosophical Publishing House, 1976.

Graves, Robert, trans. *The Transformations of Lucius, Otherwise Known as The Golden Ass.* New York: Farrar, Straus and Giroux, 1951.

———. *The Greek Myths.* New York: George Braziller, 1957.

———. *The White Goddess: A Historical Grammar of Poetic Myth.* New York: Farrar, Straus and Giroux, 1986 (originally written in 1948).

Greer, Mary K. *The Essence of Magic: Tarot, Ritual, and Aromatherapy.* North Hollywood, CA: Newcastle Publishing, 1993.

———. *Women of the Golden Dawn: Rebels and Priestesses.* Rochester, VT: Park Street Press, 1995.

Grey, Morgan, and Julia Penelope. *Found Goddesses: Asphalta to Viscera.* Norwich, CT: New Victoria Publishers, 1988.

Griffin, Susan. *Woman and Nature: The Roaring Inside Her.* New York: Harper and Row, 1978.

Hall, Manly P. *The Symbolism of Light and Color.* Los Angeles: Philosophical Research Association, 1976.

Harding, M. Esther. *Woman's Mysteries: Ancient and Modern.* New York: Harper Colophon Book, Harper and Row, 1971 (originally published in 1933).

Harp, David, and Nina S. Feldman. *MetaPhysical Fitness!: The Complete 30 Day Plan for Your Mental, Emotional and Spiritual Health.* Novato, CA: Mind's I Press, 1989.

Hart, Mickey, and Fredric Lieberman, Ph.D. *Drumming at the Edge of Magic: A Journey into the Spirit of Percussion.* San Francisco: HarperSanFrancisco, 1990.

Haskins, Susan. *Mary Magdalen: Myth and Metaphor.* New York: Riverhead Books, 1993.

Heyob, Sharon Kelly. *The Cult of Isis Among Women in the Greco-Roman World. Etudes Preliminaires aux Religions Orientales dans L'Empire Romain.* Leyden: E.J. Brill, 1975.

Hirshfield, Jane, ed. *Women in Praise of the Sacred: 43 Centuries of Spiritual Poetry by Women.* New York: HarperCollins, 1994.

Holy Bible From Ancient Eastern Manuscripts, Containing the Old and New Testaments Translated from the Peshitta, the Authorized Bible of the Church of the East. Trans. by George M. Lamsa. Philadelphia: A.,J. Holman Company, 1968 (originally published in 1933).

Houston, Jean. *The Passion of Isis and Osiris, A Union of Two Souls.* New York: Ballantine Books, 1996.

Humphrey, Naomi. *Meditation the Inner Way: How to Use Meditation as a Powerful Force for Self-Improvement.* London: Aquarian Press, 1987.

Jade. *To Know: A Guide to Women's Magic and Spirituality.* New York: Delphi Press, 1991.

Janeway, Elizabeth. *Between Myth and Morning: Women Awakening.* New York: William Morrow, 1975.

Johnson, Buffie. *Lady of the Beasts: Ancient Images of the Goddess and Her Sacred Animals.* New York: Harper and Row, 1988.

Johnson, Cait and Maura D. Shaw. *Celebrating the Great Mother: A Handbook of Earth-Honoring Activities for Parents and Children*. Rochester, VT: Destiny Books, 1995.

Judith, Anodea. *Wheels of Life: A User's Guide to the Chakra System*. St. Paul: Llewellyn, 1988.

———, and Selene Vega. *The Sevenfold Journey: Reclaiming the Mind, Body and Spirit Through the Chakras*. Freedom, CA: Crossing Press, 1993.

Kabat-Zinn, Jon. *Wherever You go, There You Are: Mindfulness Meditation in Everyday Life*. Westport, CT: Hyperion, 1994.

Karas, Sheryl Ann. *The Solstice Evergreen: The History, Folklore and Origin of the Christmas Tree*. Boulder Creek, CA: Aslan Publishing, 1991.

Lamsa, George M. *Gospel Light: From Aramaic on the Teachings of Jesus*. Philadelphia: A. J. Holman, 1967.

———. *Old Testament Light: A Spiritual Commentary based on the Aramaic of the ancient Peshitta Text*. Philadelphia: A.J. Holman Company, 1978.

Larousse Encyclopedia of Mythology. Ed. Robert Graves. London: Paul Hamlyn, 1959.

LaTour, Kathy. *The Breast Cancer Companion: From Diagnosis Through Treatment to Recovery: Everything You Need to Know for Every Step Along the Way*. New York: Avon, 1994.

Leadbeater, C. W. *The Chakras*. Wheaton, IL: Quest Book, Theosophical Publishing House, 1974 (originally written in 1927).

———. *Man Visible and Invisible*. Wheaton, IL: Quest Book, Theosophical Publishing House, 1975 (originally written in 1925).

LeShan, Lawrence. *How to Meditate: A Guide to Self-Discovery*. New York: Little, Brown, 1974.

Leviton, Charles D., Ed.D. *There is No Bad Truth: The Search for Self*. Iowa: Kendall/Hunt Publishing Co., 1990.

Lindbergh, Anne Morrow. *Gifts from the Sea, 20th Anniversay Edition*. New York: Vintage Books, Random House, 1978.

Linn, Denise. *Sacred Space: Clearing and Enhancing the Energy of Your Home*. New York: Ballantine Books, 1995.

Long, Asphodel P. *In a Chariot Drawn by Lions: The Search for the Female in Deity*. Freedom, CA: Crossing Press, 1993.

Mann, John, and Lar Short. *The Body of Light: History and Practical Techniques for Awakening Your Subtle Body*. Yorktown, NY: Globe Press Books, 1990.

Marcus, Clare Cooper. *House As a Mirror of Self: Exploring the Deeper Meaning of Home*. Emeryville, CA: Conari Press, 1995.

Matthews, John, ed. *The World Atlas of Divination*. New York: Little, Brown and Co., 1992.

Merton, Thomas. *Contemplative Prayer*. Herder and Herder, 1969.

Metzner, Ralph. *The Well of Remembrance: Rediscovering the Earth Wisdom Myths of Northern Europe*. Boston: Shambhala Publications, 1994.

Monaghan, Patricia. *The Book of Goddesses and Heroines*. St. Paul: Llewellyn Publications, 1990.

———. *O Mother Sun! A New View of the Cosmic Feminine*. Freedom, CA: Crossing Press, 1994.

Muten, Burleigh, ed. *Return of the Great Goddess*. Boston: Shambhala, 1994.

Nadel, Laurie, et al. *Sixth Sense: The Whole-Brain Book of Intuition, Hunches, Gut Feelings, and Their Place in Your Everyday Life*. New York: Prentice Hall, 1990.

Neihardt, John H. *Black Elk Speaks: Being the Life Story of a Holy Man of the Oglala Sioux*. Lincoln: University of Nebraska Press, 1961.

Nhat Hanh, Thich. *A Guide to Walking Meditation*. Philadelphia: Fellowship Publications, 1985.

Noble, Vicki. *Motherpeace: A Way to the Goddess Through Myth, Art, and Tarot*. New York: Harper and Row, 1983.

————. *Shakti Woman: Feeling Our Fire, Healing Our World, The New Female Shamanism*. San Francisco: HarperSanFrancisco, 1991.

Olson, Carl, ed. *The Book of the Goddess, Past and Present: An Introduction to Her Religion*. New York: Crossroad Publishing Co., 1987.

Opie, Iona, and Moira Tatem, eds. *A Dictionary of Superstitions*. Oxford: Oxford University Press, 1989.

Orenstein, Gloria. *The Reflowering of the Goddess*. Elmsford, NJ: Athene Series, Pergamon Press, 1990.

Pagels, Elaine. *The Gnostic Gospels*. New York: Random House, 1979.

Palmer, Martin, and Jay Ramsay, with Man-Ho Kwok. *Kuan Yin: Myths and Prophecies of the Chinese Goddess of Compassion*. New York: Thorsons, HarperCollins, 1995.

Paxon, Diana L. *Brisingamen*. New York: Berkeley Books, 1984.

————. *The Serpent's Tooth*. New York: Avon Books, 1993.

Perera, Sylvia Brinton. *Descent to the Goddess: A Way of Initiation for Women*. Inner City Books, 1981.

Ram Dass. *Journey of Awakening: A Meditator's Guidebook*. New York: Bantam Books, 1978.

Ranke-Heinemann, Uta. *Eunuchs for the Kingdom of Heaven: Women, Sexuality and the Catholic Church*. Trans. Peter Heinegg. New York: Doubleday, 1990.

Regardie, Israel. *The Art of True Healing*, ed. Marc Allen. San Rafael, CA: New World Library, 1991 (originally written in 1932).

Roderick, Timothy. *Dark Moon Mysteries: Wisdom, Power and Magic of the Shadow World*. St. Paul: Llewellyn, 1996.

————. *The Once Unknown Familiar: Shamanic Paths to Unleash Your Animal Powers*. St. Paul: Llewellyn, 1994.

Rose, Jeanne. *Herbs and Things*. New York: GD/Perigee Book, Putnam Publishing Group, 1972.

Ryall, Rhiannon. *West Country Wicca: A Journal of the Old Religion*. Custer, WA: Phoenix Publishing, 1989.

de Saint Exupery, Antoine. *The Little Prince*. Trans. Katherine Woods. New York: Harvest/HBJ Book, Harcourt Brace Jovanovich, 1971 (originally written in 1943).

Sams, Jamie, and David Carson. *Medicine Cards: The Discovery of Power Through the Ways of Animals*. Illus. by Angela C. Werneke. Santa Fe, NM: Bear and Co., 1988.

Schaef, Anne Wilson. *Native Wisdom for White Minds: Daily Reflections Inspired by the Native Peoples of the World*. New York: Ballantine Books, 1995.

Shapiro, Deane H. *Meditation, Self-Regulation Strategy and Altered State of Consciousness: A Scientific/Personal Exploration*. Hawthorne, NY: Aldine Press, 1980.

Siuda-Legan, Tamara. *The Neteru of Kemet*. Chicago: Eschaton Productions, 1994.

Sjoo, Monica, and Barbara Mor. *The Great Cosmic Mother: Rediscovering the Religion of the Earth*. New York: Harper and Row, 1987.

Somé, Malidoma Patrice. *Ritual: Power, Healing and Community*. New York: Penguin/Arkana, 1993.

Spear, William. *Feng Shui Made Easy: Designing Your Life with the Ancient Art of Placement*. San Francisco: HarperSanFrancisco, 1995.

Spretnak, Charlene. *Lost Goddesses of Early Greece: A Collection of Pre-Hellenic Myths*. Boston: Beacon Press, 1978.

Starhawk. *The Spiral Dance: A Rebirth of the Ancient Religion of the Great Goddess*. 10th Anniversary Ed. New York: Harper and Row, 1989.

———. *Truth or Dare: Encounters with Power, Authority, and Mystery*. New York: Harper and Row, 1976.

Stark, Marcia and Gynne Stern. *The Dark Goddess: Dancing with the Shadow*. Freedom, CA: Crossing Press, 1993.

Stein, Diane. *Essential Reiki: A Complete Guide to an Ancient Healing Art*. Freedom, CA: Crossing Press, 1995.

Steinem, Gloria, ed. *Wonder Woman. A Ms. Book*. New York: Holt, Rinehart and Winston, 1972.

Stone, Merlin. *Ancient Mirrors of Womanhood: A Treasury of Goddess and Heroine Lore from Around the World*. Boston: Beacon Press, 1979.

———. *When God Was a Woman*. New York: Harcourt Brace Jovanovich, 1976.

Swain, Sally. *Oh My Goddess*. New York: Penguin Books, 1994.

Teish, Luisah. *Jambalaya: The Natural Woman's Book*. New York: Harper and Row, 1985.

——— . *Carnival of the Spirit: Seasonal Celebrations and Rites of Passage*. San Francisco: HarperSanFrancisco, 1994.

Walker, Barbara G. *The Woman's Dictionary of Symbols and Sacred Objects*. New York: Harper and Row, 1983.

Warner, Marina. *From the Beast to the Blonde: On Fairy Tales and Their Tellers*. New York: Noonday Press, Farrar, Straus and Giroux, 1996.

Watkins, Mary. *Invisible Guests: The Development of Imaginal Dialogues*. Boston: Sigo Press, 1990.

Welwood, John, ed. *Ordinary Magic: Everyday Life as Spiritual Path*. Boston: Shambhala, 1992.

White, Stewart Edward, *The Unobstructed Universe*. New York: E. P. Dutton, 1940.

Wilbur, Ken. *The Spectrum of Consciousness*. Wheaton, IL: Quest Book, Theosophical Publishing House, 1977.

Wolf, Fred Alan. *Taking the Quantum Leap: The New Physics for Nonscientists*. New York: Harper and Row, 1981.

Woolger, Jennifer Barker and Roger J. *The Goddess Within: A Guide to the Eternal Myths That Shape Women's Lives*. New York: Fawcett, 1987.

Zukav, Gary. *The Dancing Wu Li Masters: An Overview of the New Physics*. New York: William Morrow, 1979.

Goddess Index

General Index

☽ REACH FOR THE MOON

Llewellyn publishes hundreds of books on your favorite subjects! To get these exciting books, including the ones on the following pages, check your local bookstore or order them directly from Llewellyn.

ORDER BY PHONE

- Call toll-free within the U.S. and Canada, 1-800-THE MOON
- In Minnesota, call (612) 291-1970
- We accept VISA, MasterCard, and American Express

ORDER BY MAIL

- Send the full price of your order (MN residents add 7% sales tax) in U.S. funds, plus postage & handling to:

  Llewellyn Worldwide
  P.O. Box 64383, Dept. K034-5
  St. Paul, MN 55164–0383, U.S.A.

POSTAGE & HANDLING

(For the U.S., Canada, and Mexico)

- $4.00 for orders $15.00 and under
- $5.00 for orders over $15.00
- No charge for orders over $100.00

We ship UPS in the continental United States. We ship standard mail to P.O. boxes. Orders shipped to Alaska, Hawaii, The Virgin Islands, and Puerto Rico are sent first-class mail. Orders shipped to Canada and Mexico are sent surface mail.

International orders: Airmail—add freight equal to price of each book to the total price of order, plus $5.00 for each non-book item (audio tapes, etc.).

Surface mail—Add $1.00 per item.

Allow 2 weeks for delivery on all orders.
Postage and handling rates subject to change.

DISCOUNTS

We offer a 20% discount to group leaders or agents. You must order a minimum of 5 copies of the same book to get our special quantity price.

FREE CATALOG

Get a free copy of our color catalog, *New Worlds of Mind and Spirit*. Subscribe for just $10.00 in the United States and Canada ($30.00 overseas, airmail). Many bookstores carry *New Worlds*—ask for it!

Visit our web site at www.llewellyn.com for more information.

The New Book of Goddesses and Heroines

Patricia Monaghan

They come out in your dreams, your creativity, your passion, and in all of your relationships. They represent you in all your glory and complexity, and you represent them. They are the goddesses and heroines that form our true history. Your history. Let these mythic stories nourish your soul as they speak to you on a level as deep and mysterious as the source of life itself.

The third edition of this classic reference offers a complete, shining collection of goddess myths from around the globe. Discover more than 1,500 goddesses in Australia, Africa, North and South America, Asia, Europe—and experience her as she truly is. This new edition also adds hundreds of new entries to the original text—information found only in rare or limited editions and obscure sources.

There is a new section on Cultures of the Goddess, which provides the location, time and general features of the major religious system detailed in the myths. A comprehensive index, titled "Names of the Goddess," provides all available names, with variants. Stories, rites, invocations, and prayers are recorded in the Myths section, as well as a list of common symbols. Never before has such a vast panorama of female divinity been recorded in one source.

1-56718-465-0, 8½ x 11, 384 pp., illus., photos, softcover   **$19.95**